MW01273999

# *Solaris 2.6*

## ADMINISTRATOR CERTIFICATION TRAINING GUIDE, *Part I*

MACMILLAN
TECHNICAL
PUBLISHING
U·S·A

*Bill Calkins*

| | |
|---|---|
| Publisher | Jim LeValley |
| Executive Editor | Alicia Buckley |
| Managing Editor | Patrick Kanouse |
| Acquisitions Editor | Alicia Buckley |
| Development Editor | Tina Oldham |
| Technical Reviewer | Janice Winsor |
| Project Editor | Theresa Wehrle |
| Copy Editor | Malinda McCain |
| Proofreader | Megan Wade |
| Indexer | Chris Barrick |
| Aquisitions Coordinator | Amy Lewis |
| Manufacturing Coordinator | Brook Farling |
| Book Designer | Gary Adair |
| Cover Designer | Sandra Schroeder |
| Production Team Supervisor | Daniela Raderstorf |
| Production | Darin Crone |

# Copyright © 1999 by Macmillan Technical Publishing

## Trademark Acknowledgments

All terms mentioned in this book that are known to be trademarks or service marks have been appropriately capitalized. Macmillan Technical Publishing cannot attest to the accuracy of this information. Use of a term in this book should not be regarded as affecting the validity of any trademark or service mark.

## Warning and Disclaimer

This book is designed to provide information about Solaris 2.6. Every effort has been made to make this book as complete and as accurate as possible, but no warranty or fitness is implied.

The information is provided on an as-is basis. The authors and Macmillan Technical Publishing shall have neither liability nor responsibility to any person or entity with respect to any loss or damages arising from the information contained in this book or from the use of the discs or programs that may accompany it.

## Feedback Information

At Macmillan Technical Publishing, our goal is to create in-depth technical books of the highest quality and value. Each book is crafted with care and precision, undergoing rigorous development that involves the unique expertise of members from the professional technical community.

Readers' feedback is a natural continuation of this process. If you have any comments regarding how we could improve the quality of this book, or otherwise alter it to better suit your needs, you can contact us at `alewis@mcp.com`. Please make sure to include the book title and ISBN in your message.

# ABOUT THE AUTHOR

**B**ill Calkins is owner and president of Pyramid Design, Inc., a computer consulting firm specializing in the implementation of client-server technologies on UNIX and Windows NT operating systems. Bill has 15 years of experience in system administration and consulting at more than 75 different companies. He has worked as a trainer in both corporate and university settings. He speaks frequently at international user conferences and has written white papers on TCP/IP networking and UNIX system administration and management. Bill draws on his many years of experience in system administration and training to provide a unique approach to conducting computer training.

# ABOUT THE TECHNICAL REVIEWER

**J**anice Winsor is a senior technical writer with 13 years experience in documenting UNIX systems. She worked at Sun Microsystems for seven years. For the past three years, she worked at the Filoli Information Systems Company as a project leader and manager. She is now working as a freelance author. Janice has received 10 writing awards from the Society for Technical Communications. Her published works include *UNIX Book of Games*, *Jumping JavaScript*™, and the first edition of both the *Solaris System Administrator's Guide* and *Solaris Advanced System Administrator's Guide*, published by Sun Microsystems Press.

Janice contributed considerable practical, hands-on expertise to the entire development process for *Solaris 2.6 Administrator Certification Training Guide, Part 1*. As the book was being written, Janice reviewed all the material for technical content, organization, and flow. Her feedback was critical to ensuring that *Solaris 2.6 Administrator Certification Training Guide, Part 1* fits our readers' needs for the highest quality technical information.

# DEDICATION

To Glenda, for helping me maintain a balance between too much work and having fun.

To William, for keeping me company while you played computer games in the office.

To Nicole, for the great snacks and good coffee.

To Neil, well…for going to bed on time.

# INTRODUCTION

**W**elcome to *Solaris 2.6 Administrator Certification Training Guide, Part I.* My goal with this book is to teach you Solaris system administration and, specifically, to help you become certified. Sun offers two examinations for the Solaris system administrator. This book prepares you for Part 1 of the Solaris administrator examination; it is the single best reference for learning the information necessary to pass the certification exam. Each chapter opens with specific test objectives. In addition, I provide the background information you'll need to better understand each topic.

Whether your goal is to become certified or to simply learn more about administering a Solaris system, *Solaris 2.6 Administrator Certification Training Guide, Part I* provides an easy-to-follow format. This book begins at system installation and boot up. It then takes you through the tasks of installing patches and additional software packages; setting up file systems and user accounts; customizing the CDE environment; setting up printers; and configuring the network. It will even introduce you to shell scripts. I describe each topic as though you are new to system administrating, and I walk you through the advanced topics slowly. The only assumption I make is that you have some basic UNIX experience. I assume that you know how to log in and out, copy and remove files, and perform simple tasks with the VI editor.

I am in a good position to help you get through this learning process. I have conducted UNIX training for corporations for more than seven years. I have worked with SunOS and Solaris since the early 1980s, and I have worked as a system administrator for a large site of Sun systems for 14 years. For the past six years, I have worked independently as a system administration consultant and trainer on all flavors of UNIX, helping users like you with system administration. I have spent hundreds of hours training system administrators who had no prior UNIX experience as well as administrators who had many years of experience.

Putting this book together was a great experience. I always learn something when going back over the basics, just as I do every time I teach an introductory class. I invite even the most experienced system administrator to read this book—I guarantee you'll find something new. I also urge you to take the certification exam, if you have not done so already. Certification provides a measure and validation of your technical skills, gives you credibility in your job, and is a great way to advance your career.

The following guidelines apply when reading this book. The following list outlines the test objectives for the exam and then recommends the chapter(s) you should study to gain a firm grasp of those objectives.

- System Concepts

  Study Appendixes A and B and Chapters 2 and 10

- Booting the Workstation

  Study Chapter 1

- Solaris Installation

  Study Chapters 1, 2, 3, 6, and 13

- User Security

  Study Chapters 4 and 5

- Adding Users and Software with Admintool

  Study Chapters 5 and 6

- Software Package Administration

  Study Chapter 6

- Maintaining Patches

  Study Chapter 6

- Administration of Initialization Files

  Study Chapters 1 and 5

- File Permissions

  Study Chapter 4

- Administration and Configuration of CDE

  Study Chapter 7

- File Systems

  Study Chapter 3

- Disk Management

  Study Chapters 2, 3, and 11

- Script Writing

  Study Chapter 8

- Networks

  Study Chapter 13

- LP Print Service and Print Manager

  Study Chapter 9

- Process Control

  Study Chapter 10

- Backup and Recovery

  Study Chapter 11

- Device Administration

  Study Chapter 12

- The Service Access Facility

  Study Chapter 12

- Adding Terminals and Modems

  Study Chapter 12

When you feel prepared to take the exam, you first must buy a voucher from Sun Educational Services (call 1-800-422-8020). Then, call Sylvan Prometric at 1-800-792-3926 with your voucher number in hand to register for an exam. The test will cost $150 and has approximately 72 questions, which consist of multiple choice and short-answer, fill-in questions. You'll take the exam at a local Sylvan Prometric testing center and you'll have 90 minutes to complete the test. You'll find out right away if you passed or failed. When finished, you'll receive a report showing the percentage of items you answered correctly in each section. Keep this report so you know what areas you need to improve. You must answer at least 75% of the questions correctly to pass the exam. If you need to retake the exam, don't feel bad—it takes an average of two tries to pass the exam.

The sections you will be graded on, and the chapter(s) in this book that cover them, are as follows:

- System Concepts (Appendixes A and B and Chapters 2 and 10)

- Solaris Installation (Chapters 1, 2, 3, 6, 12, and 13)

- File Systems (Chapters 3 and 11)

- Navigating the File System (Chapter 3)

- Metacharacters and Redirection (Chapter 8)

- Shell Features (Chapter 8)

- File Security (Chapters 4 and 11)

- User Security (Chapters 4 and 5)

- Networks (Chapter 13)

- LP Print Service and Print Manager (Chapters 9 and 12)

- Print Commands (Chapter 9)

- Utilities (Covered throughout the book)

You'll also be graded on three areas not covered in this book: File Commands (cp, mv, rm, and so on), Visual Text Editor (basic editing tasks), and electronic communications (using UNIX email, talk, and wall commands). These are basic UNIX topics that you should be familiar with before taking the exam. As I stated earlier, this book covers system administration topics; basic UNIX topics are not within that scope. If you are not familiar with these three areas, I suggest you learn about them before taking the exam. There are many excellent books that cover basic UNIX topics and commands.

Also, watch my Web site, www.pdesigninc.com. I'll keep it up to date with any late breaking changes Sun might make to the exam or the objectives. Once you're confident, get certified and send me your comments by emailing me at wcalkins@pdesigninc.com.

# Conventions Used in This Book

**Commands**   In the steps and examples, the commands you enter are boldface and in a monospaced font. For example: `ls -l <return>`. The `<return>` means to press the Enter key to enter the command. Only press Enter when instructed to do so.

**Arguments and Options**   When describing command syntax, command options and arguments are in an italic monospaced font, and they are enclosed within angle brackets (< >). For example,

```
lp -d<printer name> <filename> <return>
```

**Using the Mouse**   When using menus and windows, you'll be selecting items with the mouse. Here is the default mapping for a three-button mouse:

Left button          Selects objects or activates controls

Middle button        Moves or adjusts objects

Right button         Displays pop-up menus

# CONTENTS AT A GLANCE

# TABLE OF CONTENTS

# CHAPTER

# 1

# Booting the Workstation

The following are the test objectives for this chapter:

- Booting the system

- Using OpenBoot PROM commands to record basic system configuration information

- Using OpenBoot PROM commands to alter the system boot device

- Using OpenBoot PROM commands to perform basic hardware testing

- Booting a system from more than one device

- System run states and startup scripts

- System shutdown

**B**ootstrapping is the process the computer follows to load and execute the bootable operating system. The name is coined from the phrase "pulling yourself up by your own bootstraps." The instructions for the bootstrap procedure are stored in the boot PROM (programmable read-only memory).

The boot process goes through the following phases:

1. **Boot PROM Phase**. The PROM displays system identification information and runs self-test diagnostics to verify the system's hardware and memory. Then the PROM loads the primary boot program, called `bootblk`.

2. **Boot Programs Phase**. The `bootblk` program finds and executes the secondary boot program (called `ufsboot`) from the ufs file system and loads it into memory. After the `ufsboot` program is loaded, it loads the kernel.

3. **Kernel Initialization Phase**. The kernel initializes itself and begins loading modules, using `ufsboot` to read the files. When the kernel has loaded enough modules to mount the root file system, it unmaps the `ufsboot` program and continues, using its own resources. The kernel starts the UNIX operating system, mounts the necessary file systems, and runs `/sbin/init` to bring the system to the "initdefault" state specified in /etc/inittab.

4. **Init Phase**. The kernel creates a user process and starts the `/sbin/init` process, which starts other processes by reading the /etc/inittab file.

   The `/sbin/init` process starts the run control (rc) scripts, which execute a series of other scripts. These scripts (`/sbin/rc*`) check and mount file systems, start various processes, and perform system maintenance tasks.

## Boot PROM and Program Phases

The bootstrap process begins after power-up when information located in the hardware's PROM chip is accessed. Sun calls this the *OpenBoot* firmware, and it is executed immediately after you turn on your system. The primary task of the OpenBoot firmware is to boot the operating system either from a mass storage device or from a network.

OpenBoot contains a program called the *monitor*, which controls the operation of the system before the kernel is available. When a system is turned on, the monitor runs a quick self-test that checks such things as the hardware and memory on the system. If no errors are found, the system begins the automatic boot process. OpenBoot contains a set of instructions that locate and start up the system's boot program and eventually start up the UNIX operating system. The boot program is stored in a predictable area on the system hard drive, CD-ROM, or other bootable device and is referred to as the *bootblock*. The bootblock is responsible for loading the UNIX kernel into memory and passing control of the system to the kernel. The kernel is a file named /kernel/unix, located on the bootable device.

The OpenBoot firmware was first introduced on the Sun SPARCstation 1. This chapter describes Version 2 of the firmware, which first appeared on the SPARCstation 2 system. Version 2 of the OpenBoot architecture provides a significant increase in functionality over the boot PROMs in earlier Sun systems. One notable feature of the OpenBoot firmware is a programmable user interface, based on the interactive programming language Forth. In Forth, sequences of user commands can be combined to form complete programs. This capability provides a powerful tool for debugging hardware and software.

You can enter the OpenBoot environment in the following ways:

- By halting the operating system with the various UNIX shutdown commands.

- By using the Stop-A key sequence from the keyboard (simultaneously press the Stop key and the A key).

**CAUTION!** *Using the Stop-A key sequence abruptly breaks execution of the operating system and should be used only as a last effort to restart the system.*

- By resetting the power to the system.

**NOTE.** *If your system is configured to boot automatically, you can enter the OpenBoot environment by pressing Stop-A after the display console banner appears but before the system starts booting the operating system. This procedure is not the same as the method described above, in which the Stop-A sequence is pressed after the system has booted. If automatic booting is not enabled, the system enters the OpenBoot environment on its own instead of booting the operating system.*

- When the system hardware detects an error from which it cannot recover. (The system halts and puts you at the OpenBoot prompt. This system failure is known as a Watchdog Reset.)

## OpenBoot Interface

The OpenBoot firmware provides a command line interface for the user at the system console, which has two modes: the Restricted Monitor and the Forth Monitor.

The *Restricted Monitor* provides a simple set of commands to initiate booting of the system, resume system execution, or enter the Forth Monitor. The Restricted Monitor is also used to implement system security.

The Restricted Monitor prompt is >. When you enter the Restricted Monitor, the following screen is displayed, showing the commands you can enter:

```
Type b (boot), c (continue), or n (new command mode) >
```

The Restricted Monitor commands are:

b *specifiers*         Boot the operating system.

c              Resume the execution of a halted program.

n              Enter the Forth Monitor (commonly referred to as "new command mode").

The *Forth Monitor*, the default mode in OpenBoot, is an interactive command interpreter that gives you access to an extensive set of functions for hardware and software diagnosis. These functions are available to anyone who has access to the system console.

The Forth Monitor prompt is ok. When you enter the Forth Monitor mode, the following screen is displayed:

```
Type help for more information ok
```

If you want to leave the Forth Monitor mode and get into the Restricted Monitor mode, type:

**ok old-mode**

**NOTE.** *When the system is halted, the PROM monitor prompt is displayed. The type of prompt depends on your system type. Older Sun systems, such as the Sun4/nnn series, use the greater than sign (>) as the PROM prompt. Newer Sun systems use* ok *as the PROM prompt but support the > prompt. To switch from the > prompt to the* ok *prompt on newer Sun systems, type* n *at the > prompt.*

## How to Find the PROM Release for a System

For Solaris 2.6 to work properly, your PROM release must be revision 1.1 or higher. To get the PROM release on your system, type **banner** at the ok PROM prompt and press Enter. Hardware configuration information, including the release number of the PROM, is displayed:

```
ok banner
        SPARCstation 2, Type 4 Keyboard
        ROM Rev. 2.2, 16 MB memory installed, Serial #426751
        Ethernet address 8:0:20:e:fd:7c HostID 55411df8
```

The OpenBoot PROM monitor supports three security modes (nonsecure, command secure, and fully secure) and an authentication password. Access to monitor commands is controlled by these security modes. In nonsecure mode, all monitor commands are allowed. In command secure mode, only the b (boot) command with no arguments and the c (continue) command with no arguments may be entered without supplying the authentication password. In fully secure mode, only the c (continue) command with no arguments may be entered without supplying the authentication password. Note that systems do not auto-reboot in fully secure mode. The authentication password must be entered before booting takes place.

## OpenBoot Parameters

The OpenBoot PROM supports several parameters, which are user-definable (superuser only). The following list provides a few common ones you should remember. The only time you should need to modify these parameters is if you want to boot from a SCSI disk other than target 3, in which case you might want to turn off automatic booting (auto-boot). Another reason you might want to change an OpenBoot parameter is for setting security. Don't change OpenBoot parameters unless absolutely necessary. Not all OpenBoot systems support all parameters, and defaults can vary, depending on the system and the PROM revision.

### Version 2 OpenBoot Parameters

Table 1–1 describes some of the OpenBoot parameters. For a more complete listing, refer to the OpenBoot Command Reference Manual for the version of OpenBoot on your system.

### Table 1–1   OpenBoot Parameters

| Parameter | Description |
| --- | --- |
| auto-boot? | If true, boots automatically after power-on or reset. Default=true. |
| boot-device | Device from which to boot. Defaults to disk. Note: Disk is an alias that can be user-defined. |
| input-device | Power-on input device (usually keyboard, ttya, or ttyb). Default=keyboard. |
| output-device | Power-on output device (usually screen, ttya, or ttyb). Default=screen. |
| security-#badlogins | Number of incorrect security password attempts. |
| security-mode | Firmware security level (options: none, command, or full). If set to command or full, system prompts for PROM security password. Default=none. |
| security-password | Firmware security password (never displayed). Can be set only when security-mode is set to command or full. |
| watchdog-reboot? | If true, reboots after watchdog reset. Default=false. |

The following example demonstrates the method for setting the `auto-boot?` parameter to false. At the `ok` prompt, type `auto-boot?=false`.

An OpenBoot parameter can also be changed from the UNIX command line by using the `eeprom` command without being at the `openboot` prompt. After a parameter is changed, it

remains that way even after a reboot. To change the OpenBoot parameter `security-password` from the command line, use the following:

```
example# eeprom security-password=
Changing PROM password:
New password:
Retype new password:
```

**C A U T I O N !** *Setting the security mode and password can leave a system unable to boot if you forget the password. There is no way to break in without sending the CPU to Sun to have the PROM reset.*

## PROM Device Names, Addresses, and Arguments

Sun's firmware deals directly with hardware devices in the system. Each device has a unique name, representing the type of device and a path to that device's location in the hardware hierarchy or the system addressing structure. The following example shows a full device pathname:

```
/sbus@1,f8000000/esp@0,40000/sd@3,0:a
```

A full device pathname consists of information, or node names, separated by slashes (/). The root of the tree is the machine node, which is not named explicitly but is indicated by a leading slash (/). Each node name has the form

```
name@address:arguments
```

Table 1–2 describes the parameters in the node name.

**Table 1–2    Full Device Path Node Name Parameters**

| Node Name Parameter | Description |
| --- | --- |
| name | A text string that, ideally, has some mnemonic value (for example, sd represents "SCSI disk"). Many names, especially names of plug-in modules, include the name or stock symbol of the device's manufacturer (for example, SUNW is the stock symbol for Sun Microsystems). |
| @ | Separates the name from the address parameter. |
| address | A text string representing an address, usually of the form *hex_number,hex_number*. (Numbers are given in hexadecimal format.) |
| : | Must precede the argument's parameter. |
| arguments | A text string whose format depends on the particular device. It can be used to pass information to the device's software. |

OpenBoot commands require the full device pathname to locate and distinguish between different devices. This means you can specify a particular device without ambiguity.

Example:

`/sbus@1,f8000000/esp@0,40000/sd@3,0:a`

`1,f8000000` represents an address on the main system bus because the SBus interface is directly attached to the main system bus.

`0,40000` is an SBus slot number. The esp device is in SBus slot 0 at offset 40000. (In this example, the device is a SCSI host adapter, although the name does not say so directly.)

`3,0` is a SCSI target and logical unit number. The sd device is attached to a SCSI bus at target 3, logical unit 0.

See Appendix C, "Overview of SCSI Devices," for more information on SCSI host adapters, targets, and logical units.

The `:arguments` part of the node name is optional. In the previous example, the argument for the sd device is the string a. The Solaris software driver for sd interprets the argument as a disk partition, so the device pathname refers to partition a on that disk.

## PROM Device Aliases

OpenBoot recognizes two kinds of device pathnames:

- Full device (discussed in the previous section), such as
  /sbus@1,f8000000/esp@0,40000/sd@3,0:a

- Device aliases, such as *disk*

An alias is shorthand representing a long device pathname. An alias represents an entire device pathname, not a component of it. For example, the alias *disk* might represent the device pathname

`/sbus@1,f8000000/esp@0,40000/sd@3,0:a`

OpenBoot has the following predefined device aliases for commonly used devices, so you rarely need to type a full device pathname.

| Alias | Device Pathname |
|---|---|
| disk | /sbus@1,f8000000/esp@0,40000/sd@3,0:a |
| disk1 | /sbus@1,f8000000/esp@0,40000/sd@1,0:a |
| disk2 | /sbus@1,f8000000/esp@0,40000/sd@2,0:a |
| disk3 | /sbus@1,f8000000/esp@0,40000/sd@3,0:a |

Table 1–3 describes the `devalias` command, which is used in OpenBoot to examine, create, and change aliases.

**Table 1–3    devalias Examples**

| Command | Description |
| --- | --- |
| devalias | Displays all current device aliases. |
| devalias alias | Displays the device pathname corresponding to alias. |
| devalias alias *device-path* | Defines an alias representing a device path. |

## Getting Help in OpenBoot

Whenever you see the `ok` prompt on the display, you can ask the system for help by typing one of the help commands described in Table 1–4.

**Table 1–4    Help Commands**

| Command | Description |
| --- | --- |
| help | Displays instructions about using the help system and lists the available help categories. |
| help category | Shows help for all commands in the category. Use only the first word of the category description. |
| help command | Shows help for the individual command. |

Because of the large number of commands, help is available only for commands that are used frequently.

If you want to see the help messages for all commands in the category `diag`, for example, type

**ok help diag**

Help responds with

```
ok help diag
 Category: Diag
test      device-specifier (--) run selftest method for specified device
      examples:
      test /memory      -test memory
      test /iommu/sbus/ledma@f,400010/le      -test net
      test floppy      -test floppy disk drive
```

```
      test net            - test net
      test scsi        - test scsi
watch-clock      (--)      show ticks of real-time clock
watch-net      (--)     monitor broadcast packets using auto-selected interface
watch-aui      (--)      monitor broadcast packets using AUI interface
watch-net-all      (--)       monitor broadcast packets on all net interfaces
probe-scsi      (--)        show attached SCSI devices
probe-scsi-all      (--)      show attached SCSI devices for all host adapters
test-all            (--)        execute test for all devices with selftest method
test-memory      (--)       test all memory if diag-switch? is true, otherwise
                  test memory specified by selftest-#megs
ok
```

If you want help for a specific command, type

**ok help test net**

Help responds with the following:

```
Category: Diag
test      device-specifier (--) run selftest method for specified device
examples:
test /memory                      -test memory
test/iommu/sbus/ledma@f,400010/le    -test net
test floppy                      -test floppy disk drive
test net                         -test net
test scsi                        -test scsi
```

The message also shows the format of the command.

## Testing and Booting the System

The most common commands in OpenBoot are those that verify the system hardware and those that boot the operating system. After the system power is turned on, the ok prompt appears, indicating the system is ready for your input.

### Testing the Hardware

The OpenBoot diagnostics command used to check all major components of the system is

**ok testall**

The system tests the video components and performs various other tests.

Another command used to check the physical connection to SCSI devices such as tape drives and disk drives is

**ok probe-scsi**

The system responds with

```
Target 1
    Unit 0    Disk      SEAGATE ST1120N      833400093849
                        Copyright ©     1992 Seagate
                        All rights reserved 0000
Target 3
    Unit 0    Disk      MAXTOR LXT-213S SUN2074.20
```

Probe-scsi inspects all SCSI devices for connectivity. Devices are not recognized if they are not connected properly or if they share the same target ID.

**TIP.** *Use the* probe-scsi *command to obtain an open SCSI target ID number before adding a tape unit, CD-ROM drive, disk drive, or any other SCSI peripheral. Use this command after installing a SCSI device to ensure it has been connected properly and the system can see it. Also, use this command if you suspect a faulty cable or connection.*

## Kernel Initialization Phase

The OpenBoot PROM automatically issues the boot command if the OpenBoot parameter auto-boot is set to true (default) and the OpenBoot PROM is not in fully secure mode. The system automatically starts the boot process after power has been turned on and you do not see the ok prompt displayed. To interrupt the auto-boot process, press Stop-A. The ok prompt appears. Table 1–5 lists the boot command options.

**Table 1–5**  *boot* **Command Options**

| Option | Description |
|--------|-------------|
| -a | An interactive boot |
| -s | Boots into a single user state |
| -r | Reconfigure |
| -v | Boots in verbose mode |

ok boot -v, for example, boots the system in verbose mode, which displays a full listing of system messages during the boot phase.

The boot program is responsible for loading the UNIX kernel into memory and passing the control of the system to it. The kernel (covered in detail later in this chapter) is the part of the operating system that remains running at all times until the system is shut down.

The boot command must access the OpenBoot parameter `boot-device`. The alias assigned to the boot device (disk or disk#) tells the boot device where to find the kernel and how to start it up. For example, the alias *disk* provides the boot path /sbus@1,f8000000/ esp@0,40000/sd@3,0:a.

## The *boot* Command

A noninteractive boot (`boot`) automatically boots the system using default values for the boot path.

```
ok boot
```

An interactive boot (`boot -a`) stops and asks for input during the boot process. The system provides a dialog box in which it displays the default boot values and gives you the option to change them. You might want to boot interactively to make a temporary change to the system file or the kernel. Booting interactively enables you to test your changes and recover easily if you have any problems.

The following provides detail of the interactive boot process:

1. At the `ok` PROM prompt, type **boot -a** and press Enter. The boot program prompts you interactively.

2. Press Enter to use the default kernel (/kernel/unix) as prompted, or type the name of the kernel to use for booting and press Enter.

3. Press Enter to use the default /etc/system file as prompted, or type the name of the system file and press Enter.

4. Press Enter to use the default modules directory path as prompted, or type the path for the modules directory and press Enter.

5. Press Enter to use the default /etc/path_to_inst file as prompted, or type an alternate file and press Enter.

6. Press Enter to use the default root file system type as prompted—`ufs` for local disk booting or `nfs` for diskless clients.

7. Press Enter to use the default physical name of the root device as prompted, or type the device name.

The following output shows an example of an interactive boot session:

```
ok boot -a
Enter filename [/kernel/unix]:
(Copyright notice)
Name of system file [/etc/system]:
Name of default directory for modules [/kernel /usr/kernel]:
```

```
Enter name of device instance number file [/etc/path_to_inst]:
root filesystem type [ufs]
Enter physical name of root device  [/sbus@1,f8000000/esp@0,800000/sd@0,0:a]:
Configuring network interfaces:  le0
Hostname: sol
(fsck messages)
The system is coming up.  Please wait
(More messages)
sol login:
```

Boot information is displayed on the system console as the system boots. If you are not at the system console to watch the boot information, you can use the UNIX dmesg command to redisplay information that was displayed during the boot process or view the information in the /var/adm/messages file.

To view messages displayed during the boot process, use one of the following methods:

- At a UNIX prompt, type **/usr/sbin/dmesg** and press Enter. The boot messages are displayed.

- At a UNIX prompt, type **more /var/adm/messages** and press Enter.

## System Run States

After the kernel is initiated by the boot command, it begins several phases of the startup process. The first task is for OpenBoot to load the kernel. By default, the kernel is named /kernel/unix and is located in the /root partition on the disk, with its path defined in an OpenBoot PROM alias named *disk*. The kernel consists of a small static core and many dynamically loadable kernel modules. Many kernel modules are loaded automatically at boot time, but for efficiency, others—such as device drivers—are loaded in from the disk as needed by the kernel. When the kernel loads, the system reads a file named /etc/system. Parameters in this file modify how the kernel gets loaded. Occasionally, kernel parameters in this file need to be adjusted.

**CAUTION!** *Do not modify the /etc/system file unless you are certain of the results. A good practice is always to make a backup copy of any system file you modify in case the original needs to be restored. Incorrect entries could prevent your system from booting.*

After control of the system gets passed to the kernel, the system begins initialization and enters one of eight run states—also called init states—described in Table 1–6. The init state in which the system is running defines the services and resources available to users. When preparing to do a system administration task, you need to determine which init state is appropriate for the task. Use Table 1–7 in determining what init state to use for a particular task. A system can run in only one init state at a time.

## Table 1–6    System Run States

| Run State | Description |
| --- | --- |
| 0 | Power-down state; halted |
| 1,S,s | System administrator state, single-user state |
| 2 | Multiuser state, resources such as printers and file systems are not exported |
| 3 | Multiuser state, resources exported |
| 4 | (currently not used) |
| 5 | Reboot and turn off power to computer |
| 6 | Reboot |

## Table 1–7    System Run States Defined

| Init State | When to use it |
| --- | --- |
| 0 | To shut down the system so it is safe to turn off the power system administrator state. |
| 1 | When performing administrative tasks that require you to be the only user on the system. / and /usr are the only file systems mounted, and you can access only minimum kernel utilities. The terminal from which you issue this command becomes the console. No other users are logged in. |
| s or S | To run as a single user with all file systems mounted and accessible. |
| 2 | For normal operations. Multiple users can access the system and the entire file system. All daemons are running except NFS server and syslog. |
| 3 | For normal operations, with NFS resource sharing available. |
| 4 | (currently not used) |
| 5 | When you want to be prompted for a device other than the default boot devices. You can also change to this level by using the boot -a command. |
| 6 | To shut down the system to run level 0 and then reboot to multiuser level (or whatever level is the default in the inittab file). |

## Swapper

The first task for the kernel is to start up the *swapper* process. The swapper process is the part of the kernel that schedules all other processes. The swapper has a process ID of zero. Its first job is to start up the init process.

# INIT Phase

The init process is the parent of all other processes. Init examines the contents of the /etc/inittab file to determine the order for starting up other processes and what to do when one of these processes ends. Each entry in the /etc/inittab file has the following fields:

```
id:runlevel:action:process
```

Table 1–8 provides a more detailed description of each field.

**Table 1–8    Fields in the inittab File**

| Field | Description |
| --- | --- |
| id | A unique identifier |
| runlevel | The run level |
| action | How the process is to be run |
| process | The name of the command to execute |

The following example shows a default /etc/inittab file:

```
ap::sysinit:/sbin/autopush -f /etc/iu.ap
fs::sysinit:/sbin/bcheckrc                  >/dev/console 2>&1 </dev/console
is:3:initdefault:
p3:s1234:powerfail:/sbin/shutdown -y -i0 -g0 >/dev/console 2>&1 </dev/console
s0:0:wait:/sbin/rc0 off                     >/dev/console 2>&1 </dev/console
s1:1:wait:/sbin/shutdown -y -iS -g0         >/dev/console 2>&1 </dev/console
s2:23:wait:/sbin/rc2                        >/dev/console 2>&1 </dev/console
s3:3:wait:/sbin/rc3                         >/dev/console 2>&1   </dev/console
s5:5:wait:/sbin/rc5 ask                     >/dev/console 2>&1   </dev/console
s6:6:wait:/sbin/rc6 reboot                  >/dev/console 2>&1 </dev/console
of:0:wait:/sbin/uadmin 2 0                  >/dev/console 2>&1 </dev/console
fw:5:wait:/sbin/uadmin 2 2                  >/dev/console 2>&1 </dev/console
RB:6:wait:/sbin/sh -c 'echo "\nThe system is being restarted."'  >/dev/ \
console 2>&1
sc:234:respawn:/usr/lib/saf/sac -t 300
co:234:respawn:/usr/lib/saf/ttymon -g -h -p "'uname -n' console  login: " -T \
sun -d \ /dev/console -l
console -m ldterm,ttcompat
```

When the system is first booted, init starts all processes labeled sysinit in the inittab file. The initdefault entry in /etc/inittab identifies the default run level. In this example, the default is run level 3 (multiuser mode with network file sharing). The init daemon runs each process associated with this run level (each entry that has a 3 in its run-level field). Each process is run using the entry from the action field. The action field can have one of the following values:

| | |
|---|---|
| powerfail | The system has received a powerfail signal. |
| wait | Wait for the command to be completed. |
| respawn | Restart the command. |

## /etc/bcheckrc

The first script set to run by the /etc/inittab file is the /etc/bcheckrc script, which prepares the root file system and other critical file systems such as /usr. Solaris uses a state flag, stored on the hard drive, to record the condition of the file systems. The flag is checked by the /etc/bcheckrc script during booting to determine the state of a file system—clean or unclean. File systems and their states are discussed in Chapter 3, "Introduction to File Systems."

**NOTE.** *Many of the Solaris startup scripts can be identified by their "rc" prefix or suffix, which means "run control."*

## rc Scripts

For each init state, there is a corresponding series of rc scripts, located in the /sbin directory, to control each init state:

```
rc0
rc1
rc2
rc3
rc5
rc6
rcS
```

For each rc script in the /sbin directory, a corresponding directory named /etc/rcn.d contains scripts to perform various actions for that run level. For example, /etc/rc2.d contains files used to start and stop processes for run level 2. rc scripts are run in numerical order until the desired run level is reached; for example, to get to run level 3, /sbin/rc1, /sbin/rc2, and /sbin/rc3 are run.

All run-control scripts are also located in the /etc/init.d directory. These files are linked to corresponding run-control scripts in the /etc/rc*.d directories.

**NOTE.** *On other UNIX systems, startup scripts are sometimes found in /sbin/rc*.d and sometimes in the /etc/rc*.d directories. Links were put into Solaris so users who are accustomed to other flavors of UNIX (HP-UX, SunOS, and so on) can locate the startup files easily. Also, any scripts they might have ported over that reference these startup files are compatible without modification.*

The following is a listing of the scripts located in /etc/rc2.d:

```
ls /etc/rc2.d

sol% ls /etc/rc2.d
        K20lp               S21perf             S72inetsvc          S89bdconfig
        K60nfs.server       S30sysid.net        S73nfs.client       S90xtl
        K65nfs.client       S47asppp            S74autofs           S91gsconfig
        K92volmgt           S69inet             S74syslog           S91gtconfig
        README              S70uucp             S75cron             S91leoconfig
        S01MOUNTFSYS        S71rpc              S80PRESERVE         S92rtvc-config
        S05RMTMPFILES       S71sysid.sys        S80lp               S92volmgt
        S18setuname         S72autoinstall      S88sendmail         S99audit
        S20sysetup
```

The /etc/rcn.d scripts are always run in ASCII sort order. The scripts have names of the form

```
[K,S][0-9][0-9][A-Z]
```

Files beginning with K are run to terminate (kill) some system process. Files beginning with S are run to start up a system process. The actions of each run-control–level script are summarized in the following lists.

The /sbin/rc0 script

- Stops system services and daemons

- Terminates all running processes

- Unmounts all file systems

The /sbin/rc1 script runs the /etc/rc1.d scripts and

- Stops system services and daemons

- Terminates all running processes

- Unmounts all file systems

- Brings the system up in single-user mode

**TIP.** *Use the init 1 run level to perform system administration tasks when you want to ensure that other users cannot log in and access the system.*

The /sbin/rc2 script sets the TIMEZONE variable, runs the /etc/rc2.d scripts, and

- Mounts all file systems

- Enables disk quotas if at least one file system was mounted with the quota option

- Saves editor temporary files in /usr/preserve
- Removes any files in the /tmp directory
- Creates device entries in /dev for new disks (only if `boot -r` is run)
- Prints system configuration (the default is not to save a core file)
- Configures system accounting
- Configures the default router
- Sets the NIS domain
- Sets the ifconfig netmask
- Starts `inetd`
- Starts `named`, if appropriate
- Starts `rpcbind`
- Starts the Kerberos client-side daemon, `kerbd`
- Starts NIS daemons (`ypbind`) and NIS+ daemons (`rpc.nisd`), if appropriate
- Starts `keyserv`
- Starts `statd`, `lockd`
- Mounts all NFS entries
- Starts `automount`
- Starts `cron`
- Starts the LP daemons
- Starts the `sendmail` daemon

The `/sbin/rc3` script runs the /etc/rc3.d scripts and

- Cleans up sharetab
- Starts `nfsds`
- Starts `mountd`
- If boot server, starts `rarpd` and `rpc.bootparamd`

The `/sbin/rc5` script runs the /etc/rc0.d scripts and

- Kills the printer daemons
- Unmounts local file systems

- Kills the syslog daemon
- Unmounts remote file systems
- Stops NFS services
- Stops NIS services
- Stops RPC services
- Stops cron services
- Stops NFS client services
- Kills all active processes
- Initiates an interactive boot

The /sbin/rc6 script runs /etc/rc0.d/K* and

- Kills all active processes
- Unmounts the file systems
- Runs the initdefault entries in /etc/inittab

The /sbin/rcS script runs the /etc/rcS.d scripts to bring the system up to single-user mode and

- Establishes a minimal network
- Mounts /usr, if necessary
- Sets the system name
- Checks the / and /usr file systems
- Checks and mounts the /usr/kvm file system, if necessary
- Mounts pseudo file systems (/proc and /dev/fd)
- For reconfiguration boots, rebuilds the device entries
- Checks and mounts other file systems to be mounted in single-user mode

Run level init S is similar to run level 1 except all file systems get mounted and are accessible.

# Using the Run-Control Scripts to Stop or Start Services

The advantage of having individual scripts for each init is that you can run these scripts individually to turn off processes in Solaris without rebooting or changing init states.

For example, you can turn off NFS server functionality by typing `/etc/init.d/nfs.server stop` and pressing Enter. After you have changed the system configuration, you can restart the functionality by typing `/etc/init.d/nfs.server start` and pressing Enter.

## Adding Scripts to the Run-Control Directories

If you add a script, put the script in the /etc/init.d directory and create a link to the appropriate rc*.d directory. Assign appropriate numbers and names to the new scripts so they will be run in the proper sequence.

**TIP.** *If you do not want a particular script to run when entering a corresponding init state, change the uppercase prefix (S or K) to lowercase (s or k). Only files with an uppercase prefix are run. For example, change* `S99mount` *to* `s99mount` *to disable the script.*

# System Shutdown

Solaris has been designed to run continuously, 7 days a week, 24 hours a day. Occasionally, however, you need to shut down the system to carry out administrative tasks. At other times, an application might cause the system to go awry and the operating system must be stopped to kill off run-away processes and then be restarted. You can shut down the system in many ways, using various UNIX commands. With Solaris, taking down the operating system in an orderly fashion is important. When the system booted, several processes were started and must be shut down before you power off the system. In addition, information has been cached in memory and not yet written to disk. The process of shutting down Solaris involves shutting down processes and flushing data from memory to the disk. Remember that shutting down the system improperly can result in loss of data and the risk of corrupting the file systems.

**TIP.** *To avoid having your system shut down improperly during a power failure, use a UPS (uninterruptable power supply) capable of shutting down the system before the power is shut off.*

## Commands to Shut Down the System

When preparing to shut down a system, you need to determine which of the following commands is appropriate for the system and the task at hand:

```
/usr/sbin/shutdown
/sbin/init
/usr/sbin/halt
/usr/sbin/reboot
Stop-a or L1-a (to be used as a last resort; see warning earlier in this chapter)
```

The first four commands initiate shutdown procedures, kill all running processes, write data to disk, and shut down the system software to the appropriate run level. The last command, which is really a series of keystrokes, stops the system unconditionally.

### /usr/sbin/shutdown

Use the shutdown command when shutting down a system with multiple users. The shutdown command sends a warning message to all users who are logged in, waits for 60 seconds (the default), and then shuts down the system to single-user state. A command option (-g) lets you choose a different default wait time.

The shutdown command performs a clean system shutdown, which means all system processes and services are terminated normally and file systems are synchronized. You need superuser privileges to use the shutdown command.

When the shutdown command is initiated, all logged-in users and all systems mounting resources receive a warning about the impending shutdown, and then a final message. For this reason, the shutdown command is recommended over the init command on a server.

**TIP.** *When using either command, you might want to give users more advanced notice by sending an email message about any scheduled system shutdown.*

The following are the recommended steps for shutting down the system:

1. As superuser, type the following to find out if users are logged in to the system.

   ```
   # who
   ```

2. A list of all logged-in users is displayed. You might want to send mail or broadcast a message to let users know the system is being shut down.

3. Shut down the system by using the shutdown command.

   ```
   # shutdown -i<init-state> -g<grace-period> -y
   ```

The following describes the `shutdown` command:

| | |
|---|---|
| `-i<init-state>` | Brings the system to an init state different from the default of S. The choices are 0, 1, 2, 5, and 6. |
| `-g<grace-period>` | Indicates a time (in seconds) before the system is shut down. The default is 60 seconds. |
| `-y` | Continues to shut down the system without intervention; otherwise, you are prompted to continue the shutdown process after 60 seconds. If you used the shutdown -y command, you are not prompted to continue; otherwise, you are asked, "Do you want to continue? (y or n)." |

### /sbin/init

Use the `init` command to shut down a single-user system or to change its run level. You can use `init` to place the system in power-down state (init 0) or in single-user state (init1).

### /usr/sbin/halt

Use the `halt` command when the system must be stopped immediately and it is acceptable not to warn any current users. The `halt` command shuts down the system without any delay. It does not warn any other users on the system.

### /usr/sbin/reboot

Use the `reboot` command to shut down a single-user system and bring it into multiuser state. `Reboot` does not warn other users on the system.

The Solaris `reboot` and `halt` commands do an unconditional shutdown of system processes. These commands shut down the system much more quickly than the `shutdown` command, but not as gracefully. No messages are sent to users. `Reboot` and `halt` do not notify all logged-in users and systems mounting resources of the impending shutdown; however, the two commands do synchronize file systems.

**N O T E .** `init` *and* `shutdown` *are the most reliable ways to shut down a system because they use rc scripts to kill running processes and shut down the system with minimal data loss. The* `halt` *and* `reboot` *commands do not run the rc scripts properly and are not the preferred method for shutting down the system.*

## How to Stop the System for Recovery Purposes

Occasionally the system might not respond to the init commands specified earlier. A system that doesn't respond to anything is called a "crashed" or "hung" system. After trying the above commands with no response, you can press Stop-A or L1-A to get back to the boot

PROM (the specific stop-key sequence depends on your keyboard type). On terminals, press the Break key.

1.  Use the abort key sequence for your system (Stop-A or L1-A).

    The monitor displays the ok PROM prompt.

2.  Type the sync command to synchronize the disks.

    ```
    ok sync
    ```

3.  When you see the syncing file systems message, press the abort key sequence for your system again.

4.  Type the appropriate boot command to start the boot process.

    ```
    ok boot
    ```

5.  Type the following to  verify the system is booted to the specified run level.

    ```
    # who -r
    ```

6.  The system responds with

    ```
    .        run-level 3  Jun  9 09:19    3      0  S
    ```

## Turning Off Power

Only after shutting down the file systems can you turn off the power on the hardware. Turn off power to all devices after the system is shut down. If necessary, also unplug the power cables. When power can be restored, use the following steps to turn on the system and devices:

1.  Plug in the power cables.

2.  Turn on the monitor.

3.  Turn on disk drives, tape drives, and printers.

4.  Turn on the CPU.

## System Failures

This chapter reviewed the Solaris boot-up and shutdown procedures. In the upcoming chapters, you'll learn more about the Solaris operating system and—just as important—the computer hardware. Thorough knowledge of these two system components is essential before you can adequately troubleshoot system problems.

# CHAPTER

# 2

# Installing the Solaris 2.x Software

The following are the test objectives for this chapter:

- Requirements for installing the Solaris 2.x software

- Preparation for the installation

- Disk storage systems

- Device drivers

- Software configurations, clusters, and packages

- Methods of installing the Solaris 2.x software

The installation process consists of three phases: system configuration, system installation, and post-installation tasks, such as setting up printers, users, and networking. This chapter describes the various system configurations and the installation of the Solaris operating system. Later chapters cover post-installation topics.

The first step in the installation is to determine whether your system type is supported under Solaris 2.6. Second, you'll need to decide on the system configuration you want to install and whether you have enough disk space to support that configuration.

In preparation for installing Solaris 2.6 on a system, use Table 2–1 to check if your system type is supported. Also, make sure you have enough disk space for Solaris and all of the packages you plan to install. The section on software configuration clusters will help you estimate the amount of disk space required to hold the Solaris operating system.

To determine your system type, use the uname -m command. The system will respond with the platform group and the platform name for your system. Compare the system response to the platform group column in Table 2–1. For example, to check for Sun platforms that support the Solaris 2.6 environment, use the command uname -m. The system returns sun4m as the platform name.

### Table 2–1    Sun Platforms that Support the Solaris 2.6 Environment

| System | Platform Name | Platform Group |
|---|---|---|
| x86 based | i86pc | i86pc |
| SPARCstation 1 | SUNW, Sun_4_60 | sun4c |
| SPARCstation 1+ | SUNW, Sun_4_65 | sun4c |
| SPARCstation SLC | SUNW, Sun_4_20 | sun4c |
| SPARCstation ELC | SUNW, Sun_4_25 | sun4c |
| SPARCstation IPC | SUNW, Sun_4_40 | sun4c |
| SPARCstation IPX | SUNW, Sun_4_50 | sun4c |
| SPARCstation 2 | SUNW, Sun_4_75 | sun4c |
| SPARCserver 1000 | SUNW, SPARCserver-1000 | sun4d |
| SPARCcenter 2000 | SUNW, SPARCcenter-2000 | sun4d |
| SPARCstation 5 | SUNW, SPARCstation-5 | sun4m |

*continues*

**Table 2–1    Sun Platforms that Support the Solaris 2.6 Environment (continued)**

| System | Platform Name | Platform Group |
| --- | --- | --- |
| SPARCstation 10 | SUNW, SPARCstation-10 | sun4m |
| SPARCstation 10SX | SUNW, SPARCstation-10SX | sun4m |
| SPARCstation 20 | SUNW, SPARCstation-20 | sun4m |
| SPARCstation LX | SUNW, SPARCstation-LX | sun4m |
| SPARCstation LX+ | SUNW, SPARCstation-LX+ | sun4m |
| SPARCclassic | SUNW, SPARCclassic | sun4m |
| SPARCclassic X | SUNW, SPARCclassic-X | sun4m |
| SPARCstation Voyager | SUNW, S240 | sun4m |
| SPARCstation 4 | SUNW, SPARCstation-4 | sun4m |
| Ultra 1 systems | SUNW, Ultra-1 | sun4u |
| Ultra Enterprise 1 systems | SUNW, Ultra-1 | sun4u |
| Ultra 30 | SUNW, Ultra-30 | sun4u |
| Ultra 2 systems | SUNW, Ultra-2 | sun4u |
| Ultra Enterprise 2 systems | SUNW, Ultra-2 | sun4u |
| Ultra Enterprise 150 | SUNW, Ultra-1 | sun4u |
| Ultra 450 | SUNW, Ultra-4 | sun4u |
| Ultra Enterprise 450 | SUNW, Ultra-4 | sun4u |
| Ultra Enterprise 3000, 4000, 5000, 6000, 10000 | SUNW, Ultra-Enterprise | sun4u |

Check partition C by using the format command to determine if the size of your disk drive is large enough to load Solaris. As you might recall, partition C represents the entire disk. The format command is covered in detail in Chapter 3, "Introduction to File Systems."

## Minimum System Requirements

The computer must meet the following requirements before you can install Solaris 2.6:

- The system must have a minimum of 16MB of RAM.

- The media is distributed on CD-ROM only, so a CD-ROM is required either locally or on the network.

- The system must have at least 300MB of available disk space; 1GB is recommended.

- The programmable read-only memory (PROM) must be level 1.1 or later.

# System Configurations

Before installing the OS, you'll need to determine the system configuration to be installed. System configurations, or types, are defined by the way they access the root (/), the /usr file systems, and the swap area. The five system configurations are server, standalone, diskless client, dataless client, and AutoClient.

## Server

A server system has the following file systems installed locally:

- The root (/) and /usr file systems, plus swap space

- The /export, /export/swap, and /export/home file systems, which support client systems and provide home directories for users

- The /opt directory or file system for storing application software

Servers can also contain the following software to support other systems:

- OS services for diskless clients and AutoClient systems

- Solaris CD image and boot software for networked systems to perform remote installations

- JumpStart directory for networked systems to perform custom JumpStart installations

## Standalone

On a standalone system, the OS is loaded on a local disk and the system is set to run independent of other systems for portions of the OS. It might be networked to other standalone systems. A networked standalone system can share information with other systems on the network, but it can function autonomously because it has its own hard disk with enough space to contain the root (/), /usr, and /home file systems and swap space. The standalone system has local access to operating system software, executables, virtual memory space, and user-created files.

## Diskless Client

A diskless client is a system with no local disk that is dependent on a server for all of its software and storage area. The OS is located on a server on the network. The diskless client boots from the server, remotely mounts its root (/), /usr, and /home file systems from a server, and gets all of its data from the server. Any files created are stored on the server.

A diskless client generates significant network traffic because of its need to continuously access the server for operating system functions and to access virtual memory space across the network. A diskless client cannot operate if it is detached from the network or if its server is not available.

## Dataless Client

In a dataless client system, the root file system and swap are on a local disk and the /usr and /home file systems are located on another system's disk somewhere on the network. If the dataless client is detached from the network, it cannot function because its executables (/usr) and user files (/home) are missing.

**N O T E .** *SunSoft has begun plans to remove support for dataless clients; therefore, AutoClient systems are recommended over dataless clients.*

## Solstice AutoClient

An AutoClient system is nearly identical to a diskless client. It has the following characteristics:

- Requires a 100MB or larger local disk for swapping. Its root (/) file system and the /usr file system are on a server somewhere on the network.

- Can be set up so it can continue to access its cached (/) root and /usr file system when the server is unavailable.

- Relies on servers to provide other file systems and software applications.

- Contains no permanent data, making it a field-replaceable unit (FRU).

An AutoClient system has a local disk. It caches (locally stores copies of data as it is referenced) all of its needed system software from a server. AutoClient systems use Solaris diskless and cache file system (CacheFS) technologies. CacheFS is a general-purpose file-system caching mechanism that improves performance and scalability by reducing server and network load. An AutoClient system uses its local disk for swap space and to cache its individual root (/) file system and the /usr file system from a server's file systems. With the AutoClient configuration, administration is streamlined because the system administrator can maintain many AutoClient systems from a central location. Changes do not have to be made on individual systems.

Table 2–2 gives a brief overview of each system configuration. It outlines which file systems are local and which file systems are accessed over the network.

### Table 2–2   System Configurations

| System Type | Local File Systems | Local Swap | Remote File Systems |
| --- | --- | --- | --- |
| Server | root (/), /usr, /home, /opt/export, /export/home | Yes | Optional |
| Standalone | root (/), /usr, /export/home | Yes | Optional |
| Dataless Client | root (/) | Yes | /usr, /home |
| Diskless Client | None | No | root (/), swap, /usr, /home |
| AutoClient System | cached root (/), cached /usr | Yes | root (/), /usr, /home |

## Performance of Clients Relative to a Standalone System

A system administrator decides which system configuration to use, based on available hardware, and how much to streamline the administration of the network. For example, does the system have a large enough local disk to hold all of the operating system? Also, would the features of the AutoClient, diskless, or dataless system configurations facilitate the administration of remote systems? For the most part, AutoClient configurations are used to ease system administration in a large network of systems. Because the OS is downloaded from a server at bootup, maintaining the workstation's OS from a centralized location is easy. Diskless clients, on the other hand, are used when disk space on the workstation is limited.

Table 2–3 compares the various system configurations for performance and ease of administration.

### Table 2–3   System Configuration Performance

| System Type | Centralized Admin | Performance | System Disk Usage | Network Use |
| --- | --- | --- | --- | --- |
| AutoClient | Better | Similar | Better | Similar |
| Diskless client | Better | Worse | Better | Worse |
| Dataless client | Similar | Worse | Better | Worse |

# Disk Storage Systems

Before you begin to install a system, you need to spend some time thinking about how you want data stored on your system's disks. With one disk, the decision is easy. When multiple disks are installed, you must decide which disks to use for the OS, the swap area, and the user data. Solaris breaks up disks into pieces, called partitions or slices. A Solaris disk can be divided into one to seven partitions.

Why would you want to divide the disk into multiple partitions? Some administrators don't; they use the entire disk with no partitions. The following list describes why you might want to consider partitioning disks:

- Partitions allow finer control over such tasks as creating backups. UNIX commands, such as ufsdump, work on entire file systems. For backups, you might want to separate data and swap space from the application software so only data gets backed up with a ufsdump. Partitions containing system software and swap can be backed up much less frequently.

- If one file system gets corrupted, the others remain intact. If you need to perform a recovery operation, restoring a smaller file system can be done more quickly. Also, when data is separated from system software, you can modify file systems without shutting down the system or reloading operating system software.

- Partitions enable you to control the amount of disk storage allocated to an activity or type of use.

- If file systems are mounted remotely from other systems, you can share only the data that needs to be accessed, not the entire system disk.

The installation process gives you the option of creating partitions. Start with the default partition scheme supplied through the installation program. This scheme sets up the required partitions and provides you with the sizes required, based on the software you select to install. The following is a typical partitioning scheme for a system with a single disk drive:

- root (/) and /usr—Solaris normally creates two partitions for itself, called root (/) and /usr. The installation program determines how much space you need. Most of the files in these two partitions are static. Information in these file systems will not increase in size unless you add additional software packages later. If you plan to add third-party software after the installation of Solaris, make sure you increase this partition to accommodate the additional files you plan to load. If the root (/) file system fills up, the system will not operate properly.

- swap—This area on the disk doesn't have any files in it. In UNIX you're allowed to have more programs than will fit into memory. The pieces that aren't currently needed in memory are transferred into swap to free up physical memory for other active processes. Swapping into a dedicated partition is a good idea for two reasons. Swap partitions are isolated so they don't get put on tape with the daily backups, and a swap partition can be laid out on a disk in an area to optimize performance.

- home—On a single disk system, everything not in root, /usr, or swap should go into a separate partition. Third-party applications are a good example. This is also where you would put user-created files.

- /var (optional)—This area is used by Solaris for system log files, sprint spoolers, and email. The name /var is short for variable because this file system contains system files that are not static but variable in size. One day the print spooler directory might be empty; another day it might contain several 1MB files. This separate file system is created to keep the root and /usr directories from filling up with these files. If the /var file system does not exist, make sure you make root (/) larger.

- /opt (optional)—By default, the Solaris installation program loads optional software packages here. If this file system does not exist, install puts the optional software in the root file system. If the /opt file system does not exist, make sure you make root (/) larger.

File systems provide a way to segregate data, but when a file system runs out of space, you can't increase it or "borrow" from a file system that has some unused space. Therefore, the best plan is to create a minimal number of file systems with adequate space for expansion. See Chapter 3, "Introduction to File Systems," for additional information on planning and creating file systems.

## Basic Considerations for Planning Partition Sizes

Planning disk and partition space depends on many factors: the number of users, application requirements, and the number and size of files and databases. What follows are some basic considerations for determining your disk space requirements:

- Allocate additional disk space for each language selected (for example, Chinese, Japanese, Korean).

- If you need printing or mail support, create a partition for the /var file system and allocate additional disk space. You need to estimate the number and size of email messages and print files to size this partition properly.

- Allocate additional disk space on a server that is going to provide home file systems for users. Again, the number of users and the size of their files will dictate the size of this file system. By default, home directories are usually located in the /export file system.

- Allocate additional disk space on an OS server for diskless clients or Solstice AutoClient systems.

- Make sure you allocate enough swap space. Factors that dictate the amount of swap space are number of users and application requirements. Consult with your application vendor for swap-space requirements. Usually vendors give you a formula for determining the amount of swap space you need for each application.

■ Determine the software packages you will be installing and calculate the total amount of disk space required. When planning disk space, remember the Solaris Interactive Installation program enables you to add or remove individual software packages from the software cluster you select.

■ Create a minimum number of file systems. By default, the Solaris Interactive Installation program creates only root (/), /usr, and swap, although /export is also created when space is allocated for OS services. Creating a minimum number of file systems helps with future upgrades and file system expansion, because separate file systems are limited by their slice boundaries. Be generous on the size of your file systems, especially root (/) and /usr. These file systems cannot be increased without completely reloading the operating system.

■ Calculate additional disk space for co-packaged or third-party software.

## Partition Arrangements on Multiple Disks

Although a single large disk can hold all partitions and their corresponding file systems, two or more disks are often used to hold a system's partitions and file systems.

**NOTE.** *You cannot split a partition between two or more disks.*

For example, a single disk might hold the root (/) file system, a swap area, and the /usr file system, and a second disk might be used for the /export/home file system and other file systems containing user data. In a multiple disk arrangement, the disk containing the root (/), /usr file systems, and swap space is referred to as the system disk. Disks other than the system disk are called secondary disks or non-system disks.

Locating a system's file systems on multiple disks enables you to modify file systems and partitions on the secondary disks without shutting down the system or reloading the operating system software. Also, multiple disks enable you to distribute the workload as evenly as possible among different I/O systems and disk drives. They also enable you to distribute /home and swap directories evenly across disks.

Having more than one disk increases input/output (I/O) volume. By distributing the I/O load across multiple disks, you can avoid I/O bottlenecks.

## Device Drivers

A computer typically uses a wide range of peripheral and mass-storage devices, such as a SCSI disk drive, a keyboard, a mouse, and some kind of magnetic backup medium. Other commonly used devices include CD-ROM drives, printers, and plotters. Solaris communicates with peripheral devices through files called device files. Before Solaris can communicate with a device, the device must have a device driver, a low-level program that enables the kernel to communicate with a specific piece of hardware. The driver serves as the operating system's "interpreter" for that piece of hardware.

When a system is booted for the first time, the kernel creates a device hierarchy to represent all devices connected to the system. Devices are described in three ways in the Solaris environment, using three distinct naming conventions: the physical device name, the instance name, and the logical device name.

System administrators need to understand the device names when using commands to manage disks, file systems, and other devices.

## Physical Device Name

A physical device name represents the full device pathname of the device. Physical device files are found in the /devices directory and have the following naming convention:

```
/devices/sbus@1,f8000000/esp@0,40000/sd@3,0:a
```

You can display physical device names by using one of the following commands:

- prtconf—Displays system configuration information, including total amount of memory and the device configuration as described by the system's hierarchy. The output displayed by this command depends on the type of system.

- sysdef—Displays device configuration information, including system hardware, pseudo devices, loadable modules, and selected kernel parameters.

- dmesg—Displays system diagnostic messages and a list of devices attached to the system since the last reboot.

**TIP.** *Use the output of the* prtconf *and* sysdef *commands to identify which disk, tape, and CD-ROM devices are connected to the system. The output of these commands displays the* driver not attached *messages next to the device instances. Because these devices are always being monitored by some system process, the* driver not attached *message is usually a good indication that there is no device at that device instance.*

If you need to remind yourself of the meanings of the fields of a physical device name, refer to Chapter 1, "Booting the Workstation," for a detailed discussion.

## Instance Name

The instance name represents the kernel's abbreviated name for every possible device on the system. For example, sd0 and sd1 represent the instance names of two SCSI disk devices. Instance names are mapped in the /etc/path_to_inst file and are displayed by using the commands dmesg, sysdef, and prtconf.

## Logical Device Name: Test Item

Logical device names are used with most of the Solaris file system commands to refer to devices. Logical device files in the /dev directory are symbolically linked to physical device files in the /devices directory. Logical device names are used to access disk devices in the following circumstances:

- Adding a new disk to the system

- Moving a disk from one system to another

- Accessing (or mounting) a file system residing on a local disk

- Backing up a local file system

- Repairing a file system

Logical devices are organized in subdirectories under the /dev directory by their device types:

| | |
|---|---|
| /dev/dsk | Block interface to disk devices |
| /dev/rdsk | Raw or character interface |
| /dev/rmt | Tape devices |
| /dev/term | Serial line devices |
| /dev/cua | Dial-out modems |
| /dev/pts | Pseudo terminals |
| /dev/fbs | Frame buffers |
| /dev/sad | STREAMS administrative driver |

Logical device files have major and minor numbers that indicate device drivers, hardware addresses, and other characteristics. Furthermore, a device filename must follow a specific naming convention. A logical device name for a disk drive has the following format:

`/dev/[r]dsk/cxtxdxsx`

where

| | |
|---|---|
| cx | Refers to the controller number |
| tx | Refers to the SCSI bus target number |
| dx | Refers to the disk number (always 0 except on storage arrays) |
| sx | Refers to the slice or partition number |

Here are a few examples of logical device filenames for disk drives:

- `/dev/dsk/c0t3d0s0`—Refers to slice 0 on a SCSI disk drive with a target ID of 3 on SCSI controller 0. Buffered device.

- `/dev/rdsk/c0t3d0s0`—Refers to slice 0 on a SCSI disk drive with a target ID of 3 on SCSI controller 0. Raw device.

## Block and Character Device Files

Some devices, such as disk drives, have an entry under both the /dev/dsk directory and the /dev/rdsk directory. The /dsk directory refers to the block or buffered device file, and the /rdsk directory refers to the character or raw device file. The "r" in rdsk stands for "raw." Disk and file administration commands require the use of either a raw device interface or a block device interface. The device file used specifies whether I/O is to be handled in block or character mode, commonly referred to as I/O type.

Block device files transfer data, using system buffers to speed up I/O transfer. Storage devices, such as tape drives, disk drives, and CD-ROMs, use block device files. Under most circumstances, Solaris accesses the disk via the block device. Data is buffered or cached in memory until the buffer is full and then it is written to disk.

Character device interfaces transfer only small amounts of data, one character at a time. With a character device file, data is written directly to the disk, bypassing system I/O buffers. Buffering is controlled by the application program. Terminals, printers, plotters, and storage devices use character I/O.

Different commands require different device file interfaces. When a command requires the character device interface, specify the /dev/rdsk subdirectory. When a command requires the block device interface, specify the /dev/dsk subdirectory. When you're not sure whether a command requires the use of /dev/dsk or /dev/rdsk, check the online manual page for that command.

## Software Terminology

The Solaris operating system comes on a CD-ROM and is bundled in packages. Packages are grouped into clusters. The following sections describe the Solaris bundling scheme.

### Software Package

A software package is a group of files and directories that describe a software application, such as manual pages and line printer support. Solaris 2.6 contains approximately 80 software packages that total approximately 300MB of disk space.

A Solaris software package is a standard way to deliver bundled and unbundled software. Packages are administered by using the package administration commands and are generally identified by a SUNWxxx naming convention.

## Software Clusters

Software packages are grouped into software clusters, which are logical collections of software packages. For example, the online manual pages cluster contains one package. Some clusters contain multiple packages.

## Software Configuration Clusters

Clusters are grouped together into four configuration clusters to make the software installation process easier. During the installation process, you will be asked to install one of the four configuration clusters. These four configuration clusters are end-user support, developer system support, entire distribution, and entire distribution plus OEM system support.

- End-User System Support, 281MB.

  - Windowing software

  - Common Desktop Environment (CDE)

  - OpenWindows

  - Motif runtime libraries

  - Energy-saving software (Power Management)

  - Basic networking support (telnet, rlogin, ftp)

  - Basic language and partial locale support

  - Removable media support (Volume Management)

  - Standard UNIX utilities (sed, awk, nroff, troff, grep, pipes, ld, ldd, spell)

  - Basic printer support (lp, lpstat, lpr)

  - System support for audio playback and recording

  - Java VM (capability to run Java applications)

  - Patch utilities

  - Additional hardware support (PCMCIA)

- Developer System Support, 537MB. Contains the end-user software plus the following:

  - Development support

  - CDE/Motif Developer software, runtimes, and manuals

- Java VM (capability to develop Java applications)

- OS demo code

- Power Management GUI tools

- Online manual pages

- Solaris 1.x compatibility tools

- Kernel probing support (TNF)

- Extended language and partial locale support

- Programming tools and libraries

- Extended terminal support (`terminfo`)

- Extended X support (XGL, XIL, XCU4)

- Graphics header (for graphics application development)

- ISO 8859 required fonts

- Entire distribution, 608MB. Contains the end-user and developer software plus the following:

    - AnswerBook2 (online documentation)

    - Full audio tools and demos

    - Enhanced security

    - UUCP networking (UNIX-to-UNIX copy)

    - DHCP server (Dynamic Host Configuration Protocol)

    - Additional language and partial locale support (Eastern European)

    - Additional hardware support (Leo, SX/CG14, SunVideo, SunButtons, SunDials, TCX)

    - Enhanced networking support (NIS server, point-to-point protocol)

    - Solstice Launcher

    - System recovery tools

    - Additional X features (complete fonts, PEX)

    - ISO 8559 optional fonts

- Entire distribution plus OEM system support, 616MB. Contains the end-user, developer, and entire distribution software plus extended hardware support, which includes the following:

  - Voyager drivers and modules

  - sun4u (X server modules, VIS/XIL)

  - SunFastEthernet/FastWide SCSI adapter drivers

  - PCI drivers

  - M64 graphics accelerator

  - A-10 (PFU) and Fujitsu device drivers and system support

## Methods for Installing Solaris Software

You can use one of four methods to install the Solaris software: Interactive, Custom JumpStart, Web Start, and installation over the network.

### Interactive

The Solaris Interactive Installation program guides you step by step in installing the Solaris software. The Solaris Interactive Installation program does not enable you to install all of the software (Solaris software and co-packaged software) in your product box at once; it only installs the SunOS software. After you install the Solaris software, you have to install the other co-packaged software by using the co-packaged installation programs.

### Custom JumpStart

This method, formerly called Auto-Install, enables you to automatically—and identically—install many systems with the same configuration without having to configure each of them individually. JumpStart requires up-front setup of configuration files before the systems can be installed, but it's the most cost-effective way to automatically install Solaris software for a large installation.

All new SPARC-based systems have the JumpStart software (a pre-installed boot image) pre-installed on its boot disk. JumpStart enables you to install the Solaris software on a new SPARC-based system just by inserting the Solaris CD into the system and powering on the system. You can install the JumpStart software on existing systems by using the `re-preinstall` command.

**NOTE.** *On a new system shipped by Sun, the install software is specified by a default profile that is based on the system's model and the size of its disks; you don't have a choice of the software that gets installed. Make sure this JumpStart configuration is suited to your environment. The system loads the end-user distribution group and sets up minimal swap space. Partitions and their sizes are set up by using default parameters that might not be suitable for the applications you plan to install.*

When might you want to use JumpStart? For example, suppose you need to install the Solaris software on 50 systems. Of these 50 systems to be installed, 25 are in engineering as standalone systems with the entire distribution software group and 25 are in the IS group with the developer distribution software group. JumpStart enables you to set up a configuration file for each department and install the OS identically on all the systems. The process facilitates the install by automating it and ensures consistency between systems.

## Web Start

Solaris Web Start is Sun's browser-based "virtual assistant" for installing software. Using Solaris Web Start and Sun's Web browser, you select either a default installation or a customize option to install only the software you want, including the Solaris software group, Solstice utilities, and other co-packaged software. From Sun's Web browser, an installation profile is created that is used by Solaris JumpStart to install the Solaris software and the other selected software products with minimal intervention. Web Start simplifies the creation of the JumpStart configuration file.

## Installing Over the Network

Because the Solaris software is distributed on a CD, a system has to have access to a CD-ROM drive to install it. However, if you don't have a local CD-ROM, you can set up the system to install from a remote CD or CD image on a remote disk drive. The remote Solaris CD image must be provided by an install server that has either the Solaris CD copied to its hard disk or the Solaris CD mounted from its CD-ROM drive. Installing the OS across the network is handy when a local CD-ROM is not available.

## The Solaris Installation Process

Solaris is installed by using the Solaris Install tool—a GUI that is friendly and easy to use. The installation brings up various menus and asks for your input. The tool enables you to go back to previous screens if you make a mistake, and it doesn't actually do anything to your system until the install program gets to the end and tells you it is about to start the loading process. During the installation, help is always available via the Help button.

**CAUTION!** *The following procedure reinstalls your operating system. This means it destroys all data on the target file systems.*

If you're upgrading or installing Solaris on a new system, shut down the system. Then use the following steps to complete the installation:

1. Become root.

2. Issue the shutdown command. This the command brings the system to a single-user state by halting the window system and leaving you with a single root prompt on the console. It takes about a minute.

3. Issue the halt command. This command puts you into the PROM. You'll know you're in the PROM when you receive either an ok or a > prompt.

4. Put the Solaris installation CD into the CD player and boot from the CD. The correct way to do this depends on your system type. If the screen displays the > prompt instead of the ok prompt, type n and press Enter.

5. At the ok prompt, type **boot cdrom**.

**N O T E .** *On Sun systems with older EEPROMs, the process of booting from CD is different. For your particular system, boot to the CD-ROM as follows:*

*For a Sun 4/1nn, 4/2nn, 4/3nn, or 4/4nn system, type* b sd(0,30,1).

*For a SPARCstation 1(4/60), 1+(4/65), SLC(4/20), or IPC(4/40) system, type* boot sd(0,6,2).

The system boots from the CD-ROM. The process is slow, but the flashing light on the CD player shows activity. Eventually the system starts the GUI and presents you with the Solaris Installation program. Follow the instructions on the screen to install the software on the system. Have the following information available; the installation tool will ask for it:

- *Hostname*—The name for the system. Hostnames should be short, easy to spell, lowercase, and have no more than 64 characters. If the system is on a network, the hostname should be unique.

- *IP address*—This information must come from your site IP coordinator. 192.9.200 is one example of an IP address. IP addresses must be unique for every system on your network. For a large site, or a site that has a presence on the Internet, you should apply for a unique IP address from the NIC to ensure that no other network shares your address.

- *NIS or NIS+*—You'll need to specify which your system will be using.

When the installation program is finished gathering information, it asks you if it's okay to begin the installation. When the installation is complete, you are asked to supply a root password. Make sure you complete this step and supply a secure password.

This completes the installation of the Solaris operating system. Other chapters in this book will discuss post-installation procedures such as setting up print queues, adding users, and setting up a backup procedure.

# 3

# Introduction to
# File Systems

The following are the test objectives for
this chapter:

- Defining and understanding the
  Solaris 2.x file system structure,
  parameters, and utilities

- Identifying utilities used to create,
  check, mount, and display file
  systems

- Comparing the Logical Volume
  Manager to standard Solaris file
  systems

- Understanding disk geometry and
  disk slicing

- Managing and controlling disk-
  space use

- Defining Volume Manager

**A**ll disk-based computer systems have a file system. In UNIX, file systems have two basic components: files and directories. A file is the actual information as it is stored on the disk, and a directory is a listing of the filenames. In addition to keeping track of filenames, the file system must also keep track of files' access dates and of file ownership. Managing the UNIX file systems is one of the system administrator's most important tasks. Administration of the file system involves:

- Ensuring users have access to data. This means that systems are up and operational, file permissions are set up properly, and data is accessible.

- Protecting file systems against file corruption and hardware failures. This is accomplished by checking the file system regularly and maintaining proper system backups.

- Securing file systems against unauthorized access. Only authorized users should have access to them. The data must be protected from intruders.

- Providing users with adequate space for their files.

- Keeping the file system file clean. In other words, data in the file system must be relevant and not wasteful of disk space. Procedures are needed to make sure users follow proper naming conventions and data is stored in an organized manner.

This chapter discusses the basic structures that make up the file system, the utility that creates file systems, and how Solaris accesses the file system.

## A File System Defined

A file system is a structure of directories used to organize and store files on disk. It is a collection of files and directories stored on disk in a standard UNIX file system format. You'll see the term "file system" used in several ways. Usually *file system* describes a particular type of file system (disk-based, network-based, or pseudo file system). It might also describe the entire file tree from the root directory downward. In another context, the term "file system" might be used to describe the structure of a disk slice, described later in this chapter.

The Solaris system software uses the virtual file system (VFS) architecture, which provides a standard interface for different file system types. The VFS architecture enables the kernel to handle basic operations, such as reading, writing, and listing files, without requiring the user or program to know about the underlying file system type. Furthermore, Solaris provides file-system administrative commands that enable you to maintain file systems.

# Defining a Disk's Geometry

Before creating a file system on a disk, you need to understand the basic geometry of a disk drive. Disks come in many shapes and sizes. The number of heads, tracks, and sectors and the disk capacity vary from one model to another.

A *hard disk* consists of several separate disks mounted on a common spindle. Data stored on each disk surface is written and read by *disk heads*. The circular path a disk head traces over a spinning disk is called a *track*.

Each track is made up of a number of sectors laid end to end. A *sector* consists of a header, a trailer, and 512 bytes of data. The header and trailer contain error-checking information to help ensure the accuracy of the data. Taken together, the set of tracks traced across all of the individual disk surfaces for a single position of the heads is called a *cylinder*.

## Disk Controller

Associated with every disk is a *controller*, an intelligent device responsible for organizing data on the disk. Some disk controllers are located on a separate circuit board and some are embedded in the disk drive.

## Defect List

Disks might contain areas where data cannot be written and retrieved reliably. These areas are called *defects*. The controller uses the error-checking information in each disk block's trailer to determine whether a defect is present in that block. When a block is found to be defective, the controller can be instructed to add it to a defect list and avoid using that block in the future. The last two cylinders are set aside for diagnostic use and for storing the disk defect list.

## Disk Labels

A special area of every disk is set aside for storing information about the disk's controller, geometry, and slices. This information is called the disk's label or Volume Table of Contents (VTOC). To *label a disk* means to write slice information onto the disk. You usually label a disk after defining its slices. If you fail to label a disk after creating slices, the slices will be unavailable because the operating system has no way of "knowing" about the slices.

## Partition Table

An important part of the disk label is the partition table that identifies a disk's slices, the slice boundaries (in cylinders), and the total size of the slices. A disk's partition table can be displayed by using the `format` utility.

# Solaris File System Types

Solaris file systems can be put into three categories: disk-based, network-based, and pseudo.

## Disk-Based File Systems

Disk-based file systems reside on the system's local disk. The four types of disk file systems are

- *UFS*—The UNIX file system, which is based on the BSD FAT Fast file system (the traditional UNIX file system). The UFS file system is the default disk-based file system used in Solaris.

- *HSFS*—The High Sierra and ISO 9660 file system. The HSFS file system is used on CD-ROMs and is a read-only file system.

- *PCFS*—The PC file system, which allows read/write access to data and programs on DOS-formatted disks written for DOS-based personal computers.

- *S5*—The System V file system, which is seldom used. It is supported for backward compatibility purposes only.

## Network-Based File Systems

Network-based file systems are file systems accessed over the network. Typically, network-based file systems reside on one system and are accessed by other systems across the network.

The Network File System (NFS) or remote file systems are systems made available from remote systems. NFS is the only available network-based file system.

## Pseudo File Systems

Pseudo file systems are virtual or memory-based file systems that provide access to special kernel information and facilities. Most pseudo file systems do not use file-system disk space, although a few exceptions exist. Cache File Systems, for example, use a file system to contain the cache. Some pseudo file systems, such as the temporary file system, might use the swap space on a physical disk.

- *SWAPFS*—A file system or one used by the kernel for swapping.

- *PROCFS*—The Process File System resides in memory. It contains a list of active processes, by process number, in the /proc directory. Information in the /proc directory is used by commands such as ps. Debuggers and other development tools can also access the address space of the processes by using file system calls.

- *LOFS*—The Loopback File System enables you to create a new virtual file system. You can access files by using an alternative path name. The entire file system hierarchy looks as though it is duplicated under /tmp/newroot, including any file systems mounted from NFS servers. All files are accessible with either a pathname starting from / or a pathname starting from /tmp/newroot.

- *CacheFS*—The Cache File System enables you to use disk drives on local workstations to store frequently used data from a remote file system or CD-ROM. The data stored on the local disk is the cache.

- *TMPFS*—The temporary file system uses local memory for file system reads and writes. Because TMPFS uses physical memory and not the disk, access to files in a TMPFS file system is typically much faster than to files in a UFS file system. Files in the temporary file system are not permanent; they are deleted when the file system is unmounted and when the system is shut down or rebooted. TMPFS is the default file system type for the /tmp directory in the SunOS system software. You can copy or move files into or out of the /tmp directory just as you would in a UFS /tmp file system. The TMPFS file system uses swap space as a temporary backing store as long as adequate swap space is present.

## Disk Slices

Disks are divided into regions called disk slices or disk partitions. This book attempts to use the term slice whenever possible; however, certain interfaces, such as the `format` utility, refer to slices as partitions. A *slice* is composed of a single range of contiguous blocks. It is a physical subset of the disk (except for slice 2, which represents the entire disk). A UNIX file system is built within these disk slices. The boundaries of a disk slice are defined when a disk is formatted by using the Solaris `format` utility. Each disk slice appears to the operating system (and to the system administrator) as though it is a separate disk drive.

**N O T E .** *Solaris device names use the term "slice" (and the letter "s" in the device name) to refer to the slice number. Slices were called "partitions" in SunOS 4.x.*

A physical disk consists of a stack of circular platters. Data is stored on these platters in a cylindrical pattern. Cylinders can be grouped and isolated from one another. A group of cylinders is referred to as a slice. A slice is defined with start and end points, defined from the center of the stack of platters, which is called the spindle. To define a slice, the administrator provides a starting cylinder and an ending cylinder. A disk can have up to eight slices, named 0–7. See Chapter 2, "Installing the Solaris 2.x Software," for a discussion of disk-storage systems and sizing partitions.

When setting up slices, remember these rules:

- Each disk slice holds only one file system.

- No file system can span multiple slices.

- After a file system is created, its size cannot be increased or decreased without repartitioning the entire disk and restoring all data from a backup.

- Slices cannot span multiple disks; however, multiple swap slices on separate disks are allowed.

Also follow these guidelines when planning the layout of file systems:

- Distribute the workload as evenly as possible among different I/O systems and disk drives. Distribute /home and swap directories evenly across disks.

- Keep projects or groups within the same file system.

- Use as few file systems per disk as possible. On the system (or boot) disk, you usually have three slices: /, /usr, and a swap area. On other disks, create one or—at most—two slices. Fewer, roomier slices cause less file fragmentation than many small, overcrowded slices. Higher-capacity tape drives and the capability of ufsdump to handle multiple volumes facilitate backing up larger file systems.

- It is not important for most sites to be concerned about keeping similar types of user files in the same file system.

- Infrequently, you might have some users who consistently create very small or very large files. You might consider creating a separate file system with more inodes for users who consistently create very small files. See the sections on inodes and changing the number of bytes per inode later in this chapter.

## Displaying Disk Configuration Information

As described earlier, disk configuration information is stored in the disk label. If you know the disk and slice number, you can display information for a disk by using the prtvtoc (print volume table of contents) command. You can specify the volume by specifying any non–zero-size slice defined on the disk (for example, /dev/rdsk/c0t3d0s2 for all of disk 3 or /dev/rdsk/c0t3d0s5 for the sixth slice of disk 3). If you know the target number of the disk but do not know how it is divided into slices, you can show information for the entire disk by specifying either slice 2 or slice 0. The following steps show how you can examine information stored on a disk's label by using the prtvtoc command.

1. Become superuser.

2. Type **prtvtoc** **/dev/rdsk/cntndnsn** and press Enter.

Information for the disk and slice you specify is displayed. In the following steps, information is displayed for all of disk 3:

1. Become superuser.

2. Type **prtvtoc /dev/rdsk/c0t3d0s2** and press Enter.

   The system responds with:

```
* /dev/rdsk/c0t3d0s2 (volume "") partition map
*
* Dimensions:
*     512 bytes/sector
*      36 sectors/track
*       9 tracks/cylinder
*     324 sectors/cylinder
*    1272 cylinders
*    1254 accessible cylinders
*
* Flags:
*    1: unmountable
*   10: read-only
*
*                        First    Sector   Last
* Partition Tag   Flags  Sector   Count    Sector   Mount Directory
     2      5      01     0        406296   406295
     6      4      00     0        242352   242351
     7      0      00     242352   163944   406295   /files7
```

The prtvtoc command shows the number of cylinders and heads, as well as how the disk's slices are arranged.

## Using the *format* Utility to Create Slices

Before you can create a file system on a disk, the disk must be formatted and you must divide it into slices by using the Solaris format utility. Formatting involves two separate processes:

- *Formatting*—Writing format information to the disk

- *Surface analysis*—Compiling an up-to-date list of disk defects

When a disk is formatted, header and trailer information is superimposed on the disk. When the format utility runs a surface analysis, the controller scans the disk for defects. It needs to be noted that defects and formatting information reduce the total disk space available for data. This is why a new disk usually holds only 90–95% of its capacity after formatting. This percentage varies according to disk geometry and decreases as the disk ages and develops more defects.

The need for performing a surface analysis on a disk drive has dropped as more manufacturers ship their disk drives formatted and partitioned. You should not need to use the format utility when adding a disk drive to an existing system unless you think disk defects are causing problems or you want to change the partitioning scheme.

**C A U T I O N !** *Formatting and creating slices is a destructive process, so make sure user data is backed up before you start.*

The format utility searches your system for all attached disk drives and reports the following information about the disk drives it finds:

- Target location
- Disk geometry
- Whether the disk is formatted
- Whether the disk has mounted partitions

In addition, the format utility is used in disk repair operations to do the following:

- Retrieve disk labels
- Repair defective sectors
- Format and analyze disks
- Partition disks
- Label disks (write disk name and configuration information to the disk for future retrieval)

The Solaris installation program partitions and labels disk drives as part of installing the Solaris release. However, you might need to use the format utility when

- Displaying slice information
- Dividing a disk into slices
- Adding a disk drive to an existing system
- Formatting a disk drive
- Repairing a disk drive

The main reason a system administrator uses the format utility is to divide a disk into disk slices. The process of creating slices is as follows:

1. Become superuser.
2. Type format.

The system responds with

```
AVAILABLE DISK SELECTIONS:
0. c0t0d0 at scsibus0 slave 24
sd0: <SUN0207 cyl 1254 alt 2 hd 9 sec 36>
1. c0t3d0 at scsibus0 slave 0: test
sd3: <SUN0207 cyl 1254 alt 2 hd 9 sec 36>
```

3. Specify the disk (enter its number).

The system responds with

```
FORMAT MENU:
    disk - select a disk
    type - select (define) a disk type
    partition - select (define) a partition table
    current - describe the current disk
    format - format and analyze the disk
    repair - repair a defective sector
    label - write label to the disk
    analyze - surface analysis
    defect - defect list management
    backup - search for backup labels
    verify - read and display labels
    save - save new disk/partition definitions
    inquiry - show vendor, product and revision
    volname - set 8-character volume name
    quit
```

4. Type **partition** at the format prompt and the partition menu is displayed.

```
format> partition

PARTITION MENU:
    0 - change '0' partition
    1 - change '1' partition
    2 - change '2' partition
    3 - change '3' partition
    4 - change '4' partition
    5 - change '5' partition
    6 - change '6' partition
    7 - change '7' partition
    select - select a predefined table
    modify - modify a predefined partition table
    name - name the current table
    print - display the current table
    label - write partition map and label to the disk
    quit
```

5. Type **print** to display the current partition map.

The system responds with

```
partition> print
Volume: test
Current partition table (original sd3):
    Part     Tag         Flag    Cylinders      Size        Blocks
     0       root        wm      0 - 39         14.06MB     (40/0/0)
     1       swap        wu      40 - 199       56.25MB     (160/0/0)
     2       backup      wm      0 - 1150       404.65MB    (1151/0/0)
     3       unassigned  wm      0              0           (0/0/0)
     4       unassigned  wm      0              0           (0/0/0)
     5       -           wm      0              10.20MB     (29/0/0)
     6       usr         wm      200 - 228      121.29MB    (345/0/0)
     7       home        wm      574 - 1150     202.85MB    (577/0/0)
```

6. After partitioning the disk, it must be labeled by typing **label** at the partition prompt.

```
partition> label
```

7. After labeling the disk, type **quit** to exit the partition menu.

```
partition> quit
```

8. Type **quit** again to exit the format utility.

```
format> quit
```

## Logical Volumes

On a large server with many disk drives, standard methods of disk slicing are inadequate and inefficient. Limitations imposed by standard file systems include the inability to be larger than the size of the file system that holds them. Because file systems cannot span multiple disks, the size of the file system is limited to the size of the disk. Another problem with standard file systems is that they cannot be increased in size without destroying data on the file system. Sun has addressed these issues with two unbundled Sun packages: Solstice DiskSuite and Sun Enterprise Volume Manager. Both packages allow file systems to span multiple disks and provide for improved I/O and reliability compared to the standard Solaris file system. We refer to these types of file systems as logical volumes (LVMs). Both Sun packages are purchased separately and are not part of the standard Solaris operating system distribution. Typically, DiskSuite is used on Sun's multipacks and the Enterprise Volume Manager package is used on the SparcStorage arrays.

The following is an overview of the primary elements of a logical volume:

- Concatenation and striping

  Concatenations and stripes work much the way the UNIX cat(1) command program is used to concatenate two or more files to create one larger file. When partitions are concatenated, the addressing of the component blocks is done on the components sequentially. The file system can use the entire concatenation.

  Striping is similar to concatenation, except the addressing of the component blocks is interlaced on the slices rather than sequentially. Striping is used to gain performance. When data is striped across disks, multiple controllers can access data simultaneously.

- Mirroring (mirrors and submirrors)

  Mirroring replicates all writes to a single logical device (the mirror) and then to multiple devices (the submirrors), and distributes read operations. This provides redundancy of data in the event of a disk or hardware failure.

- UFS logging (journaled file system)

  UFS logging records UNIX file system (UFS) updates in a log (the logging device) before the updates are applied to the UNIX file system. With this technique, the risk of file system corruption due to a power failure or unsafe shutdown is greatly reduced.

- Hot spare pools

  A hot spare pool is a group of spare disk drives that automatically replace failed components.

- Disksets

  A diskset is an association of two hosts (servers) and a group of disk drives in which all of the drives are accessible by each host. If one host fails, the other takes over. This scenario is used where high availability is critical.

- RAID devices

  RAID is an acronym for "redundant arrays of inexpensive disks." Many disks are housed in a cabinet to provide large amounts of disk space.

- Ability to expand mounted file systems

  On a server requiring high availability, disk space can be added to a file system without shutting down the system or unmounting the file system.

Logical volumes can be made up of one or more component slices. You can configure the component slices of one disk or use slices from multiple disks. After you create the logical volumes, they are used like physical disk slices. Logical volumes provide increased capacity, higher availability, and better performance. To gain increased capacity, you create logical volumes that are concatenations, stripes, or RAID devices. Disk concatenations and

stripes can help performance and address capacity issues. Mirroring, UFS logging, and RAID devices provide higher availability. Logical volumes are transparent to the application software and to the hardware.

## Parts of a UFS File System

UFS is the default disk-based file system used in the Solaris system software. It provides the following features:

- *State flags*—Shows the state of the file system as clean, stable, active, or unknown. These flags eliminate unnecessary file system checks. If the file system is "clean" or "stable," fsck (file system check) is not run when the system boots.

- *Extended fundamental types (EFT)*—32-bit user ID (UID), group ID (GID), and device numbers.

- *Large file systems*—A UFS file system can be as large as 1 terabyte (1TB) and can have regular files up to 2 gigabytes (2GB). By default, the Solaris system software does not provide striping, which is required to make a logical slice large enough for a 1TB file system. Optional software packages, such as Solstice DiskSuite, provide this capability.

During the installation of the Solaris software, several UFS file systems are created on the system disk. These default file systems and their contents are described in Table 3–1.

**Table 3–1    Solaris Default File Systems**

| Slice | File System | Description |
|-------|-------------|-------------|
| 0 | root | Root (/) is the top of the hierarchical file tree. Root holds files and directories that make up the operating system. The root directory contains the directories and files critical for system operation, such as the kernel, the device drivers, and the programs used to boot the system. It also contains the mount point directories, in which local and remote file systems can be attached to the file tree. The root (/) file system is always in slice 0. |
| 1 | swap | Provides virtual memory or swap space. Swap space is used when running programs too large to fit in a computer's memory. The Solaris operating environment then "swaps" programs from memory to the disk and back, as needed. The swap slice is always located in slice 1 unless /var is set up as a file system. If /var is set up, /var uses slice 1 and swap is put on slice 4. The /var file system is for files and directories likely to change or grow over the life of the local system. These include system logs, vi and ex backup files, and uucp files. On a server, a good idea is to have these files in a separate file system. |
| 2 | | Refers to the entire disk and is defined automatically by Sun's format utility and the Solaris installation programs. The size of this slice should not be changed. |

*continues*

**Table 3–1    Solaris Default File Systems (continued)**

| Slice | File System | Description |
| --- | --- | --- |
| 3 | /export | Holds alternate versions of the operating system. These alternate versions are required by client systems whose architectures differ from that of the server. Clients with the same architecture type as the server obtain executables from the /usr file system, usually slice 6. |
| 4 | /export/swap | Provides virtual memory space for client systems if the system is set up for client support. |
| 5 | /opt | Holds optional third-party software added to a system. If a slice is not allocated for this file system during installation, the /opt directory is put in slice 0. |
| 6 | /usr | Holds operating system commands—also known as executables—designed to be run by users. This slice also holds documentation, system programs (init and syslogd, for example), and library routines. The /usr file system also includes system files and directories that can be shared with other users. Files (such as man pages) that can be used on all types of systems are in /usr/share. |
| 7 | /home | Holds files created by users (also named /export/home). |

You only need to create (or re-create) a UFS file system when you

- Add or replace disks
- Change the slices of an existing disk
- Do a full restore on a file system
- Change the parameters of a file system, such as block size or free space

When you create a UFS file system, the disk slice is divided into cylinder groups. The slice is then divided into blocks to control and organize the structure of the files within the cylinder group. A UFS file system has the following four types of blocks, with each performing a specific function in the file system:

- *Boot block*—Stores information used when booting the system
- *Superblock*—Stores much of the information about the file system
- *Inode*—Stores all information about a file except its name
- *Storage or data block*—Stores data for each file

## The Boot Block

The boot block stores the procedures used in booting the system. Without a boot block, the system does not boot. If a file system is not to be used for booting, the boot block is left blank. The boot block appears only in the first cylinder group (cylinder group 0) and is the first 8KB in a slice.

## The Superblock

The superblock stores much of the information about the file system. A few of the more important things contained in a superblock are

- Size and status of the file system

- Label (file system name and volume name)

- Size of the file system's logical block

- Date and time of the last update

- Cylinder group size

- Number of data blocks in a cylinder group

- Summary data block

- File system state: clean, stable, or active

- Pathname of the last mount point

Without a superblock, the file system becomes unreadable. The superblock is located at the beginning of the disk slice and is replicated in each cylinder group. Because the superblock contains critical data, multiple superblocks are made when the file system is created. A copy of the superblock for each file system is kept up-to-date in memory. If the system gets halted before a disk copy of the superblock gets updated, the most recent changes to the superblock are lost and the file system becomes inconsistent. The sync command forces every superblock in memory to write its data to disk. The file system check program fsck can fix problems that occur when the sync command hasn't been used before a shutdown.

A summary information block is kept with the superblock. It is not replicated but is grouped with the first superblock, usually in cylinder group 0. The summary block records changes that take place as the file system is used, listing the number of inodes, directories, fragments, and storage blocks within the file system.

## Inodes

An inode contains all of the information about a file except its name, which is kept in a directory. An inode is 128 bytes. The inode information is kept in the cylinder information block and contains the following:

- The type of the file (regular, directory, block special, character, link, and so on)

- The mode of the file (the set of read/write/execute permissions)

- The number of hard links to the file

- The user-id of the owner of the file

- The group-id to which the file belongs

- The number of bytes in the file

- An array of 15 disk-block addresses

- The date and time the file was last accessed

- The date and time the file was last modified

- The date and time the file was created

The maximum number of files per UFS file system is determined by the number of inodes allocated for a file system. The number of inodes depends on how much disk space is allocated for each inode and the total size of the file system. By default, one inode is allocated for each 2KB of data space. You can change the default allocation by using the -i option of the newfs command.

## Storage Blocks

The rest of the space allocated to the file system is occupied by storage blocks, also called data blocks. The size of these storage blocks is determined at the time a file system is created. Storage blocks are allocated, by default, in two sizes: an 8KB logical block size and a 1KB fragmentation size.

For a regular file, the storage blocks contain the contents of the file. For a directory, the storage blocks contain entries that give the inode number and the filename of the files in the directory.

## Free Blocks

Blocks not currently being used as inodes, indirect address blocks, or storage blocks are marked as free in the cylinder group map. This map also keeps track of fragments to prevent fragmentation from degrading disk performance.

## How to Create a UFS File System

Use the newfs command to create UFS file systems. newfs is a convenient front-end to the mkfs command, the program that creates the new file system on a disk slice. On Solaris 2.x systems, information used to set some of the parameter defaults, such as number of tracks per cylinder and number of sectors per track, is read from the disk label. newfs determines the file system parameters to use, based on the options you specify and information provided in the disk label. Parameters are then passed to the mkfs (make file system) command, which builds the file system. Although you can use the mkfs command directly, it's more difficult to use and you must supply many of the parameters manually. The use of the newfs command is discussed later in this chapter.

The disk must be formatted and divided into slices before you can create UFS file system on it. newfs removes any data on the disk slice and creates the skeleton of a directory structure, including the directory named lost+found. After you run newfs successfully, the slice is ready to be mounted as a file system.

To create a UFS file system on a formatted disk that has already been divided into slices, you need to know the raw device filename of the slice that will contain the file system. If you are re-creating or modifying an existing UFS file system, back up and unmount the file system before performing these steps:

1. Become superuser.

2. Type **newfs /dev/rdsk/*device-name*** and press Enter. You are asked if you want to proceed. The newfs command requires the use of the raw device name and not the buffered device name.

**CAUTION!** *Be sure you have specified the correct device name for the slice before performing the next step. You will erase the contents of the slice when the new file system is created, and you don't want to erase the wrong slice.*

3. Type **y** to confirm.

The following example creates a file system on /dev/rdsk/c0t3d0s7:

1. Become superuser, type **su**, and enter the root password.

2. Type **newfs /dev/rdsk/c0t3d0s7**.

   The system responds with

   ```
   newfs: construct a new file system /dev/rdsk/c0t3d0s7 (y/n)? y
   /dev/rdsk/c0t3d0s7:     163944 sectors in 506 cylinders of 9 tracks, 36 sectors
   83.9MB in 32 cyl groups (16 c/g, 2.65MB/g, 1216 i/g)
   super-block backups (for fsck -b #) at:
   32, 5264, 10496, 15728, 20960, 26192, 31424, 36656, 41888,
   47120, 52352, 57584, 62816, 68048, 73280, 78512, 82976, 88208,
   93440, 98672, 103904, 109136, 114368, 119600, 124832, 130064, 135296,
   140528, 145760, 150992, 156224, 161456,
   ```

The newfs command uses optimized default values to create the file system. The default parameters used by the newfs command are

- File system block size = 8,192.

- File system fragment size (the smallest allocatable unit of disk space) = 1,024 bytes.

- Percentage of free space = 10%.

- Number of inodes or bytes per inode = 2,048. This controls how many inodes are created for the file system (one inode for each 2KB of disk space).

# Understanding Custom File System Parameters

Before you choose to alter the default file system parameters assigned by the newfs command, you need to understand them. This section describes each of these parameters:

- Block size
- Fragment size
- Minimum free space
- Rotational delay
- Optimization type
- Number of inodes

## Logical Block Size

The logical block size is the size of the blocks the UNIX kernel uses to read or write files. The logical block size is usually different from the physical block size (usually 512 bytes), which is the size of the smallest block the disk controller can read or write.

You can specify the logical block size of the file system. After the file system is created, you cannot change this parameter without rebuilding the file system. You can have file systems with different logical block sizes on the same disk.

By default, the logical block size is 8,192 bytes (8KB) for UFS file systems. The UFS file system supports block sizes of 4,096 or 8,192 bytes (4 or 8KB, with 8KB the recommended logical block size).

To choose the best logical block size for your system, consider both the performance desired and the available space. For most UFS systems, an 8KB file system provides the best performance, offering a good balance between disk performance and use of space in primary memory and on disk.

As a general rule, a larger logical block size increases efficiency for file systems in which most of the files are very large. Use a smaller logical block size for file systems in which most of the files are very small. You can use the quot -c file system command on a file system to display a complete report on the distribution of files by block size.

## Fragment Size

As files are created or expanded, they are allocated disk space in either full logical blocks or portions of logical blocks called fragments. When disk space is needed to hold data for a file, full blocks are allocated first and then one or more fragments of a block are allocated for the remainder. For small files, allocation begins with fragments.

The ability to allocate fragments of blocks to files, rather than just whole blocks, saves space by reducing fragmentation of disk space resulting from unused holes in blocks.

You define the fragment size when you create a UFS file system. The default fragment size is 1KB. Each block can be divided into 1, 2, 4, or 8 fragments, resulting in fragment sizes from 8,192 bytes to 512 bytes (for 4KB file systems only). The lower bound is actually tied to the disk sector size, typically 512 bytes.

**N O T E .** *The upper bound might equal the full block size, in which case the fragment is not a fragment at all. This configuration might be optimal for file systems with very large files when you are more concerned with speed than with space.*

When choosing a fragment size, look at the trade-off between time and space: a small fragment size saves space but requires more time to allocate. As a general rule, a larger fragment size increases efficiency for file systems in which most of the files are large. Use a smaller fragment size for file systems in which most of the files are small.

## Minimum Free Space

The minimum free space is the percentage of the total disk space held in reserve when you create the file system. The default reserve is 10%. Free space is important because file access becomes less and less efficient as a file system gets full. As long as there is an adequate amount of free space, UFS file systems operate efficiently. When a file system becomes full, using up the available user space, only root can access the reserved free space.

Commands such as df report the percentage of space available to users, excluding the percentage allocated as the minimum free space. When the command reports that more than 100% of the disk space in the file system is in use, some of the reserve has been used by root.

If you impose quotas on users, the amount of space available to the users does not include the free space reserve. You can change the value of the minimum free space for an existing file system by using the tunefs command.

## Rotational Delay (Gap)

The rotational delay is the expected minimum time (in milliseconds) it takes the CPU to complete a data transfer and initiate a new data transfer on the same disk cylinder. The default delay depends on the type of disk and is usually optimized for each disk type.

When writing a file, the UFS allocation routines try to position new blocks on the same disk cylinder as the previous block in the same file. The allocation routines also try to optimally position new blocks within tracks to minimize the disk rotation needed to access them.

To position file blocks so they are "rotationally well behaved," the allocation routines must know how fast the CPU can service transfers and how long it takes the disk to skip over a block. By using options to the mkfs command, you can indicate how fast the disk rotates and how many disk blocks (sectors) it has per track. The allocation routines use this information to figure out how many milliseconds the disk takes to skip a block. Then, by using the expected transfer time (rotational delay), the allocation routines can position or place blocks so the next block is just coming under the disk head when the system is ready to read it.

**NOTE.** *It is not necessary to specify the rotational delay (*-d *option to* newfs*) for some devices.*

Place blocks consecutively only if your system is fast enough to read them on the same disk rotation. If the system is too slow, the disk spins past the beginning of the next block in the file and must complete a full rotation before the block can be read, which takes a lot of time. You should try to specify an appropriate value for the gap so the head is located over the appropriate block when the next disk request occurs.

You can change the value of this parameter for an existing file system by using the tunefs command. The change applies only to subsequent block allocation, not to blocks already allocated.

## Optimization Type

The optimization type is either space or time.

When you select space optimization, disk blocks are allocated to minimize fragmentation and optimize disk use. Space is the default when you set the minimum free space to less than 10%.

When you select time optimization, disk blocks are allocated as quickly as possible, with less emphasis on their placement. Time is the default when you set the minimum free space to 10% or greater. With enough free space, the disk blocks can be allocated effectively with minimal fragmentation.

You can change the value of the optimization type parameter for an existing file system by using the tunefs command.

## Number of Bytes per Inode

The number of inodes determines the number of files you can have in the file system: one inode for each file. The number of bytes per inode determines the total number of inodes created when the file system is made: the total size of the file system divided by the number of bytes per inode. After the inodes are allocated, you cannot change the number without re-creating the file system.

The default number of bytes per inode is 2,048 bytes (2KB), which assumes the average size of each file is 2KB or greater. Most files are larger than 2KB. A file system with many symbolic links will have a lower average file size. If your file system is going to have many small files, you can give this parameter a lower value. Note, however, that having too many inodes is much better than running out of them. If you have too few inodes, you could reach the maximum number of files on a disk slice that is practically empty.

# File System Operations

This section describes the Solaris utilities used for creating, checking, repairing, and mounting file systems. Use these utilities to make file systems available to the user and to ensure their reliability.

## Synchronizing a File System

The UFS file system relies on an internal set of tables to keep track of inodes and used and available blocks. When a user performs an operation that requires data to be written out to the disk, the data to be written is first copied into a buffer in the kernel. Normally, the disk update is not handled until long after the write operation has returned. At any given time, the file system, as it resides on the disk, might lag behind the state of the file system represented by the buffers located in physical memory. The internal tables finally get updated when the buffer is required for another use or when the kernel automatically runs the fsflush daemon (at 30-second intervals). If the system is halted without writing out the memory-resident information, the file system on the disk will be in an inconsistent state. If the internal tables are not properly synchronized with data on a disk, inconsistencies result and file systems need repairing. File systems can be damaged or become inconsistent because of abrupt termination of the operating system in these ways:

- Power failure
- Accidental unplugging of the system
- Turning off the system without the proper shutdown procedure
- A software error in the kernel

To prevent unclean halts, the current state of the file system must be written to disk (that is, "synchronized") before you halt the CPU or take a disk offline.

## Repairing File Systems

During normal operation, files are created, modified, and removed. Each time a file is modified, the operating system performs a series of file system updates. When a system is booted, a file system consistency check is automatically performed. Most of the time, this file system check repairs any problems it encounters. File systems are checked with the fsck (file system check) program.

The Solaris `fsck` command uses a state flag, which is stored in the superblock, to record the condition of the file system. This flag is used by the `fsck` command to determine whether a file system needs to be checked for consistency. The flag is used by the `/etc/bcheckrc` script during booting and by the `fsck` command when run from a command line using the `-m` option. The possible state values are

- *FSCLEAN*—If the file system was unmounted properly, the state flag is set to FSCLEAN. Any file system with an FSCLEAN state flag is not checked when the system is booted.

- *FSSTABLE*—The file system is (or was) mounted but has not changed since the last check point—`sync` or `fsflush`—which normally occurs every 30 seconds. For example, the kernel periodically checks to see if a file system is idle and, if so, flushes the information in the superblock back to the disk and marks it FSSTABLE. If the system crashes, the file system structure is stable, but users might lose a small amount of data. File systems marked FSSTABLE can skip the checking before mounting.

- *FSACTIVE*—When a file system is mounted and then modified, the state flag is set to FSACTIVE and the file system might contain inconsistencies. A file system is marked as FSACTIVE before any modified data is written to the disk. When a file system is unmounted gracefully, the state flag is set to FSCLEAN. A file system with the FSACTIVE flag must be checked by `fsck` because it might be inconsistent. The system does not mount a file system for read/write unless the file system state is FSCLEAN or FSSTABLE.

- *FSBAD*—If the root file system is mounted when its state is not FSCLEAN or FSSTABLE, the state flag is set to FSBAD. The kernel does not change this file system state to FSCLEAN or FSSTABLE. A root file system flagged FSBAD as part of the boot process is mounted read-only. You can run `fsck` on the raw root device and then remount the `root` file system as read/write.

`fsck` is a multipass file system check program that performs successive passes over each file system, checking blocks and sizes, pathnames, connectivity, reference counts, and the map of free blocks (possibly rebuilding it) and performing some cleanup. The phases (passes) performed by the UFS version of `fsck` are

Initialization

| | |
|---|---|
| Phase 1 | Check blocks and sizes. |
| Phase 2 | Check pathnames. |
| Phase 3 | Check connectivity. |
| Phase 4 | Check reference counts. |
| Phase 5 | Check cylinder groups. |

Normally, fsck is run noninteractively at bootup to preen the file systems after an abrupt system halt in which the latest file system changes were not written to disk. Preening automatically fixes any basic file system inconsistencies and does not try to repair more serious errors. While preening a file system, fsck fixes the inconsistencies it expects from such an abrupt halt. For more serious conditions, the command reports the error and terminates. It then gives the operator a message to run fsck manually.

## How to Determine If a File System Needs Checking

File systems must be checked periodically for inconsistencies to avoid unexpected loss of data. As stated in the previous section, checking the state of a file system is automatically done at bootup; however, it is not necessary to reboot a system to check if the file systems are stable. The following procedure outlines a method for determining the current state of the file systems and whether they need to be fixed.

1. Become superuser.

2. Type fsck -m /dev/rdsk/cntndnsn and press Enter. The state flag in the superblock of the file system you specify is checked to see whether the file system is clean or requires checking. If you omit the device argument, all the UFS file systems listed in /etc/vfstab with a fsck pass value of greater than 0 are checked.

In this example, the first file system needs checking; the second file system does not:

```
fsck -m /dev/rdsk/c0t0d0s6
** /dev/rdsk/c0t0d0s6
ufs fsck: sanity check: /dev/rdsk/c0t0d0s6 needs checking
fsck -m /dev/rdsk/c0t0d0s7
** /dev/rdsk/c0t0d0s7
ufs fsck: sanity check: /dev/rdsk/c0t0d0s7 okay
```

## To Run *fsck* Manually

You might need to manually check file systems when they cannot be mounted or when you've determined that the state of a file system is unclean. Good indications that a file system might need to be checked are error messages displayed in the console window or system crashes for no reason.

When you run fsck manually, fsck reports each inconsistency found and fixes innocuous errors. For more serious errors, the command reports the inconsistency and prompts you to choose a response. Sometimes corrective actions performed by fsck result in some loss of data. The amount and severity of data loss can be determined from the fsck diagnostic output.

To check a file system manually, follow these steps:

1.  Become superuser.

2.  Unmount the file system.

3.  Type `fsck` and press Enter.

    All file systems in the `/etc/vfstab` file with entries greater than zero in the `fsck` pass field are checked. You can also specify the mount point directory or `/dev/rdsk/cntndnsn` as arguments to `fsck`. The `fsck` command requires the raw device filename.

    Any inconsistency messages are displayed. The only way to successfully change the file system and correct the problem is to answer "yes" to these messages.

**NOTE.** *The `fsck` command has an option `-y` that will automatically answer yes to every question. But be careful: if `fsck` asks to delete a file, it will answer yes and you will have no control over it. If it doesn't delete the file, however, the file system remains unclean and cannot be mounted.*

4.  If you corrected any errors, type `fsck` and press Enter. `fsck` might not be able to fix all errors in one execution. If you see the message FILE SYSTEM STATE NOT SET TO OKAY, run the command again and continue to run `fsck` until it runs clean with no errors.

5.  Rename and move any files put in `lost+found`. Individual files put in the `lost+found` directory by `fsck` are renamed with their inode numbers, and figuring out what they were named originally can be difficult. If possible, rename the files and move them where they belong. You might be able to use the `grep` command to match phrases with individual files and the `file` command to identify file types, ownership, and so on. When whole directories are dumped into `lost+found`, it is easier to figure out where they belong and move them back.

## Mounting File Systems

After you create a file system, you need to make it available. You make file systems available by mounting them. Using the `mount` command, you attach a file system to the system directory tree at the specified mount point and it becomes available to the system. The root file system is mounted at boot time and cannot be unmounted. Any other file system can be mounted or unmounted from the root file system at any time.

The various methods used to mount a file system are described in the next sections.

### Creating an Entry in the /etc/vfstab File to Mount File Systems

The /etc/vfstab (virtual file system table) file contains a list of file systems to be automatically mounted when the system is booted to the multiuser state. The system administrator

places entries in the file, specifying what file systems are to be mounted at bootup. The following is an example of the /etc/vfstab file:

```
#device            device          mount   FS     fsck   mount    mount
#to mount          to fsck         point   type   pass   at boot  options
/dev/dsk/c0t0d0s0  /dev/rdsk/c0t0d0s0  /       ufs    1      no       -
/proc              -               /proc   proc          no       -
/dev/dsk/c0t0d0s1  -               -       swap          no       -
swap               -               /tmp    tmpfs  -      yes      -
/dev/dsk/c0t0d0s6  /dev/rdsk/c0t0d0s6  /usr    ufs    2      no       -
/dev/dsk/c0t3d0s7  /dev/rdsk/c0t3d0s7  /data   ufs    2      no       -
```

Each column of information follows this format:

- device to fsck—The raw (character) special device that corresponds to the file system being mounted. This determines the raw interface used by fsck. Use a dash (–) when there is no applicable device, such as for a read-only file system or a network-based file system.

- mount point—The default mount point directory.

- FS type—The type of file system.

- fsck pass—The pass number used by fsck to decide whether to check a file. When the field contains a dash (–), the file system is not checked. When the field contains a value of 1, the file system is checked sequentially. When fsck is run on multiple UFS file systems that have fsck pass values of greater than one, fsck automatically checks the file systems on different disks in parallel to maximize efficiency. Otherwise, the value of the pass number does not have any effect.

**NOTE.** *In SunOS system software, the* fsck pass *field does not specify the order in which file systems are to be checked. During bootup, a preliminary check is run on each file system to be mounted from a hard disk, using the boot script* /sbin/rcS, *which checks the /, /usr, and /usr/kvm file systems. The other rc shell scripts then use the* fsck *command to check each additional file system sequentially. They do not check file systems in parallel. File systems are checked sequentially during booting even if the* fsck *pass numbers are greater than 1. The values can be any number greater than 1.*

- mount at boot—Specify whether the file system should be automatically mounted when the system is booted.

- mount options—A list of comma-separated options (with no spaces) used when mounting the file system. Use a dash (–) to show no options.

## Using the Command Line to Mount File Systems

File systems can be mounted from the command line by using the mount command. The following commands are used from the command line to mount and unmount file systems:

| | |
|---|---|
| mount | Mounts specified file systems and remote resources |
| mountall | Mounts all file systems specified in a file system table (vfstab) |
| umount | Unmounts specified file systems and remote resources |
| umountall | Unmounts all file systems specified in a file system table |

CD-ROMs containing file systems are automatically mounted when the CD-ROM is inserted. Disks containing file systems are mounted by running the volcheck command.

As a general rule, local disk slices should be included in the /etc/vfstab file so they automatically mount at bootup.

Unmounting a file system removes it from the file system mount point. Some file system administration tasks cannot be performed on mounted file systems. You should unmount a file system when

- It is no longer needed

- You check and repair it by using the fsck command

- You are about to do a complete backup of it

**NOTE.** *File systems are automatically unmounted as part of the system shutdown procedure.*

## Displaying Mounted File Systems

Whenever you mount or unmount a file system, the /etc/mnttab (mount table) file is modified to show the list of currently mounted file systems. You can display the contents of the mount table by using the cat or more commands, but you cannot edit it as you would the /etc/vfstab file. Here is an example of a mount table file:

```
/dev/dsk/c0t3d0s0       /         ufs      rw,suid 693186371
/dev/dsk/c0t1d0s6       /usr      ufs      rw,suid 693186371
/proc                   /proc     proc     rw,suid 693186371
swap                    /tmp      tmpfs    ,dev=0 693186373
```

You can also view a mounted file system by typing **/etc/mount** from the command line. The system displays the following:

```
/ on /dev/dsk/c0t3d0s0 read/write/setuid/largefiles on ...
/usr on /dev/dsk/c0t1d0s6 read/write/setuid/largefiles on ...
/proc on /proc read/write/setuid on Fri May 16 11:39:05 1997
```

```
/dev/fd on fd read/write/setuid on Fri May 16 11:39:05 1997
/export on /dev/dsk/c0t3d0s3 setuid/read/write/largefiles on ...
/export/home on /dev/dsk/c0t3d0s7 setuid/read/write/largefiles on ...
/export/swap on /dev/dsk/c0t3d0s4 setuid/read/write/largefiles on ...
/opt on /dev/dsk/c0t3d0s5 setuid/read/write/largefiles on ...
/tmp on swap read/write on Fri May 16 11:39:07 1997
```

## How to Mount a File System with Large Files

The new `largefiles` mount option enables users to mount a file system containing files larger than 2GB. The `largefiles` mount option is the default state for the Solaris 2.6 environment. The `largefiles` option means a file system mounted with this option may contain one or more files larger than 2GB.

You must explicitly use the `nolargefiles` mount option to disable this behavior. The `nolargefiles` option provides total compatibility with previous file system behavior, enforcing the 2GB maximum file size limit.

## Displaying a File System's Disk Space Use

Use the `df` command and its options to see the capacity of each disk mounted on a system, the amount available, and the percentage of space already in use. Use the `du` (directory usage) command to report the number of free disk blocks and files.

**N O T E .** *File systems at or above 90% of capacity should be cleared of unnecessary files. You can do this by moving them to a disk, or you can remove them after obtaining the user's permission.*

The following is an example of how to use the `df` command to display disk space information. The command syntax is

```
$ df directory -F fstype -g -k -t
```

The following is an explanation of the `df` command and its options:

| | |
|---|---|
| df | The df command with no options lists all mounted file systems and their device names. It also lists the number of total 512-byte blocks used and the number of files. |
| directory | Directory whose file system you want to check. The device name, blocks used, and number of files are displayed. |
| -F fstype | Displays a list of unmounted file systems, their device names, the number of 512-byte blocks used, and the number of files on file systems of type fstype. |
| -g | Displays the statvfs structure for all mounted file systems. |
| -k | Displays a list of file systems, kilobytes used, free kilobytes, percent capacity used, and mount points. |
| -t | Displays total blocks as well as blocks used for all mounted file systems. |

## Displaying Directory Size Information

By using the `df` command, you displayed file system disk use. You can use the `du` command to display the disk use of a directory and all of its subdirectories in 512-byte blocks.

The `du` command shows you the disk use of each subdirectory. To get a list of subdirectories in a file system, `cd` to the pathname associated with that file system and run the following pipeline:

```
$ du ¦ sort -r -n
```

This pipeline, which uses the reverse and numeric options of the `sort` command, pinpoints large directories. Use `ls -l` to examine the size (in bytes) and modification times of files within each directory. Old files or text files over 100KB often warrant storage offline.

## Controlling User Disk Space Use

Quotas enable system administrators to control the size of UFS file systems by limiting the amount of disk space individual users can acquire. Quotas are especially useful on the file systems where user home directories reside. After the quotas are in place, they can be changed to adjust the amount of disk space or number of inodes users can consume. Additionally, quotas can be added or removed as system needs change. In addition, quota status can be monitored. Quota commands enable administrators to display information about quotas on a file system or to search for users who have exceeded their quotas.

After you have set up and turned on disk and inode quotas, you can check for users who exceed their quotas. You can also check quota information for entire file systems by using the following commands:

| | |
|---|---|
| quota | Displays the quotas and disk use within a file system for individual users on which quotas have been activated. |
| repquota | Displays the quotas and disk use for all users on one or more file systems. |

You won't see quotas in to use much today, as the cost of disk space continues to fall. In most cases, the system administrator simply watches disk space to identify users who might be using more than their fair share. As we saw in this section, you can easily do this by using the `du` command. On a large system with many users, disk quotas can be an effective way to control disk space use.

This chapter described disk file systems and how they are managed. The system administrator will spend a great deal of time managing and fine-tuning file systems to improve system efficiency.

# CHAPTER

# 4

## System Security

The following are the test objectives for this chapter:

- Understanding the superuser account and its importance to system administration

- Understanding the format of the /etc/passwd, /etc/shadow, and /etc/group files and their importance to system security

- Changing ownership and access permissions on files and directories

- Displaying and changing default permissions (umask)

- Setting access control lists (ACLs) on files

- Monitoring system and user activity

- Modifying system defaults to control and monitor superuser access to the system

- Monitoring and restricting access to the root account

- Understanding how the setuid and setgid permissions relate to system security

- Understanding how the sticky permission protects files and directories

**K**eeping the system's information secure is one of the primary tasks for the system administrator. System security involves protecting data against loss due to a disaster or system failure. In addition, it is the system administrator's responsibility to protect systems from the threat of an unauthorized intruder and to protect data on the system from unauthorized users. Some of the worst disasters I've seen have come from authorized personnel—even system administrators—destroying data unintentionally. Therefore, the system administrator is presented with two levels of security: protecting data from accidental loss and securing the system against intrusion or unauthorized access.

The first scenario, protecting data from accidental loss, is easy to achieve with a full system backup scheme you run regularly. Regular backups provide protection in the event of a disaster. If a user accidentally destroys data, the hardware malfunctions, or a computer program simply corrupts data, the system administrator can restore files from the backup media.

The second form of security, securing the system against intrusion or unauthorized access, is more complex. This chapter cannot cover every security hole or threat, but it does discuss UNIX security fundamentals. Protection against intruders involves

- *Physical security*—Limiting physical access to the computer equipment

- *Access to data*—Limiting user access via passwords and permissions

- *Network security*—Protecting against access through phone lines, serial lines, or the network

- *Superuser access*—Reserving superuser access for system administration use only

## Physical Security

Physical security is simple: Lock the door. Limit the people who have physical access to the computer equipment to prevent theft or vandalism. In addition, limit access to the system console. Anyone who has access to the console ultimately has access to the data. If the computer contains sensitive data, keep it locked in a controlled environment with clean power and adequate protection against fire, lightning, flood, or other building disasters. Restrict access to protect against tampering with the system and its backups. Anyone with access to the backup media could steal it and access the data. Furthermore, if a system is logged in and left unattended, anyone who can use that system can gain access to the operating system and the network. Make sure your users log out or "lock" their screens before walking away. In sum, you need to be aware of your users' computer surroundings and you need to physically protect them from unauthorized access.

# Controlling System Access

Controlling access to systems involves using passwords and appropriate file permissions. To control access, all logins must have passwords, and the passwords must be changed frequently. Password aging is a system parameter set by the system administrator requiring users to change their passwords after a specific number of days. Password aging enables you to force users to change their passwords periodically or to prevent users from changing a password before a specified interval. Set an expiration date for a password to prevent an intruder from gaining undetected access to the system through an old and inactive account. For a high level of security, you should require users to change their passwords every six weeks. Once every three months is adequate for lower levels of security. Change system administration logins (such as root and sys) monthly, or whenever a person who knows the root password leaves the company or is reassigned.

Several files that control default system access are stored in the /etc/default directory. These files limit access to specific systems on a network. Table 4–1 summarizes the files in the /etc/default directory.

## Table 4–1   Files in /etc/default Directory

| | |
|---|---|
| /etc/default/login | Controls system login policies, including root access. The default is to limit root access to the console. |
| /etc/default/passwd | Controls default policy on password aging. |
| /etc/default/su | Specifies where attempts to su to root are logged and where these log files are located. The file also specifies whether attempts to su to root are displayed on a named device (such as a system console). |

You can set default values in the /etc/default/passwd file to control user passwords. See Table 4–2 for the list of options that can be controlled through the /etc/default/passwd file.

## Table 4–2   Flags in /etc/default/passwd

| | |
|---|---|
| MAXWEEKS | Maximum time period password is valid |
| MINWEEKS | Minimum time period before the password can be changed |
| PASSLENGTH | Minimum length of password, in characters |
| WARNWEEKS | Time period until warning of password's ensuing expiration date |

The system administrator's job is to ensure that all users have secure passwords. Improper passwords can be broken by a system cracker and could put the entire system at risk.

Enforce the following guidelines on passwords:

- Combinations of six to eight letters, numbers, or special characters
- Phrases (beammeup)
- Nonsense words made up of the first letters of every word in a phrase (swotrb for SomeWhere Over The RainBow)
- Words with numbers or symbols substituted for letters (sn00py for snoopy)

On the other hand, poor choices for passwords include:

- Proper nouns, names, login names, and other passwords a person might guess just by knowing something about you (the user)
- Your name forwards, backwards, or jumbled
- Names of family members or pets
- Car license numbers
- Telephone numbers
- Social Security numbers
- Employee numbers
- Names related to a hobby or interest
- Seasonal themes, such as Santa in December
- Any word in the dictionary
- Simple keyboard patterns (asdfgh)
- Passwords you've used previously

# Where User Account Information is Stored

User account and group information is stored in files located in the /etc directory.

Most of the user account information is stored in the /etc/passwd file; however, password encryption and password aging are stored in the /etc/shadow file. Group information is stored in the /etc/group file. Users are put together into groups based on their file access needs; for example, the "acctng" group might be users in the accounting department.

Fields in the /etc/passwd file are separated by colons and contain the following information:

```
username:password:uid:gid:comment:home-directory:login-shell
```

Each line in the /etc/passwd file contains several fields, separated by a colon (:) and defined in Table 4–3.

## Table 4–3   Fields in the /etc/passwd file

| Field Name | Description |
| --- | --- |
| username | Contains the information user or login name. User names should be unique and consist of 1–8 letters (A–Z, a–z) and numerals (0–9) but no underscores or spaces. The first character must be a letter, and at least one character must be a lowercase letter. |
| password | Contains an x, which is a placeholder for the encrypted password that is stored in the /etc/shadow file. |
| uid | Contains a user identification (UID) number that identifies the user to the system. UID numbers for regular users should range from 100 to 2147483647. All UID numbers should be unique. UIDs less than 100 are reserved. To minimize security risks, avoid reusing the UIDs from deleted accounts. |
| gid | Contains a group identification (GID) number that identifies the user's primary group. Each GID number must be a whole number between 0 and 2147483647 (60001 and 60002 are assigned to nobody and noaccess, respectively). |
| comment | Usually contains the full name of the user. |
| home-directory | Contains the user's home directory path name. |
| login-shell | Contains the user's default login shell. |

Fields in the /etc/shadow file are separated by colons and contain the following information:

```
username:password:lastchg:min:max:warn:inactive:expire
```

Each line in the /etc/shadow file contains several fields separated by colons (:) and defined in Table 4–4.

## Table 4–4   Fields in the /etc/shadow file

| Field Name | Description |
| --- | --- |
| username | Contains the user or login name. |
| password | Might contain the following entries: a 13-character encrypted user password; the string *LK*, which indicates an inaccessible account; or the string NP, which indicates no password on the account. |
| lastchg | Indicates the number of days between January 1, 1970, and the last password modification date. |
| min | Contains the minimum number of days required between password changes. |
| max | Contains the maximum number of days the password is valid before the user is prompted to specify a new password. |
| inactive | Contains the number of days a user account can be inactive before being locked. |
| expire | Contains the absolute date when the user account expires. Past this date, the user cannot log into the system. |

The fields in the group file are separated by colons and contain the following information:

```
group-name:group-password:gid:user-list
```

Each line in the /etc/group file contains several fields, separated by colons (:) and defined in Table 4–5.

## Table 4–5    Fields in the /etc/group File

| Field Name | Description |
| --- | --- |
| group-name | Contains the name assigned to the group. For example, members of the accounting department might be called acct. Group names can have a maximum of nine characters. |
| group-password | Usually contains an asterisk or is empty. The group-password field is a relic of earlier versions of UNIX. |
| gid | Contains the group's GID number. It must be unique on the local system and should be unique across the entire organization. Each GID number must be a are whole number between 0 and 60002. Numbers under 100 are reserved for system default group accounts. User-defined groups can range from 100 to 60000 (60001 and 60002 are reserved and assigned to nobody and noaccess, respectively). |
| user-list | Contains a list of groups and a comma-separated list of user names, representing the user's secondary group memberships. Each user can belong to a maximum of 16 secondary groups. |

By default, all Solaris 2.x systems have the following groups already defined in the /etc/group file. Do not use the following groups for users and do not remove them.

```
root::0:root
other::1:
bin::2:root,bin,daemon
sys::3:root,bin,sys,adm
adm::4:root,adm,daemon
uucp::5:root,uucp
mail::6:root
tty::7:root,tty,adm
lp::8:root,lp,adm
nuucp::9:root,nuucp
staff::10:
daemon::12:root,daemon
sysadmin::14:
nobody::60001:
noaccess::60002:
nogroup::65534:
```

**NOTE.** *Members of the* sysadmin *group (group 14) are allowed to use the Solstice AdminSuite software. A system administrator may assign this group to a backup system administrator or power user. Unless you are a member of the UNIX* sysadmin *group, you must become superuser on your system to use Admintool.*

## Controlling File Access

After you have established login restrictions, you'll need to control access to the data on the system. Some users only need to look at files; other users need the ability to change or delete files. You might have data you do not want anyone else to see. Data access is controlled by assigning permission levels to a file. Three levels of access permission are assigned to a UNIX file to control access by the owner, the group, and all others. Display permissions with the ls -la command. The following example shows the use of the ls -la command to display permissions on files in the /public directory:

```
ls -la    /users
```

The system responds with

```
drwxr-xr-x    2 bill    staff     512   Sep 23 07:02   .
drwxr-xr-x    3 root    other     512   Sep 23 07:02   ..
-rw-r--r--    1 bill    staff     124   Sep 23 07:02   .cshrc
-rw-r--r--    1 bill    staff     575   Sep 23 07:02   .login
```

The first column of information displays the type of file and its access permissions for the user, group, and others. The r, w, and x are described in Table 4–6. The third column displays the owner of the file—usually the user who created the file. The owner of a file can decide who has the right to read it, to write to it, or—if it is a command—to execute it. The fourth column displays the group to which this file belongs.

### Table 4–6   File Access Permissions

| Symbol | Permission | Means Designated Users... |
|---|---|---|
| r | Read | Can open and read the contents of a file |
| w | Write | Can write to the file (modify its contents), add to it, or delete it |
| x | Execute | Can execute the file (if it is a program or shell script) |
| - | Denied | Cannot read, write, or execute the file |

When listing the permissions on a directory, all columns of information are the same as on a file, with one exception. The r, w, and x found in the first column are treated slightly differently than for a file and are described in Table 4–7.

**Table 4–7    Directory Access Permissions**

| Symbol | Permission | Means Designated Users... |
|---|---|---|
| r | Read | Can list files in the directory. |
| w | Write | Can add or remove files or links in the directory. |
| x | Execute | Can open or execute files in the directory. Also can make the directory and the directories beneath it current. |
| - | Denied | Neither read, write, nor execute privileges have been assigned. |

Use the following commands to modify file access permissions and ownership, but remember that only the owner of the file or root can assign or modify these values.

| chmod | Changes access permissions on a file. You can use either symbolic mode (letters and symbols) or absolute mode (octal numbers) to change permissions on a file. |
|---|---|
| chown | Changes the ownership of a file. |
| chgrp | Changes the group ownership of a file. |

## Default *umask*

When a user creates a file or directory, the default file permissions assigned to the file or directory are controlled by the user mask. The user mask should be set by the umask command in a user initialization file such as /etc/profile or .cshrc. You can display the current value of the user mask by typing umask and pressing Enter.

The user mask is set with a three-digit octal value such as 022. The first digit sets permissions for the user; the second sets permissions for the group; the third sets permissions for other. To set the umask to 022, type:

`umask 022`

By default, the system sets the permissions on a file to 666, granting read and write permission to the user, group, and others. The system sets the default permissions on a directory or executable file to 777, or rwx. The value assigned by umask is subtracted from the default. To determine the umask value you want to set, subtract the value of the permissions you want from 666 (for a file) or 777 (for a directory). The remainder is the value to use with the umask command. For example, suppose you want to change the default mode for files to 644 (rw-r--r--). The difference between 666 and 644 is 022, which is the value you would use as an argument to the umask command.

Setting the umask value has the effect of denying permissions in the same way chmod grants them. For example, the command chmod 022 grants write permission to group and others, and umask 022 denies write permission to group and others.

## Sticky Bit

The *sticky bit* is a permission bit that protects the files within a directory. If the directory has the sticky bit set, a file can be deleted only by the owner of the file, the owner of the directory, or by root. This prevents a user from deleting other users' files from public directories. A t or T in the access permissions column of a file listing indicates the sticky bit has been set.

```
drwxrwxrwt   2 uucp    uucp   512 Feb 12 07:32 /var/spool/uucppublic
```

Use the chmod command to set the sticky bit. The symbols for setting the sticky bit by using the chmod command in symbolic mode are

t       Sticky bit is on; execution bit for others is on.

T       Sticky bit is on; execution bit for others is off.

## Access Control Lists (ACLs)

ACLs (ACLs, pronounced "ackkls") can provide greater control over file permissions when the traditional UNIX file protection in the Solaris operating system is not enough. The traditional UNIX file protection provides read, write, and execute permissions for the three user classes: owner, group, and other. An ACL provides better file security by enabling you to define file permissions for the owner, owner's group, others, specific users, and groups, and default permissions for each of those categories.

For example, assume you have a file you want everyone in a group to be able to read. To give everyone access, you would give "group" read permissions on that file. Now, assume you want only one person in the group to be able to write to that file. Standard UNIX doesn't let you set that up; however, you can set up an ACL to give only one person in the group write permissions on the file. ACL entries are the way to define an ACL on a file, and they are set through the ACL commands. ACL entries consist of the following fields, separated by colons and defined in Table 4–8:

```
entry_type:uid¦gid:perms
```

**Table 4–8    ACL Entries**

| | |
|---|---|
| *entry_type* | Type of ACL entry on which to set file permissions. For example, entry_type can be user (the owner of a file) or mask (the ACL mask). |
| *uid* | User name or identification number. |
| *gid* | Group name or identification number. |
| *perms* | Represents the permissions set on entry_type. Permissions are indicated by the symbolic characters rwx or an octal number as used with the chmod command. |

The ACL mask entry indicates the maximum permissions allowed for users, other than the owner, and for groups. The mask is a quick way to change permissions on all users and groups. For example, the mask:r-- mask entry indicates users and groups cannot have more than read permissions, even though they might have write/execute permissions.

Set ACL entries on a file by using the setfacl command.

```
$ setfacl -s user::perms,group::perms,other:perms,mask:perms,acl_entry_list
filename ...
```

The -s option replaces the entire ACL with the new ACL entries, if an ACL already exists on the file.

The following example sets the user permissions to read/write, group permissions to read only, and other permissions to none on the txt1.doc file. In addition, the user Bill is given read/write permissions on the file, and the ACL mask permissions are set to read/write, which means no user or group can have execute permissions.

```
$ setfacl -s user::rw-,group::r--,other:---,mask:rw-, user:bill:rw- txt1.doc
```

Check the new file permissions with the ls -l command. The plus sign (+) to the right of the mode field indicates the file has an ACL:

```
$ ls -l
 total 210
 -rw-r-----+   1 mike   sysadmin   32100   Sep 11 13:11 txt1.doc
 -rw-r--r--    1 mike   sysadmin    1410   Sep 11 13:11 txt2.doc
 -rw-r--r--    1 mike   sysadmin    1700   Sep 11 13:11 labnotes
```

To verify which ACL entries were set on the file, use the getfacl command:

**$ getfacl txt1.doc**

The system responds with

```
 # file: txt1.doc
 # owner: mike
 # group: sysadmin
 user::rw-
 user:bill:rw-      #effective:rw-
 group::r--          #effective:r--
 mask:rw-
 other:---
```

In addition to the ACL entries for files, you can set default ACL entries on a directory that apply to files created within the directory.

## Setting the Correct Path

Setting your path variable correctly is important; otherwise, you might accidentally run a program introduced by someone else that harms the data or your system. This kind of program, which creates a security hazard, is referred to as a "Trojan horse." For example, a substitute su program could be placed in a public directory where you, as system administrator, might run it. Such a script would look just like the regular su command. The script would remove itself after execution, and you'd have trouble knowing you actually ran a Trojan horse.

The path variable is automatically set at login time through the startup files: .login, .profile, and .cshrc. Setting up the user search path so the current directory (.) comes last prevents you or your users from running this type of Trojan horse. The path variable for superuser should not include the current directory (.) at all. Solaris provides a utility called ASET (Automated Security Enhancement Tool) that examines the startup files to ensure the path variable is set up correctly and does not contain a dot (.) entry for the current directory. ASET is discussed later in this chapter.

## *setuid* and *setgid* Programs

When set-user identification (setuid) permission is set on an executable file, a process that runs this file is granted access based on the owner of the file (usually root) rather than the user who created the process. This allows a user to access files and directories normally only available to the owner. For example, the setuid permission on the passwd command makes it possible for a user to edit the /etc/passwd file to change passwords. When a user executes the passwd command, that user assumes the permissions of the root ID, which is UID 0. The setuid permission can be identified by using the ls --l command. The -s in the permissions field of the following example indicates the use of setuid.

```
ls -l /etc/passwd
  -r-sr-sr-x   1 root      sys     10332 May  3 08:23 /usr/bin/passwd
```

Many executable programs have to be run as root (that is, as superuser) to work properly. These executables run with the user ID set to 0 (setuid=0). Anyone running these programs runs them with the root ID, which creates a potential security problem if the programs are not written with security in mind.

On the other hand, the use of setuid on an executable program presents a security risk. A determined user can usually find a way to maintain the permissions granted to him by the setuid process, even after the process has finished executing. For example, a particular command might grant root privileges through the setuid. If a user can break out of this command, that user could still have the root privileges granted by the setuid on that file. Any intruder permission who accesses a system will look for any files that have the setuid.

Except for the executables shipped with Solaris with setuid to root, you should disallow the use of setuid programs—or at least restrict and keep them to a minimum.

**TIP.** *To find files with* setuid *permissions, become superuser. Then use the* find *command to find files with* setuid *permissions set:*

```
# find [directory] -user root -perm -4000 -exec ls -ldb {}\; >/tmp/filename
```

The set-group identification (setgid) permission is similar to setuid, except the process's effective group ID (GID) is changed to the group owner of the file, and a user is granted access based on permissions granted to that group. Using the ls -l command, you can see that the file /usr/bin/mail has setgid permissions:

```
-r-x--s--x  1 bin   mail   64376 Jul  16 1997  /usr/bin/mail
```

## Restricted Shells

System administrators can use restricted versions of the Korn shell (rksh) and Bourne shell (rsh) to limit the operations allowed for a particular user account. Restricted shells are especially useful for ensuring that timesharing users, or users' guests on a system, have restricted permissions during login sessions. When an account is set up with a restricted shell, users may not:

- Change directories
- Set the $PATH variable
- Specify path or command names beginning with "/"
- Redirect output

You can also provide the user with shell procedures that have access to the full power of the standard shell, but impose a limited menu of commands.

**NOTE.** *Do not confuse the restricted shell with the remote shell:*

```
/usr/lib/rsh – restricted shell
/usr/bin/rsh – remote shell
```

*When specifying a restricted shell, you should not include the user's path /bin, /sbin, or /usr/bin. Doing so allows the user to start another shell (a nonrestricted shell).*

# Monitoring Users and System Usage

As the system administrator, you'll need to monitor system resources and be on the lookout for unusual activity. Having a method to monitor the system is very useful when there is a

suspected breach in security. For example, you might want to monitor the login status of a particular user.

1. Become superuser.

2. Display a user's login status by using the `logins` command:

```
# logins -x -l username
```

For example, to monitor login status for the user calkins, type

```
# logins -x -l calkins
```

The system displays the following information:

```
calkins        200     staff           10    Bill S. Calkins
                       /export/home/calkins
                       /bin/sh
                       PS 030195 10 7 -1
```

Table 4–8 describes the information output of the `logins` command.

---

**Table 4–8   Output from the *logins* Command**

| | |
|---|---|
| Calkins | The login name |
| 200 | The UID |
| staff | The primary group |
| 10 | The group ID |
| Bill S. Calkins | The comment field of the /etc/passwd file |
| /export/home/calkins | The user's home directory |
| /bin/sh | The user's default login shell |
| PS 030195 10 7 -1 | Specifies the password aging information: last date password was changed, number of days required between changes, number of days allowed before a change is required, and warning period |

---

You'll want to monitor user logins to ensure their passwords are secure. A potential security problem is to have users without passwords (in other words, users who use a carriage return for a password). Periodically check user logins by using the following method:

1. Become superuser.

2. Display users who have no passwords by using the `logins` command:

```
# logins -p
```

The system responds with a list of users who do not have passwords.

Another good idea is to watch anyone who has tried to access the system but failed. You can save failed login attempts by creating the /var/adm/loginlog file with read and write permission for root only. After you create the `loginlog` file, all failed login activity is written to this file automatically after five failed attempts.

The loginlog file contains one entry for each failed attempt. Each entry contains the user's login name, the tty device, and the time of the failed attempt. If a person makes fewer than five unsuccessful attempts, none of the attempts is logged.

The `loginlog` file might grow quickly. To use the information in this file and to prevent the file from getting too large, you must check it and clear its contents occasionally. If this file shows a lot of activity, someone might be attempting to break into the computer system.

## Checking Who's Logged In

Use the Solaris `who` command to find out who's logged into a system. For each user logged in, the `who` command lists the user's name, the terminal she is using, when she logged in, the elapsed time since activity occurred at the terminal, and the process-ID of the shell she is using. To obtain this information, the `who` command examines the /var/adm/utmp file, which contains a history of all logins since the file was last created.

The Solaris `last` command looks in the /var/adm/wtmpx file for information about users who have logged into the system. The `last` command displays the sessions of the specified users and terminals in chronological order. For each user, `last` displays the time when the session began, the duration of the session, and the terminal where the session took place. The `last` command also indicates if the session is still active or was terminated by a reboot.

For example, the command `last root console` lists all of root's sessions as well as all sessions on the console terminal.

## Network Security

The most difficult system administration issue to administer is network security. When you connect your computer to the rest of the world via a network, someone could find an opening. A way to protect your network from unauthorized users accessing hosts on your network is to use a *firewall* or secure gateway system. A firewall is a dedicated system separating two networks, each of which approaches the other as not trusted—a secure host that acts as a barrier between your internal network and outside networks. The firewall has two primary functions. It acts as a gateway to pass data between the networks, and it acts as a barrier to block the passage of data to and from the network. In addition, the firewall system receives all incoming email and distributes it to the hosts on the internal network.

## Modems

Modems are always a potential point of entry for intruders. Anyone who discovers the phone number can attempt to log in. Low-cost computers can be turned into automatic calling devices that search for modem lines and then try endlessly to guess passwords and break in. If you must use a modem, use it for outgoing calls only. An outgoing modem will not answer the phone. If you allow calling in, implement a callback system. The callback system guarantees that only authorized phone numbers can connect to the system. Another option is to have two modems that establish a security key between one and the other. This way, only modems with the security key can connect with the system modem and gain access to the computer.

## The Trusted Host

Along with protecting the password, you need to protect your system from a root user coming in from across the network. For example, systemA is a *trusted host* from which a user can log in without being required to type a password. Be aware that a user who has root access on systemA could access the root login on systemB simply by logging in across the network if systemA is set up as a trusted host on systemB. When systemB attempts to authenticate root from systemA, it relies on information in its local files; specifically /etc/hosts.equiv and /.rhosts.

## The /etc/hosts.equiv File

The /etc/hosts.equiv file contains a list of trusted hosts for a remote system, one per line.

A hosts.equiv file has the following structure:

```
system1
system2 user_a
```

If a user (root) attempts to log in remotely by using rlogin from one of the hosts listed in this file, and if the remote system can access the user's password entry, the remote system allows the user to log in without a password.

When an entry for a host is made in hosts.equiv, such as the sample entry for system1, it means the host is trusted and so is any user at that machine. If the user name is also mentioned, as in the second entry in the same file, the host is trusted only if the specified user is attempting access. A single line of + in the /etc/hosts.equiv file indicates that every known host is trusted.

The /etc/hosts.equiv file presents a security risk. If you maintain an /etc/hosts.equiv file on your system, this file should include only trusted hosts in your network. The file should not include any host that belongs to a different network or any machines that are in public areas.

**T I P.** *Change the root login to something other than "root," and never put a system name into the /etc/hosts.equiv file without a name or several names after it.*

## The .rhosts File

The .rhosts file is the user equivalent of the /etc/hosts.equiv file. It contains a list of hosts and users. If a host-user combination is listed in this file, the specified user is granted permission to log in remotely from the specified host without having to supply a password. Note that an .rhosts file must reside at the top level of a user's home directory, because .rhosts files located in subdirectories are not consulted. Users can create .rhosts files in their home directories—another way to allow trusted access between their own accounts on different systems without using the /etc/hosts.equiv file.

The .rhosts file presents a major security problem. Although the /etc/hosts.equiv file is under the system administrator's control and can be managed effectively, any user can create an .rhosts file granting access to whomever the user chooses—without the system administrator's knowledge.

When all of the users' home directories are on a single server, and only certain people have superuser access on that server, a good way to prevent a user from using an .rhosts file is to create (as superuser) an empty file in the user's home directory. Then change the permissions in this file to 000 so changing it would be difficult, even as superuser. This would effectively prevent a user from risking system security by using an .rhosts file irresponsibly.

The only secure way to manage .rhosts files is to completely disallow them. One possible exception to this policy is the root account, which might need to have an .rhosts file to perform network backups and other remote services.

## Securing Superuser Access

The UNIX superuser identity is immune from restrictions placed on other users of the system. Any UNIX account with a UID of zero (0) is the superuser. All UNIX systems have a default superuser login named root. The user of this account can access any file and run any command. This login is valuable because any user who might have gotten himself into trouble by removing access permissions or forgetting his password, or who simply needs a file from an area to which he doesn't have access, can be helped by root. Root access, however, can be very dangerous. Root can delete anything, including the operating system (most system administrators remember deleting the entire root file system at one time or another). The root login is both dangerous and necessary. System administrators must not give this password to anyone and should use it themselves only when required.

**N O T E.** *Change the default root login to another name. The first login attempt made by any system cracker is to try logging in as "root." If this login is on the system, the cracker is halfway in and only needs to guess the password to gain access.*

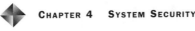

## Restricting Root Access

Root access needs to be safeguarded against unauthorized use. Assume that any intruder is looking for root access. You can protect the superuser account on a system by restricting access to a specific device through the /etc/default/login file. For example, if superuser access is restricted to the console, the superuser can only log in at the console, which should be in a locked room. Anybody who remotely logs in to the system to perform an administrative function must first log in with her user login and then use the su command to become superuser.

To restrict superuser (root) from logging in to the system console from a remote system:

1. Become superuser.

2. Edit the /etc/default/login file.

3. Uncomment the following line.

```
CONSOLE=/dev/console
```

## Monitoring Superuser Access

Solaris provides a utility for monitoring all attempts to become superuser. These logs are very useful when you're trying to track down unauthorized activity. Whenever someone issues the su command to switch from user and become root, this activity is logged in a file called /var/adm/sulog. The sulog file lists all uses of the su command, not only those used to switch user to superuser. The entries show the date and time the command was entered, whether it was successful, the port from which the command was issued, and the name of the user and the switched identity.

To monitor whom is using the su command, you must first turn on this logging utility. To turn on logging of the su command:

1. Become superuser.

2. Edit the /etc/default/su file.

3. Uncomment the following line.

```
SULOG=/var/adm/sulog
```

Through the /etc/default/su file, you can also set up the system to display a message on the console each time an attempt is made to use the su command to gain superuser access from a remote system. This is a good way to immediately detect someone trying to gain superuser access on the system on which you are working.

To display superuser (root) access attempts to the console:

1. Become superuser.

2. Edit the /etc/default/su file.

3. Uncomment the following line:

```
CONSOLE=/dev/console
```

4. Use the su command to become root, and verify that a message is printed on the system console.

## Automated Security Enhancement Tool (ASET)

SunOS 5.x system software includes the Automated Security Enhancement Tool (ASET). ASET helps you monitor and control system security by automatically performing tasks you would otherwise do manually. ASET performs the following seven tasks, each making specific checks and adjustments to system files and permissions to assure system security.

■ Verifies appropriate system file permissions

■ Verifies system file contents

■ Checks consistency and integrity of /etc/passwd and /etc/group entries

■ Checks on the contents of system configuration files

■ Checks environment files (.profile, .login, .cshrc)

■ Verifies appropriate eeprom settings

■ Builds a firewall on a router

The ASET security package the  provides automated administration tools that enable you to control and monitor your system's security. You specify a low, medium, or high security level at which ASET will run. At each higher level, ASET's file-control functions increase to reduce file access and tighten your system security.

ASET tasks are disk-intensive and can interfere with regular activities. To minimize the impact on system performance, schedule ASET to run when the system activity level is lowest—for example, once every 24 or 48 hours at midnight.

## Common Sense Security Techniques

A system administrator can have the best system security measures in place, but without the users' cooperation, system security will be compromised. The system administrator must teach common-sense rules regarding system security, such as:

- Use proper passwords. Countless sites use passwords such as "admin" or "supervisor" for their root accounts.

- Don't give your password out to anyone, no matter who they say they are. One of the best system crackers of our time would simply pose as a system support person, ask a user for his password, and have free reign to the system.

- If you walk away from the system, log out or lock the screen. Think of the damage if someone walked up to your station and sent a scathing email to the president of your company—with your name attached!

- Don't connect modems to your system without approval from the system administrator.

We've discussed fundamental concepts in system security in this chapter. Although system crackers seem to always find new ways to break into systems, the concepts described in this chapter provide a strong defense against an attack. Chapter 5, "Setting Up User Accounts," will put these concepts to practical use as you set up and manage user accounts.

# Setting Up User Accounts

The following are the test objectives for this chapter:

- Using Admintool to create and administer group and user accounts

- Setting up password aging on user accounts

- Locking or deleting a user account

- Using default environment files from /etc/skel to set up a user environment

- Customizing and administering initialization files

**A**ccess to a system is allowed only through user login accounts set up by the system administrator. A user account includes information a user needs to log in and use a system—a user login name, a password, the user's home directory, and login initialization files. User accounts can range from occasional guests needing read-only access to a few files to regular users who need to share information between several departments. Table 5–1 lists the methods and tools available in Solaris for adding new user accounts to the system.

## Table 5–1    Adding New User Accounts

| Environment | Recommended Tool | Availability |
| --- | --- | --- |
| On remote and/or local systems in a networked, name service (NIS, NIS+) environment | User and Group Manager (graphical user interface) from the Solstice AdminSuite | Available as a separate product. Refer to the *Solstice AdminSuite 2.3 Administration Guide.* |
| Local system | Admintool (graphical user interface) | Provided with Solaris 2.6. |
| Command-line | Terminal window (CDE environment) or shell tool or command tool (OpenWindows environment) | Provided with Solaris 2.6. |

One way to add user accounts is from the command line. Solaris supplies the following commands for setting up user accounts:

| | |
| --- | --- |
| useradd | Add a new user account |
| userdel | Delete a user account |
| usermod | Modify a user account |
| groupadd | Add a new group |
| groupmod | Modify a group (for example, change the group ID or name) |
| groupdel | Delete a group |

As with many UNIX commands, the command line method of adding user accounts is cumbersome and confusing. For this reason, Sun has added user account administration to the Solaris Admintool. Admintool is a graphical user interface designed to ease several routine system administration tasks. By using the Admintool, the system administrator is presented with a menu-like interface that is much easier to use than the ASCII interface supplied at the command prompt. Admintool does not change name service maps or tables when NIS or NIS+ is being used; this task is accomplished by an unbundled product called Solstice AdminSuite. For instructions on using AdminSuite, refer to the *Solstice AdminSuite 2.3 Administration Guide.*

This chapter describes how to use the Solaris Admintool to add user accounts to the system. When you're adding or modifying user accounts, the Admintool edits the files /etc/passwd, /etc/shadow, and /etc/group. As root, you could edit these files directly, but it is not recommended. Errors in any of the files could cause adverse effects on the system.

## Adding User Accounts with Admintool

To perform administrative tasks such as adding user accounts, the administrator must be logged in as superuser or be a member of GID 14. The first step in setting up a new user account is to have the user provide the information you will need to administer this account. You'll also need to set up proper permissions so the users can share information with other members of their departments. To start, you'll need to know the user's full name, department, and any groups with which the user will be working. I like to sit down with the user and fill out an information sheet like the one in Table 5–2 so I have all of the information I'll need when I set up the account.

### Table 5–2   User Information Data Sheet

| Item | Description |
| --- | --- |
| User Name: | |
| UID: | |
| Primary Group: | |
| Secondary Groups: | |
| Comment: | |
| Default Shell: | |
| Password Status and Aging: | |
| Home Directory Server Name: | |
| Home Directory Path Name: | |
| Mail Server: | |
| Department Name: | |
| Department Administrator: | |
| Manager: | |
| Employee Name: | |
| Employee Title: | |
| Employee Status: | |
| Employee Number: | |
| Start Date: | |
| Desktop System Name: | |

To add a new user login account, follow this procedure:

1. Start up Admintool as the user root by typing **admintool** at the command prompt.

   The Users main menu appears, as shown in Figure 5–1.

**Figure 5–1**

*The Users main menu.*

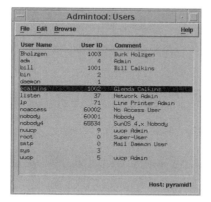

2. Choose Edit, Add to display the Add User window, as shown in Figure 5–2.

**Figure 5–2**

*The Add User window.*

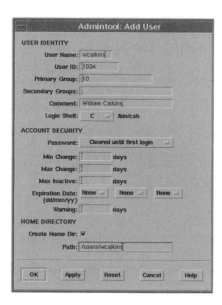

3. Fill in text boxes in the Add User window. Table 5–3 describes the information needed. If you aren't sure how to complete a field, click on the Help button to see field definitions for this window.

4. After entering the information, click on OK. The current list of user accounts is displayed in the Users main window.

---

## Table 5–3　Add User Fields

| Item | Description |
| --- | --- |
| User Name | Enter the login name that will be entered at the Solaris login prompt. Choose a name unique to your organization. The name can contain from two to eight letters and numerals, but no underscores. The first character must be a letter, and at least one character must be a lowercase letter. |
| User ID | Enter the unique user ID (discussed in Chapter 4, "System Security"). Admintool automatically assigns the next available UID; however, in a networked environment, make sure this number is not duplicated by another user on another system. All UIDs must be consistent across the network. |
| Primary Group | Enter the primary group name or GID (group ID) number for the group to which the user will belong. This is the group the operating system will assign to files created by the user. |
| Secondary Groups | (Optional) Enter the names or GIDs, separated by spaces, of any additional groups to which the user belongs. A user can belong to as many as 16 secondary groups. |
| Comment | (Optional) Enter any comments, such as the full user name or phone number. |
| Login Shell | Click on this button to select the shell the user will use; for example, /bin/csh. If nothing is selected, the default shell is the Bourne shell (/bin/sh). |
| Password | Click on this button to specify the password status. Selectable options are as follows:<br><br>Cleared until first login.<br><br>[Default] Account does not have a password assigned. The user is prompted for a password on first login, unless passreq=no is set in /etc/default/login.<br><br>Account is locked.<br><br>Account is disabled with an invalid password and can be unlocked by assigning a new password. This type of account allows a user to own files but not to log in.<br><br>No password; setuid only.<br><br>Account cannot be logged into directly. This allows programs such as lp or uucp to run under an account without allowing a user to log in.<br><br>Normal password.<br><br>Account will have a password that you set in the pop-up window that appears. |

## Table 5–3 Add User Fields (continued)

| Item | Description |
| --- | --- |
| Min Change | (Optional) The minimum number of days allowed between password changes. This is intended to prevent a user from changing the password and then changing it back a few seconds later, which would defeat the concept of password aging. The default is 0. |
| Max Change | (Optional) The maximum number of days the password is valid before it must be changed; otherwise, the account is locked. Leaving the field blank means the password never has to be changed. |
| Max Inactive | (Optional) The maximum number of days an account may go without being accessed before it is automatically locked. A blank field means the account remains active no matter how long it goes unused. |
| Expiration Date | (Optional) The date when the user account expires. None means no expiration. |
| Warning | (Optional) The number of days to begin warning the user before the password expires. A blank means no warning is given. |
| Create Home Dir check box | Select this box to have the user's home directory automatically created. |
| Path | Use the Path field to point to an existing directory or to specify a new directory to create. |

**NOTE.** *Users can type the UNIX command* passwd *at the command prompt to change their passwords.*

# Deleting a User Account with Admintool

Use the Admintool to delete an existing user account. The procedure to delete a user account is as follows:

1.  Start Admintool, if it's not already running, and choose Browse, Users.

2.  Select the user account entry you wish to remove from the Users window.

3.  Choose Edit, Delete.

4.  The message is displayed to confirm the removal of the user account (see Figure 5–3).

**Figure 5–3**

*Confirmation that you want to delete the user account.*

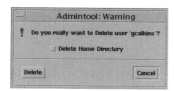

5. (Optional) Click on the Delete Home Directory check box to delete the user's home directory and its contents. If you don't check the box, the user account will be deleted but the contents of the user's home directory will remain.

6. Click on OK when you are ready to delete the user account. The user account entry is deleted from the Users main window.

## Modifying a User Account with Admintool

If a login needs to be modified—to change a password or disable an account, for example—use the Admintool to modify these user account settings. The process is as follows:

1. Start Admintool, if it's not already running, and choose Browse, Users.

2. Select the user account entry to be disabled.

3. Choose Edit, Modify.

4. The Modify Users window is displayed, containing the selected user account entry.

5. The following are descriptions of some of the modifications allowed:

   ■ Locking a login

     Choose Password: Account Is Locked, as shown in Figure 5–4.

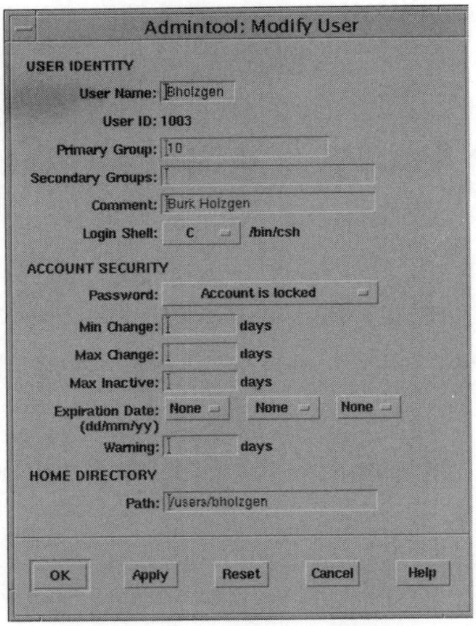

**Figure 5–4**

*The Modify User window.*

```
┌──────────────────────────────────────────┐
│  ▭        Admintool: Modify User          │
│                                            │
│  USER IDENTITY                             │
│         User Name: Bholzgen                │
│           User ID: 1003                    │
│      Primary Group: 10                     │
│   Secondary Groups: [            ]         │
│           Comment: Burk Holzgen            │
│        Login Shell:  C  ▾  /bin/csh        │
│                                            │
│  ACCOUNT SECURITY                          │
│          Password:   Account is locked  ▾  │
│        Min Change: [      ]  days          │
│        Max Change: [      ]  days          │
│       Max Inactive: [      ]  days         │
│    Expiration Date: None ▾  None ▾ None ▾  │
│         (dd/mm/yy)                         │
│           Warning: [      ]  days          │
│  HOME DIRECTORY                            │
│              Path: /users/bholzgen         │
│                                            │
│   ┌────┐  ┌──────┐ ┌──────┐ ┌──────┐ ┌──────┐ │
│   │ OK │  │Apply │ │Reset │ │Cancel│ │ Help │ │
│   └────┘  └──────┘ └──────┘ └──────┘ └──────┘ │
└──────────────────────────────────────────┘
```

■ Changing a user's password

Enable a user account by changing the password status to Normal Password or Cleared Until First Login.

6. Click on OK and the modification is made.

## Adding a Group with Admintool

You might need to add a group that does not already exist on the system. Perhaps a new group of users called "engrg" (from the engineering department) needs to be added. The following steps describe how to add the new "engrg" group.

1. Start Admintool, if it's not already running, and choose Browse, Groups.

2. The Groups window is displayed, as shown in Figure 5–5.

**Figure 5–5**

*The Groups window.*

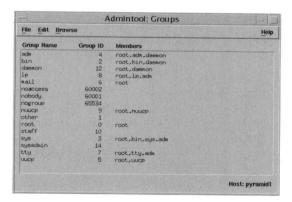

3. Choose Edit, Add.

4. The Add Group window is displayed, as shown in Figure 5–6. If you're not sure how to complete a field, click on the Help button to see field definitions for this window.

**Figure 5–6**

*The Add Group window.*

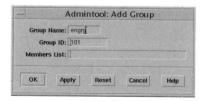

5. Type the name of the new group in the Group Name text box.

6. Type the group ID number for the new group in the Group ID text box. This should be a unique number.

7. (Optional) Type user names in the Members List text box. These are the users who belong to the new group. User names must be separated by commas. The list of users will be added to the group.

8. Click on OK. The list of groups displayed in the Groups window is updated to include the new group.

## Setting Up User Initialization Files

Part of setting up a user's home directory is providing user initialization files for the user's login shell. A user initialization file is a shell script that sets up a work environment for a user after the user logs in to a system. You can perform any task in a user initialization file that you can perform in a shell script, but its primary job is to define the characteristics of the user's work environment, such as search path, environment variables, and windowing environment. Each login shell has its own user initialization file (or files), located in the user's home directory. These files are automatically run when the user logs in.

Default user initialization files, such as .cshrc, .profile, and .login, are created automatically in the user's home directory when a new user account is added. The system administrator can predefine the contents of these files or can choose to use the system default files. The Solaris 2.x system software provides default user initialization files for each shell in the /etc/skel directory on each system. These files are named as follows:

local.cshrc          The default .cshrc file for the C shell.

local.login          The default .login file for the C shell.

local.profile        The default .profile file for the Bourne and K shells.

You can use these initialization files as a starting point and modify them to create a standard set of files that will provide a work environment common to all users. You can also modify them to provide the working environment for different types of users.

## Customizing User Initialization Files

When a user logs into a system, the user's work environment is determined by the shell initialization files. The shell start-up scripts can be modified to set environment variables and directory paths needed by a specific user. These start-up scripts are located in the user's home directory.

When you're setting up user initialization files, it might be important to allow the users to customize their own initialization files. This can be accomplished with centrally located and globally distributed user initialization files called site initialization files. Site initialization files enable you to continually introduce new functionality to all of the user work environments by editing one initialization file. A local initialization file enables users to further customize their own work environment. Site initialization files are located in the /etc directory and can be edited only by root. Site initialization files are designed to distribute site-wide changes to all user work environments. Individual user initialization files are located in each user's home directory and can be customized by the owner of that directory. When a user logs in, the site initialization file is run first, and then the initialization file located in the user's home directory is run.

**NOTE.** *Do not use system initialization files located in the /etc directory (/etc/profile, /etc/.login) to manage an individual user's work environment. These are site initialization files, considered to be global files, meant to be generic and used to set work environments for all users. The system will run this start-up file first and will then run the user's start-up file located in the home directory.*

The most common customizations to shell startup scripts are environment variables. Table 5–4 describes environment and shell variables you might want to customize in a user initialization file.

---

## Table 5–4    Shell and Environment Variable Descriptions

| Variable | Description |
| --- | --- |
| ARCH | Sets the user's system architecture (for example, sun4, i386). This variable can be set with ARCH = `uname -p` (in Bourne or Korn shells) or setenv ARCH `uname -p` (in the C shell). The shell has no built-in behavior that depends on this variable; it's just a useful variable for branching within shell scripts. |
| history | Sets history for the C shell. |
| HOME | Sets the path to the user's home directory. |
| LPDEST | Sets the user's default printer. |
| PATH (or path in the C shell) | Lists, in order, the directories the shell searches to find the program to run when the user types a command. If the directory is not in the search path, users must type the complete pathname of a command.

The default PATH is automatically defined in .profile (Bourne or Korn shell) or .cshrc (C shell) as part of the login process.

The order of the search path is important. When identical commands exist in different locations, the first command found with that name is used. For example, suppose PATH is defined (in Bourne and Korn shell syntax) as PATH=/bin:/usr/bin:/usr/sbin:$HOME/bin and a file named sample resides in both /usr/bin and /home/glenda/bin. If the user types the command sample without specifying its full pathname, the version found in /usr/bin is used. |

*continues*

**Table 5–4    Shell and Environment Variable Descriptions (continued)**

| Variable | Description |
| --- | --- |
| prompt | Defines the shell prompt for the C shell. |
| TERM (or term in the C shell) | Defines the terminal. This variable should be reset in /etc/profile or /etc/.login. When the user invokes an editor, the system looks for a file with the same name as the definition of this environment variable. The system searches the directory /usr/share/lib/terminfo to determine the terminal characteristics. |
| MAIL | Sets the path to the user's mailbox. |
| MANPATH | Sets the search path for system manual pages. |
| umask | Sets the default user mask. |

The following example illustrates how to verify a user's environment settings and how to change them.

1. Log in as the user. This step enables you to see the user's environment as the user will see it.

2. Edit the user's initialization files. The following steps suggest some changes and show the shell-specific syntax to use.

3. Set the user's default path to include the home directory and directories or mount points for the user's windowing environment and applications. To change the path setting, add or modify the line for PATH as follows:

For the Bourne or Korn shell, the syntax is:

```
PATH=/dirname1:/dirname2:/dirname3:.; export PATH
```

For example, enter the following line in the user's $HOME/.profile file:

```
PATH=$PATH:/usr/bin:/$HOME/bin:/net/glrr/files1/bin:.;export PATH
```

For the C shell, the syntax is:

```
set path =(/dirname1 /dirname2 /dirname3 .)
```

For example, enter the following line in the user's $HOME/.cshrc file:

```
set path=($path /usr/bin $HOME/bin /net/glrr/files1/bin .)
```

**N O T E .** *Prefixing $PATH (K shell) or $path (C shell) appends changes to the user's path settings already set by the site initialization file. When you set the path variable with this procedure, initial path settings are not overwritten and lost. Also note the "dot" (.) at the end of the list to denote the current working directory. The dot should always be at the end of the path, as discussed in Chapter 4.*

4. Check that the environment variables are set to the correct directories for the user's windowing environments and third-party applications. Type **env** and press Enter.

```
$ env
HOME=/home/ncalkins
HZ=100
LOGNAME=ncalkins
MAIL=/var/mail/ncalkins
MANSECTS=\1:1m:1c:1f:1s:1b:2:\3:3c:3i:3n:3m:3k:3g:3e:3x11:3
xt:3w:3b:9:4:5:7:8
PATH=/usr/bin
SHELL=/bin/sh
TERM=sun
TZ=EST5EDT
$
```

5. Add or change the settings of environment variables by entering either of the following lines.

For the Bourne or Korn shell, the syntax is:

```
VARIABLE=value;export VARIABLE
```

The following example sets the user's default mail directory:

```
MAIL=/var/mail/ncalkins;export MAIL
```

For the C shell, the syntax is:

```
setenv VARIABLE value
```

The following example sets the history to record the last 100 commands:

```
setenv HISTORY 100
```

## Directories

The home directory is the portion of a file system allocated to a user for storing private files. The amount of space you allocate for home directories depends on the kinds of files the users create and the type of work performed. An entire file system is usually allocated specifically for home directories, and the users all share this space. The system administrator needs to monitor user home directories so one user does not use more than his fair share of space. Disk quotas are used to control the amount of disk space a user can occupy and are discussed in Chapter 3, "Introduction to File Systems."

A home directory can be located either on the user's local system or on a remote file server. Although any directory name can be used, the home directory in either case is, by convention, /export/home/username. When you put the home directory in /export/home, the home

directory is available across the network in case the user logs in from several different stations. For a large site, you should store home directories on a server.

Regardless of where their home directory is located, users usually access them through a mount point named /home/username. When AutoFS is used to mount home directories, you are not permitted to create any directories under the /home mount point on any system. The system recognizes the special status of /home when AutoFS is active. For more information about AutoFS and automounting home directories, see the *NFS Administration Guide*.

To access the home directory anywhere on the network, you should always refer to it as $HOME, not as /export/home/username. The latter is machine-specific and should be discouraged. In addition, any symbolic links created in a user's home directory should use relative paths (for example, ../../../x/y/x) so the links will be valid no matter where the home directory is mounted. The location of user home directories might change. By not using machine-specific names, you maintain consistency and reduce system administration.

This concludes the discussion on how to add user login accounts to the system. By default, when users first log in, they are presented with a default desktop window environment called CDE (Common Desktop Environment). Setup and customization of CDE is described in Chapter 7, "Administration and Configuration of the CDE."

# 6

## Software
## Package
## Administration

The following are the test objectives for this chapter:

- Understanding software packages and how to display software package information

- Adding software packages

- Removing software packages

- Installing and removing software patches

The system administrator is responsible for managing all software installed on a system. Installing and removing software is a routine task that is performed frequently. In Chapter 2, "Installing the Solaris 2.x Software," I described the installation of the Solaris operating system. In this chapter, I explain how to add and remove additional applications after the operating system has already been installed.

Sun and its third-party vendors deliver software products in a form called a software *package*. The term "package" refers to a method of distributing and installing software products to systems where the products will be used. A package is a collection of files and directories in a defined format that conforms to the Application Binary Interface (ABI), a supplement to the System V Interface Definition. The Solaris operating environment provides a set of utilities that interpret the ABI format and provide the means to install or remove a package or to verify its installation.

## Tools for Managing Software

Solaris provides two tools for adding and removing software from a system. Both are shown in Table 6–1.

**Table 6–1    Tools for Managing Software**

| Command | Description |
| --- | --- |
| *Managing software from the command line* | |
| pkgadd | Adds software packages to the system |
| pkgrm | Removes software packages from the system |
| pkgchk | Checks the accuracy of a software package installation |
| pkginfo | Displays software package information |
| pkgask | Stores answers in a response file so they can be supplied automatically during an installation |
| *Managing software from the graphical user interface* | |
| Admintool™ | A GUI that is invoked from within CDE or OpenWindows |

Use the pkgadd or pkgrm commands directly from the command line to load or remove software. The pkgadd and pkgrm commands can be incorporated into scripts to automate the software installation process. Many third-party vendors use pkgadd in scripts as a means to install their software.

Admintool, on the other hand, provides an easy-to-use interface for installing or removing software. It is simply a graphical user interface to the pkgadd and pkgrm. Using the Admintool graphical interface is a convenient way to view software already installed on a system or to view the software that resides on the installation media. If you're unfamiliar with software-package naming conventions or uncomfortable using command-line options, or if you're managing software on only one system at time, you'll find Admintool an easy way to add and remove software.

## Adding and Removing Software Packages

When you add a software package, the pkgadd command uncompresses and copies files from the installation media, such as the CD-ROM, to a local system's disk. When you use packages, files are delivered in package format and are unusable as they are delivered. The pkgadd command interprets the software package's control files and then uncompresses the product files and installs them on the system's local disk.

Here are a few things you should know before installing additional application software:

- Sun packages always begin with the prefix SUNW, as in SUNWvolr, SUNWadmap, and SUNWab2m. Third-party packages usually begin with a prefix that corresponds to the company's stock symbol.

- You can use the pkginfo command or Admintool to view software already installed on a system.

- Clients might have software that resides partially on a server and partially on the client. If this is the case, adding software for the client requires adding packages to both the server and the client.

- You need to know where the software will be installed and make sure you have a file system with enough disk space to store the application software. Use the pkgparam command to determine where the package will be loaded. For example, type

  `pkgparam -d /cdrom/cdrom0/s0/Solaris_2.6   /Product SUNWvolr SUNW_PKGTYPE`

  The system responds with the location where the application will be stored:

  `root`

When you remove a package, the pkgrm command deletes all files associated with that package unless those files are also shared with other packages. Be sure you do not delete application software without using pgkrm. For example, some system administrators delete an application simply by removing the directory containing the application software. With this method, files belonging to the application that might reside in other directories are missed. With pkgrm, you'll be assured of removing all files associated with the application.

Although the `pkgadd` and `pkgrm` commands do not log their output to a standard location, they do keep track of the product installed or removed. The `pkgadd` and `pkgrm` commands store information about a package that has been installed or removed in a software product database. By updating this database, the `pkgadd` and `pkgrm` commands keep a record of all software products installed on the system.

## Adding Software Packages

The procedure for installing additional application software with Admintool is as follows:

1. Start Admintool as the user root by typing **admintool** at the command prompt.

2. The Users main menu appears, as shown in Figure 6–1.

**Figure 6–1**

*The Users main menu.*

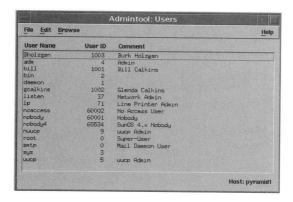

3. Choose Browse, Software. The Software window appears, as shown in Figure 6–2.

**Figure 6–2**

*The Software window.*

4.  Choose Edit, Add. The Set Source Media window appears, as shown in Figure 6–3.

**Figure 6–3**

*The Set Source Media window.*

5.  Specify the path to the installation media. The default path from which to install the application is the mounted SPARC Solaris CD. Click on OK to display the Add Software window, as shown in Figure 6–4.

**Figure 6–4**

*The Add Software window.*

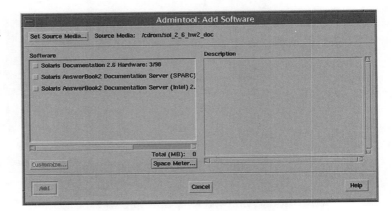

6.  In the Software portion of the window, click on the check boxes corresponding to the software you want to install. When you have selected all of the packages, click on the Add button.

A command tool window appears for each package being installed, displaying the installation output. When the installation is complete, the Software window refreshes to display the packages just added.

## Removing Software Packages

The procedure for removing application software is as follows:

1.  Start Admintool, if it's not already running, and choose Browse, Users to open the Users main menu, shown in Figure 6–5.

**Figure 6–5**

*The Users main menu.*

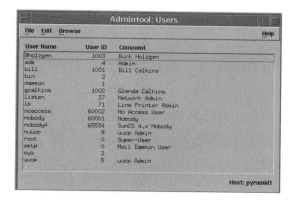

2. Choose Browse, Software. The Software window opens, as shown in Figure 6–6.

**Figure 6–6**

*The Software window.*

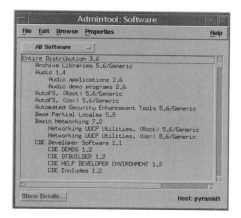

3. Select the software package you wish to remove, and choose Edit, Delete. A message appears, asking you to confirm that you want to remove the software (see Figure 6–7).

**Figure 6–7**

*Confirm the software removal.*

For each package being deleted, a command tool window is displayed, asking for confirmation before deleting the software. Type **y**, **n**, or **q**. If you choose to delete the software, the output from the removal process is displayed in the command tool window.

# Listing and Verifying Installed Packages

At any time, you can use Admintool or issue the `pkginfo` command from the command line to get a complete listing of the software installed on a system. The Software window in Admintool displays all of the installed software when you choose Software from the Browse menu (see Figure 6–8).

**Figure 6–8**

*The Software window.*

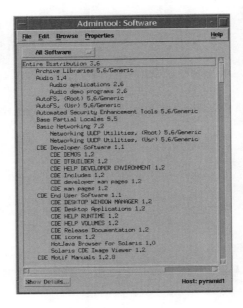

More information about individual software packages can be obtained by double-clicking any of the listed software packages in Admintool.

Figure 6–9 illustrates the `pkginfo` command used from the command line, with `more` to stop the display of information one page at a time.

**Figure 6–9**

*The* pkginfo *output.*

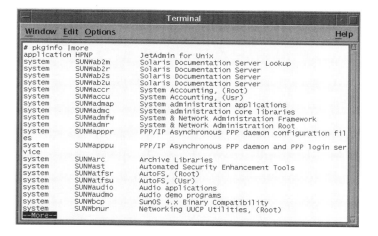

```
# pkginfo |more
application HPNP          JetAdmin for Unix
system      SUNWab2m      Solaris Documentation Server Lookup
system      SUNWab2r      Solaris Documentation Server
system      SUNWab2s      Solaris Documentation Server
system      SUNWab2u      Solaris Documentation Server
system      SUNWaccr      System Accounting, (Root)
system      SUNWaccu      System Accounting, (Usr)
system      SUNWadmap     System administration applications
system      SUNWadmc      System administration core libraries
system      SUNWadmfw     System & Network Administration Framework
system      SUNWadmr      System & Network Administration Root
system      SUNWapppr     PPP/IP Asynchronous PPP daemon configuration fil
es
system      SUNWapppu     PPP/IP Asynchronous PPP daemon and PPP login ser
vice
system      SUNWarc       Archive Libraries
system      SUNWast       Automated Security Enhancement Tools
system      SUNWatfsr     AutoFS, (Root)
system      SUNWatfsu     AutoFS, (Usr)
system      SUNWaudio     Audio applications
system      SUNWaudmo     Audio demo programs
system      SUNWbcp       SunOS 4.x Binary Compatibility
system      SUNWbnur      Networking UUCP Utilities, (Root)
--More--
```

# Software Patches

Another system administration task is managing system software patches. A *patch* is a fix to
a reported software problem. Sun will ship several software patches to customers so problems can be resolved before the next release of software. The existing software is derived
from a specified package format, which conforms to the Application Binary Interface.

Patches are identified by unique alphanumeric strings, with the patch base code first, a
hyphen, and then a number that represents the patch revision number. For example, patch
101977-04 is a Solaris 2.x patch to correct the lockd daemon.

You might want to know more about patches that have previously been installed. Table 6–2
shows commands that provide useful information about patches already installed on a
system.

## Table 6–2   Helpful Commands for Patch Administration

| Command | Function |
| --- | --- |
| showrev -p | Shows all patches applied to a system. |
| pkgparam *pkgid* PATCHLIST | Shows all patches applied to the package identified by pkgid. |
| pkgparam *pkgid* PATCH_INFO_*patch-number* | Shows the installation date and name of the host from which the patch was applied. pkgid is the name of the package: for example, SUNWadmap. |
| patchadd -R *client_root_path* -p | Shows all patches applied to a client, from the server's console. |
| patchadd -p | Shows all patches applied to a system. |
| patchrm *patchname* | Removes a specified patch. |

## Installing a Patch

All Sun customers can access security patches and other recommended patches via the World Wide Web or anonymous FTP. Sun customers who have purchased a service contract can access an extended set of patches and a complete database of patch information. This information is available via the World Wide Web or anonymous FTP and is regularly distributed on a CD-ROM. See Appendix D, "On the Web," for a listing of useful Web sites and where to access patches via the Web.

Detailed information about how to install and remove a patch is provided in the Install.info file included with each patch. Each patch also contains a README file that contains specific information about the patch.

The patchadd command is used to install directory-format patches to a Solaris 2.x system and must be run as root. The syntax is

```
patchadd [ -d ] [ -u ] [ -B backout_dir ]
```

The patchadd command is described in Table 6–3.

**Table 6–3**  *patchadd* **Command Options**

| Common Option | Description |
| --- | --- |
| -d | Does not create a backup of the files to be patched. The patch cannot be removed when this option has been used to install the patch. By default, patchadd saves a copy of all files being updated so the patch can be removed if necessary. Do not use the -d option unless you're positive the patch has been tested. |
| -p | Displays a list of the patches currently applied. |
| -u | Installs the patch unconditionally, with file validation turned off. The patch is installed even if some of the files to be patched have been modified since their original installation. |
| -B backout_dir | Saves backout data to a directory other than the package database. Specify backout_dir as an absolute pathname. |

Additional options to the patchadd command security can be found online in the Solaris system manual pages.

The following example installs a patch to a standalone machine.

```
patchadd /var/spool/patch/104945-02
```

The following example installs multiple patches. The patchlist file specifies a file containing a list of patches to install.

```
patchadd -M /var/spool/patch patchlist
```

The following example displays the patches installed on a system.

```
patchadd -R /export/root/client1 -p
```

When you're installing a patch, the `patchadd` command copies files from the patch directory to the local system's disk. More specifically, `patchadd` does two things:

- Determines the Solaris version number of the managing host and the target host.

- Updates the patch package's pkginfo file with information about patches made obsolete by the patch being installed, other patches required by this patch, and patches incompatible with this patch.

The `patchadd` command will not install a patch under the following conditions:

- The package is not fully installed on the host.

- The patch architecture differs from the system architecture.

- The patch version does not match the installed package version.

- There is already an installed patch with the same base code and a higher version number.

- The patch is incompatible with another, already installed patch. (Each installed patch keeps this information in its pkginfo file.)

- The patch being installed requires another patch that is not installed.

## Removing a Patch

Sometimes a patch does not work as planned and needs to be removed from the system. The utility used to remove or "back out" of a patch is the `patchrm` command described in Table 6–4. Its syntax is

```
patchrm [ -f ] [ -B backout_dir ]
```

The `patchrm` command removes a Solaris 2.x patch package and restores previously saved files, restoring the file system to its state before a patch was applied, unless

- The patch was installed with `patchadd -d`. The -d option instructs `patchadd` not to save copies of files being updated or replaced.

- The patch has been made obsolete by a later patch.

- The patch is required by another patch.

- The `patchrm` command calls `pkgadd` to restore packages saved from the initial patch installation.

**Table 6–4**   *patchrm* **Command Options**

| Common Options | Description |
| --- | --- |
| -f | Forces the patch removal regardless of whether the patch was superseded by another patch. |
| -B *backout_dir* | Removes a patch whose backout data has been saved to a directory other than the package database. This option is needed only if the original backout directory, supplied to the patchrm command at installation time, has been moved. Specify *backout_dir* as an absolute pathname. |

The following example removes a patch from a standalone system:

```
patchrm 104945-02
```

## General Guidelines

Some software packages do not conform to the ABI and therefore cannot be installed by using Admintool or the pkgadd command. For installation of products that do not conform to ABI, follow the vendor's specific installation instructions. Here are a few additional guidelines to follow when installing new software on a system:

- Always be cautious with third-party or public-domain software. Make sure the software has been tested and is free of viruses before installing it on a production system.

- Make sure the software package is supported under Solaris 2.6.

- Always read the vendor's release notes for special loading instructions. They might contain kernel parameters that need to be modified or suggest software patches that need to be applied.

- Do not install patches unless directed by Sun or one of your software providers. Some patches have not been tested thoroughly, especially when used in conjunction with other software patches. Adverse system performance problems could result.

Adding and removing software packages is one of the simpler tasks you will encounter in system administration. As with all computer software, you should first load new software packages on a nonproduction system for test purposes. Only after the software has been thoroughly tested should you install it on a production system.

This chapter described installing software, creating file systems, and setting up user accounts. Now it's time to start customizing what you have installed on the system. Chapter 7, "Administration and Configuration of the CDE," describes customization of the user's work environment. Looking ahead, Chapter 11, "Backup and Recovery," describes how to create a tape backup of everything you've installed. A good backup can save you time in the event of a hardware malfunction. With a good backup, you won't need to retrace the steps of reinstalling software packages or patches and setting up users.

# 7

# Administration and Configuration of the CDE

The following are the test objectives for this chapter:

- Understanding and configuring the Login Manager, Session Manager, and Front Panel

- Configuring CDE environment variables

- Understanding actions and data types

- Adding and administering applications with Application Manager

The Solaris Common Desktop Environment (CDE) is an easy-to-use interface that provides a consistent look and feel across UNIX environments. SunSoft, Inc., Hewlett-Packard Company, IBM Corporation, and Novell, Inc. each contributed "best-of-breed" technologies to establish the new standard for user and application interfaces based on the X Window System and MOTIF. While maintaining compliance with the CDE standards, Solaris CDE offers additional benefits to its users and developers. For example, you can use an image viewer to display, rotate, zoom, and convert images and PostScript files.

If you have used Sun's older windowing environment, OpenWindows, you have seen the familiar backdrops, color palettes, and pop-up Workspace menu. In CDE, a user can also run OpenWindows applications without modification. For instance, CDE supports drag-and-drop interaction between OpenWindows applications and CDE applications.

The key features available to you within CDE are CDE environment, desktop tools, and the CDE Development Environment. This chapter discusses customization of the CDE environment, which consists of

- *Login Manager*—A graphical login window that comes up after the system is booted

- *Session Manager*—A service that starts users' applications on the desktop at login and "remembers" the desktop state the next time they log in

- *Front Panel*—The set of pop-ups and icons that appear at the bottom of the CDE screen

- *Resetting User Customizations*—Setting the CDE back to its default environment

- *Actions and Data Types*—Associating commands with icons

- *Application Manager*—The desktop container displaying applications available to the user

- *dtksh shell*—kshell scripting within the desktop

## The Login Manager

The Login Manager is a server responsible for displaying a login screen, authenticating users, and starting a user's session. Displays managed by the login server can be directly attached to the login server or attached to an X terminal or workstation on the network.

The login screen, displayed by the login server, is an attractive alternative to the traditional character-mode login screen and provides capabilities beyond those provided by a character-mode login. As with a character-mode login, however, the user enters a username, followed by a password. If the user is authenticated, the login server starts a desktop session for the user. When the user exits the desktop session, the login server displays a new login screen, and the process begins again.

You can customize the login screen in the following ways:

- Change the login screen appearance
- Configure X server authority
- Change the default language
- Issue commands prior to display of the login screen
- Change the contents of the login screen Language menu
- Specify the command to start the user's session
- Issue commands prior to the start of the user's desktop session
- Issue commands after the user's session ends

Each of these customizations can be done for all displays or on a per-display basis. Refer to the *Solaris CDE Advanced User's and System Administrator's Guide* for detailed instructions on making these modifications.

## Starting the Login Server

The login server usually starts up the CDE environment when the system is booted. It can also be started from a command line. For example, to start the login server from a command line, type the following:

```
/usr/dt/bin/dtlogin -daemon; exit
```

**NOTE.** *Although you can start the login server from the command line for temporary configuration testing, you normally set up the login server to start when the system is booted.*

To set the login server CDE to start the next time the system is booted, type the following:

```
/usr/dt/bin/dtconfig -e
```

The login server will then start automatically after the user reboots the system.

## Stopping the Login Server

To disable login server CDE startup the next time the system is booted, type the following:

```
/usr/dt/bin/dtconfig -d
```

This command tells the system not to start the login server on the next reboot.

You can stop the login server immediately by killing its process ID. Type the command

`/usr/dt/bin/dtconfig -kill`

This command issues the command `kill login_server_process_ID`.

**NOTE.** *If the user is logged in to the desktop at the time you kill the login server, the desktop session immediately terminates.*

## Displaying a Login Screen on a Local Display

On startup, the login server checks the Xservers file to determine whether an Xserver needs to be started and to determine whether and how login screens should be displayed on local or network displays. The format of a line in the Xservers file is:

`display_name display_class display_type X_server_command`

Each field in the Xservers file is described in Table 7–1.

**Table 7–1    Fields in the Xservers File**

| | |
|---|---|
| display_name | Tells the login server the name to use when connecting to the Xserver (`:0` in the following example). A value of * (asterisk) is expanded to `hostname:0`. The number specified must match the number specified in the `X_server_command` connection number. |
| display_class | Identifies resources specific to this display (`Local` in the following example). |
| display_type | Tells the login server whether the display is local or network and how to manage the Command Line Login option on the login screen (`local@console` in the following example). |
| X_server_command | Identifies the command line, connection number, and other options that the login server will use to start the Xserver (`/usr/bin/X11/X: 0` in the following example). The connection number specified must match the number specified in the `display_name` field. |

The default line in the Xservers file is similar to

`:0 Local local@console /usr/bin/X11/X :0`

To modify Xservers, copy Xservers from /usr/dt/config to /etc/dt/config. The /etc/dt directory contains customized workstation-specific configuration files. If /etc/dt does not exist, you might need to create it. The system administrator can modify the system default resources by creating the /etc/dt/config/ directory. In this directory, you can create configuration files to override default resources or to specify additional resources for all desktop users. This file is merged into the desktop default resources during session startup.

Resources specified in this file take precedence over those specified in the desktop default resource file. After modifying /etc/dt/config/Xservers, tell the login server to reread Xservers by typing

`/usr/dt/bin/dtconfig -reset`

The `dtconfig -reset` issues the command `kill -HUP login_server_process_ID`.

If your login server system has a character display and not a bitmap display, you need to set `display_terminal_device` to `none` in the Xservers file to disable the login screen and enable the character-mode login screen.

# The Session Manager

A *session* is the collection of applications, settings, and resources present on the user's desktop. Session management is a set of conventions and protocols that enable Session Manager to save and restore a user's session. When a user logs in to the desktop for the first time, a default initial session is loaded. Afterward, a user is able to log in to the system and be presented with the same set of running applications, settings, and resources as were present when she last logged out.

Session Manager is responsible for starting the desktop and automatically saving and restoring running applications, colors, fonts, mouse behavior, audio volume, and keyboard click. Using Session Manager, you can

- Customize the initial session for all desktop users
- Customize the environment and resources for all desktop users
- Change the session startup message
- Change parameters for session startup tools and daemons
- Customize desktop color usage for all users

Session Manager is started through `/usr/dt/bin/Xsession`. When the user logs in, using Login Manager, `Xsession` is started by default. When Session Manager is started, it goes through the following steps to start the user's session:

1. Sources the `HomeDirectory/.dtprofile` script.
2. Sources the `Xsession.d` scripts.
3. Displays a welcome message.
4. Sets up desktop search paths.
5. Gathers available applications.
6. Optionally sources HomeDirectory/.profile or HomeDirectory/.login.

7. Starts the ToolTalk messaging daemon.

8. Loads session resources.

9. Starts the color server.

10. Starts Workspace Manager.

11. Starts the session applications.

## Sourcing the *.dtprofile* Script

At session startup, the Xsession script sources the user's HomeDirectory/.dtprofile script—a /bin/sh or /bin/ksh script that enables users to set up environment variables for their sessions. The .dtprofile accepts only sh or ksh syntax. The desktop default is /usr/dt/config/sys.dtprofile. If the HomeDirectory/.dtprofile script does not exist (for example, when a user is logging in for the first time), Xsession copies the desktop default sys.dtprofile to HomeDirectory/.dtprofile.

You can customize the sys.dtprofile script by copying it from /usr/dt/config to /etc/dt/config and editing the new file. You can set up personal environment variables in HomeDirectory/.dtprofile. For example,

```
export MYVARIABLE="value"
```

sets the variable MYVARIABLE in the user's environment at the next login.

To set system-wide environment variables, create a file in the /etc/dt/config/Xsession.d directory that sets and exports the variable. For example, if you create an executable ksh script, /etc/dt/config/Xsession.d/sitevars, containing

```
export SITEVARIABLE="value"
```

the variable SITEVARIABLE will be set in each user's environment at the next login.

**N O T E .** *Although Session Manager does not automatically read the .profile or .login files, it can be configured to use these files. To tell* Xsession *to source the* .profile *or* .login *script, set the variable* DTSOURCEPROFILE *to* True *in HomeDirectory/.dtprofile.*

## Sourcing the *Xsession.d* Scripts

After sourcing the HomeDirectory/.dtprofile script, the Xsession script sources the Xsession.d scripts. These scripts set up additional environment variables and start optional daemons for the user's session.

**CAUTION!** *Errors in any of the session startup files could prevent a user from logging in. To troubleshoot session startup problems, check the file HomeDirectory/.dt/startlog. Session Manager logs each user's session startup progress in this file.*

## The Welcome Message

After sourcing HomeDirectory/.dtprofile and the `Xsession.d` scripts, `Xsession` displays a welcome message that covers the screen. You can customize the welcome message or turn off the message entirely.

The `dthello` client is used to display the welcome message. To alter the message text, change the `dthello` options by modifying the `dtstart_hello[0]` variable. To change `dtstart_hello[0]`, create a `/usr/dt/config/Xsession.d` script that sets the new value. For example, to display the message of the day for all users, create an executable `sh` or `ksh` script called `usr/dt/config/Xsession.d/myvars` and set `dtstart_hello[0]` as follows:

```
dtstart_hello[0]="/usr/dt/bin/dthello -file /etc/motd &"
```

Users can also change the welcome message for their sessions by setting `dtstart_hello[0]` in HomeDirectory/.dtprofile. To turn off the welcome message, set `dtstart_hello[0]=" "`.

## Setting Desktop Search Paths

The desktop uses search paths, created at login, to locate applications and their associated desktop files. The desktop provides four search paths, described in Table 7–2.

**Table 7–2  Desktop Search Paths**

| Search Path | Description |
| --- | --- |
| Applications | Used to locate applications. Application Manager uses the application search path to dynamically populate its top level when a user logs in. |
| Database | Used to specify additional locations for action- and data-type definition files (*.dt files) and Front Panel files (*.fp files). |
| Icons | Used to specify additional locations for icons. |
| Help data | Used to specify additional locations for desktop help data. |

## Making Modifications to a Search Path

To make modifications to the search path for a particular user, follow these steps:

1. Open HomeDirectory/.dtprofile for editing.

2. Add or edit a line that defines and exports the personal input variable.

   For example, the following line adds a location to the user's personal application search path:

   ```
   export DTSPUSERAPPHOSTS=/projects1/editors
   ```

3. To make the change take effect, log out and then log back in.

## Gathering Available Applications

After setting up the desktop search paths, the next step is to gather available applications by using dtappgather. These are the applications that will be displayed in the Application Manager window. The dtappgather utility gathers application files for presentation by the Application Manager and is responsible for creating and refreshing the user's Application Manager subdirectory.

To alter the command-line options of dtappgather, modify the dtstart_appgather variable either in the /etc/dt/config/Xsession.d/sitevars file for all users or in the HomeDirectory/ .dtprofile for individual users. Set dtstart_appgather as follows:

```
dtstart_appgather="/usr/dt/bin/dtappgather &"
```

## Sourcing a User *.profile* or *.login* File

Xsession is able to source a user's traditional $HOME/.profile or $HOME/.login scripts but by default this capability is disabled. To tell Xsession to source the .profile or .login script, set DTSOURCEPROFILE to true in $HOME/.dtprofile.

## Starting the ToolTalk Messaging Daemon

The next task for Xsession is to start the ToolTalk messaging daemon. The ToolTalk service enables independent applications to communicate without having direct knowledge of each other. Applications create and send ToolTalk messages to communicate with each other. The ToolTalk service receives these messages, determines the recipients, and then delivers the messages to the appropriate applications. Users can change the ttsession options for their own sessions by setting the dtstart_ttsession variable in $HOME/.dtprofile as follows:

```
dtstart_ttsession="/usr/dt/bin/ttsession -s"
```

## Loading Session Resources

Resources are used by applications to set certain aspects of appearance and behavior. For example, Style Manager (dtstyle) provides resources that enable you to specify where the system looks for files containing information about color palettes:

```
dtstyle*paletteDirectories: /usr/dt/palettes/C \ HomeDirectory/.dt/palettes
```

Resources are loaded at session startup by Session Manager. The desktop default resources can be found in /usr/dt/config/language/sys.resources. These resources are made available to each user's session via the RESOURCE_MANAGER property. This file should not be edited, as it is overwritten on subsequent desktop installations. The system administrator can modify the system default resources by creating /etc/dt/config/language/sys.resources. In this file, you can override default resources or specify additional resources for all desktop users.

Users can modify the desktop default and system-wide resources through their HOME/.Xdefaults file. Resources specified in this file take precedence over those specified in the desktop default or system administrator resource files.

## Starting the Color Server

You can choose a wide range of colors for your display either by using Style Manager (as shown in Figure 7–1) or by customizing color resources used by Style Manager to control desktop color usage.

**Figure 7–1**

*The Style Manager.*

Set color server resources for all users by creating /etc/dt/config/language/sys.resources and specifying the color server resources in that file. Users can similarly set color server resources for their own sessions by specifying color server resources in $HOME/.Xdefaults.

## Starting the Workspace Manager

Session Manager is responsible for starting Workspace Manager. By default, /usr/dt/bin/dtwm is started. The Workspace Manager is the window manager provided by the desktop, which controls

- The appearance of window frame components

- The behavior of windows, including their stacking order and focus behavior

- Key bindings and button bindings

- The appearance of minimized windows

- Workspace and Window menus

In addition, the Workspace Manager controls the desktop components outlined in Table 7–3.

**Table 7–3   Desktop Components**

| | |
|---|---|
| Workspaces | The Workspace Manager controls the number of workspaces and keeps track of which windows are open in each workspace. |
| Workspace backdrops | The user can change the backdrop image by using Style Manager. Backdrop management, however, is a function of the Workspace Manager. |
| The Front Panel | Although the Front Panel uses its own configuration files, it is created and managed by the Workspace Manager. |

Additional modifications that can be made to the workspace manager include changing the number of workspaces and providing system-wide workspace names.

### Changing the Number of Workspaces on a System-Wide Basis

The default desktop configuration provides four workspaces. The user can add and delete workspaces by using the pop-up menu associated with the workspace switch.

In the /usr/dt/app-defaults/C/Dtwm file, the `workspaceCount` resource is set to the following default number of workspaces:

```
Dtwm*0*workspaceCount: 4
Dtwm*workspaceCount:    1
```

Multiple workspaces are specified on screen 0; a single workspace is specified on any other screen. You can create (or modify if it exists) the /etc/dt/config/C/sys.resources file to change the default number of workspaces for all new users on a workstation.

Use the `0*workspaceCount` resource to set the system-wide default on the primary screen:

```
Dtwm*0*workspaceCount: number
```

For example, the following resource sets the number of workspaces system-wide on the primary screen to six:

```
Dtwm*0*workspaceCount: 6
```

### Providing System-Wide Workspace Names

Internally, the workspaces are numbered by the numbering convention ws$n$, where $n$ is 0, 1, 2, and so on. For example, the default four workspaces are numbered internally ws0 through ws3.

Use the title resource to change the name of a specified workspace:

```
Dtwm*wsn: name
```

For example, the following resources set the default four workspaces to the specified names:

```
Dtwm*ws0*title:    Glenda
Dtwm*ws1*title:    Neil
Dtwm*ws2*title:    Nicole
Dtwm*ws3*title:    William
```

## Starting the Session Applications

At session startup, Session Manager restarts any applications saved in the previous session. The system default set of applications to be restored as part of the user's initial session can be found in /usr/dt/config/language/sys.session. Do not edit this file.

A system administrator can replace the set of applications started as part of the user's initial session by copying /usr/dt/config/language/sys.session to /etc/dt/config/language/sys.session and modifying the latter file. Unlike the resource files, this file is used as a complete replacement for the desktop default file.

# Customizing the Front Panel

The Front Panel contains a set of icons and pop-up menus (more like roll-up menus) that appear at the bottom of the screen. The two main elements of the Front Panel are the Main Panel and the subpanels. The Main Panel includes the workspace switch shown in Figure 7–2, which contains the buttons you use to change from one workspace to another.

**Figure 7–2**

*A Front Panel workspace switch.*

If a control in the Main Panel has an arrow button on top of it, that control has a subpanel, as shown in Figure 7–3.

**Figure 7–3**

*A subpanel.*

Users can drag and drop icons from the File Manager or Application Manager to add them to the subpanels. Up to 12 additional workspaces can be configured, each with different backgrounds and colors. Each workspace can have any number of applications running in it, and an application can be set to appear in one, more than one, or all workspaces simultaneously. In some instances, the system administrator might find it necessary to lock the Front Panel so users can't change it.

Using the desktop's interface, the Front Panel can easily be customized in the following ways:

- Customizing workspaces

- Adding and deleting workspaces

- Renaming workspaces

- Adding controls to subpanels

The System Administrator can also do more advanced customization outside of the CDE environment by editing CDE configuration files directly from the UNIX command line. For more information on advanced front-panel customization, see the *CDE Advanced User's and System Administrator's Guide*.

## Customizing Workspaces

Users can use the Front Panel workspace switch to rename or change the number of workspaces. Click on the workspace buttons to change workspaces. When the cursor is positioned on a workspace button, pressing the third mouse button displays its pop-up menu, shown in Figure 7–4.

**Figure 7–4**

*The workspace button
pop-up menu.*

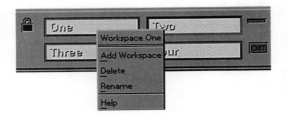

The workspace button pop-up menu includes the items described in Table 7–4.

---

**Table 7–4    Pop-up Menu Options**

| | |
|---|---|
| Add Workspace | Adds a workspace to the list of workspaces |
| Delete | Deletes the workspace |
| Rename | Changes the button into a text field for editing the name |
| Help | Displays help for the workspace switch |

---

Use the pop-up menu to modify workspace button parameters. For example, to rename a workspace, follow these steps:

1. Point to the workspace button of the workspace you want to rename.

2. Choose Rename from the button's pop-up menu (displayed by pressing the third mouse button). The workspace button turns into a text field.

3. Edit the text field.

4. Press Enter.

To add a workspace, do the following:

1. Point to any area in the workspace switch and press the third mouse button to display the pop-up menu.

2. Choose Add Workspace from the pop-up menu. The new workspace, named New, is placed at the end of the set of workspaces.

3. Rename the workspace as described earlier.

To remove a workspace, do the following:

1. Point to the workspace button of the workspace you want to remove.

2. Choose Delete from the button's pop-up menu (displayed by pressing the third mouse button).

## Customizing Workspace Controls

Customizing the controls in the workspace switch is an advanced task that requires the system administrator to create a Front Panel configuration file. This section describes some easy customizations that can be performed from the desktop. Advanced customization is covered in the *CDE Advanced User's and System Administrator's Guide*.

# The Front Panel Switch Area

The switch area shown in Figure 7–5 is the portion of the workspace switch not occupied by other controls or workspace buttons.

**Figure 7–5**

*The switch area.*

The switch area has a pop-up menu containing these items:

Add Workspace        Adds a workspace and creates a workspace button in the workspace switch

Help                         Displays help for the workspace switch

## Adding an Application or Other Icon to a Subpanel

The user can add any type of File Manager or Application Manager icon to the Front Panel. The most convenient use for this feature is adding application icons. To add an application icon to a subpanel, do the following:

1. Display the object's icon in File Manager or Application Manager.

2. Display the subpanel to which the object is to be added.

3. Drag the object to the Install Icon control, using the first mouse button, and drop it on the control.

The behavior of controls added to the Front Panel by using the Install Icon control depends on the type of icon dropped. Table 7–5 describes the control behavior for each type of icon.

**Table 7–5    Icon Control Behavior**

| Type of Icon | Behavior |
|---|---|
| File | The same behavior as the file's icon in File Manager. When the user clicks on the file icon, the Text Editor displays the contents of the file ready to be edited. |
| Folder | Opens a File Manager view of the folder. |
| Application group | Opens an Application Manager view of the application group. |
| Application icon | The same behavior as the application's icon in File Manager or Application Manager. When the user clicks on the icon, the application automatically is launched. |

## Removing All User Customizations

To reset the Front Panel and remove all user customizations, follow this procedure:

1. Open Application Manager and double-click the Desktop_Tools application group icon.

2. Double-click Restore Front Panel.

The screen goes blank for several seconds while the Workspace Manager is restarted. The Restore Front Panel action removes all customizations made by using the Install Icon control or the Front Panel's pop-up menus.

**N O T E .**  *This procedure does not affect advanced customizations made by manually editing Front Panel configuration files.*

## Actions and Data Types

Actions can be assigned to icons so associated commands are invoked when an icon is clicked. *Actions* are instructions that automate desktop tasks such as running applications and opening data files. Actions work much the same as application macros or programming functions.

An action can be created by using the Create Action menu. This menu is accessed by first bringing up the Applications pop-up menu shown in Figure 7–6.

**Figure 7–6**

*The Applications pop-up menu.*

Select Desktop_Apps from the pop-up menu shown in Figure 7–6. The Desktop Apps window appears, as shown in Figure 7–7.

**Figure 7–7**

*The Desktop Apps window.*

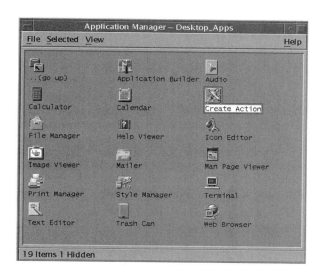

When the Desktop Apps window appears, click on the Create Action icon. The Create Action window appears, as shown in Figure 7–8.

**Figure 7–8**

*The Create Action window.*

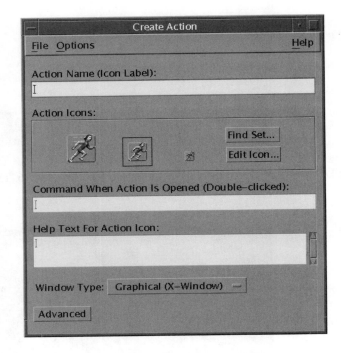

For information on filling in the appropriate fields and creating an action, click on Help, located at the top of the Create Action window.

After you define an action, you can use that action in the desktop user interface to simplify tasks. The desktop provides the capability to attach user interface components such as icons, Front Panel controls, and menu items to actions. Each of these icons runs an action when the icon is double-clicked.

Another common use for actions is in menus. Data files usually have actions in their selected menu in File Manager. For example, XWD files (files with names ending in .xwd or .wd) have an Open action that displays the screen image when you run the Xwud action.

Actions and data types are powerful components for integrating applications into the desktop. They provide a way to create a user interface for starting applications and manipulating data files. For more information on creating actions, see the *Solaris CDE Advanced User's and System Administrator's Guide*.

# The Application Manager

Application Manager is the desktop container displaying applications available to users. It is selected from the Applications pop-up menu located on the Front Panel, as shown in Figure 7–6.

When initially opened, the window displays the top level directory of the Application Manager. User interaction with the Application Manager is similar to use of the File Manager except the Application Manager contains executable modules. The user launches the Application Manager from an icon on the Front Panel, opening the window shown in Figure 7–9.

**Figure 7–9**

*The Application Manager window.*

Programs and icons can be installed in the Application Manager by the system administrator and pushed out to other workstations as part of the installation process. By default, the Application Manager comes preconfigured to include several utilities and programs (see Figure 7–9). Each of these utilities is located in a directory, which—with its contents—is called an application group. Application groups provided with the default desktop are described in Table 7–6.

**Table 7–6    Application Groups**

| | |
|---|---|
| Desktop_Apps | Desktop applications such as File Manager, Style Manager, and Calculator |
| Desktop_Tools | Desktop administration and operating system tools, such as User Registration, Reload Application, vi text editor, and Check Spelling |
| Information | Icons representing frequently used help topics |
| System_Admin | Tools used by system administrators |
| Desktop Controls | Tools to set your CDE environment, such as mouse behavior, desktop fonts, screen saver, and window behavior |
| OpenWindows | Contains several OpenWindows-style actions, such as OpenWindows-style mail tool and OpenWinwindows-style file manager |

The top level directory for the Application Manager is the directory /var/dt/appconfig/ appmanager/login-hostname-display, created dynamically each time the user logs in. For example, if user bcalkins logs in from display sparc1:0, the following Application Manager directory is created:

```
/var/dt/appconfig/appmanager/bcalkins-sparc1-0
```

The Application Manager is built by gathering application groups from directories located along the application search path. The default application search path consists of the locations shown in Table 7–7.

### Table 7–7    Default Application Search Path Locations

| Scope | Location |
|---|---|
| Built-in | /usr/dt/appconfig/appmanager/language |
| System-wide | /etc/dt/appconfig/appmanager/language |
| Personal | HomeDirectory/.dt/appmanager |

To create the top-level directory of the application Manager, links are created at login time from the application group directories to the Application Manager directory, which is /var/dt/appconfig/appmanager/login-hostname-display. The gathering operation is done by the desktop utility dtappgather, which is automatically run by Login Manager after the user has successfully logged in. For example, the desktop provides the built-in application group /usr/dt/appconfig/appmanager/language/Desktop_Tools. At login time, a symbolic link is created to /var/dt/appconfig/appmanager/login-hostname-display/Desktop_Tools.

Applications can be added to the Application Manager by copying icons from other application groups to the personal application group. To create a personal application group, follow these steps:

1. From your home folder, change to the .dt/appmanager subfolder.

2. Create a new folder. The folder name will become the name of the new application group.

3. Double-click Reload Applications in the Desktop_Apps application group.

4. Your new application group becomes registered at the top level of Application Manager.

A personal application group is an application group users can alter because they have write permission to it. For example, users can copy (by pressing the Ctrl key and dragging) the Calculator icon from the Desktop_Tools application group to a new personal application group. Another method is to create an action for an application and then place an application (action) icon in the personal application group.

## The *dtksh* Shell

Available in CDE is the Desktop KornShell (`dtksh`), which provides `kshell` scripting with the capability to easily access most of the existing Xt and MOTIF functions. The Desktop KornShell is based on `ksh-93`, which provides a powerful set of tools and commands for the shell programmer and supports the standard set of `kshell` programming commands. `dtksh` is used by developers and programmers to create MOTIF applications for the CDE environment.

## To Customize or Not to Customize

This question always arises: Should users be allowed to customize the CDE environment themselves? Most large institutions frown on letting users customize their own environments. Usually, the system administrator provides a default setup that is applied to all users. This default setup promotes consistency and prevents the "self-inflicted" problems that can occur when users incorrectly modify system files. The answer also depends on how much pain you're willing to endure for the good of your user community. Users love an administrator who allows them the flexibility to arrange their own desktops; however, you can quickly have a nightmare of problems if users are not properly trained in the use of customization utilities.

The graphical user interface available in CDE is a welcome enhancement to UNIX. With CDE, users no longer need to be exposed to the cryptic UNIX shell. Most of the routine tasks performed by users can now be done by using the menus and icons provided through CDE. As system administrator, your job is to customize CDE, using the tools provided, to facilitate tasks and maintain productivity in your specific environment.

Customization of the CDE environment is a large topic. Although this chapter introduced you to some basic customization topics, additional information can be found in publications focusing on the subject.

# 8

# Writing Shell Scripts and Programs

The following are the test objectives for this chapter:

- Understand the traditional uses of shell script types

- Learn how to set shell variables

- Understand various quoting techniques

- Understand how to redirect output and use pipes to string multiple commands

- Understand the purpose and correct use of exit status

- Understand how to use the `if` conditional statement

- Learn how to create a loop using the `for`, `while`, and `until` statements

- Understand how to use the `case` statement to control program execution flow

- Understand shell functions

**A** thorough understanding of shell programming is a must for any system administrator. The system administrator must be able to read and write shell programs because many tasks can and should be automated by using shell programs. An advantage in using a script or shell program to perform a particular task is that doing so ensures consistency—in other words, the task is performed the very same way each time. Also, many software products come with install scripts that have to be modified for your system before they will work.

A UNIX script is a sequence of UNIX commands, either in a file or typed at the command line, that perform multiple operations. Such files are also known as batch files in some systems. Another term for a script that might be familiar to you is *macro*. Usually *script* or *macro* refers to a simple command sequence, and *shell program* identifies a file containing a more complicated arrangement of commands. Shell programs use the shell's control and conditional commands, called built-ins, which will be discussed later in this chapter.

To run a file as a script, the file's execution bit must be set. This means the file looks like this when you list it:

```
% ls -l
-rwxr-xr-x  1 bcalkins      425  Jul 10 11:10     program.1
```

If the execution bit is set, what happens next depends on the first line of the file. If the first two characters on the first line are anything other than #!, the file is interpreted as a Bourne shell script. If the characters #! are followed by an explicit program location, such as /bin/csh, that program is run as an interpreter on the contents of the file. In other words, the program is run in the shell that is specified after the #! characters. To create a C shell script, for example, type in the following on the first line of the file:

```
#!/bin/csh
```

**NOTE.** *A good idea is to put scripts and shell programs into their own directory to separate them from standard UNIX programs. They are commonly put into a directory named /usr/local/bin.*

## What Shell to Use?

When writing scripts, you have your choice of using the Bourne shell, the C shell, or the Korn shell. Other shells, such as bash and tcsh, are also available. Selecting a particular shell to use is personal preference. I find most BSD UNIX users using the C shell because of its roots at Berkeley. Many of us old SunOS users still prefer to use the C shell because

we've used it for so many years. On the other hand, I find that SystemV users prefer the Korn shell. These preferences stem back to the early development days of UNIX and are discussed in Appendix A, "The History of UNIX." For system administration, the Bourne shell is best for writing your scripts. The Bourne shell is the default shell in Solaris and is the only shell found on all UNIX systems. The Bourne shell was designed from the beginning for use as a programming language, which explains its breadth of programming features. An additional reason for using the Bourne shell is that its conditionals and controls are compatible with all other shells, including the dtksh shell used in the CDE environment and discussed in Chapter 7, "Administration and Configuration of the CDE." All examples used in this chapter will use the Bourne shell.

## Bourne Shell Variables

A variable is a name that refers to a temporary storage area in memory. A value such as a text string or number is assigned to a variable and can be changed at any time. The Bourne shell uses two types of variables to store values: local and environmental. Each is described in this chapter.

A variable is either set to some particular value or is said to be "unset," which means it does not exist as a variable. Shell variables are an integral part of shell programming. The shell variable provides the capability to store and manipulate information within a shell program. The variables you use are completely under your control, and you can set or unset any number of variables as needed to perform a particular task.

A variable name must begin with a letter and may contain letters, digits, and underscores but no special characters. In the Bourne shell, environment variables are set with an assignment of NAME=value. In the following examples, the ME and BC variables are set by entering the following at a command prompt:

```
ME=bill
BC="bill calkins"
```

Be sure not to have any white space before or after the equals (=) sign. Double quotes, as used in the second example, are used when white space is present in the text string you are assigning to the variable. Whenever the shell sees a $*variable*, such as $ME, it substitutes into the command line the value stored for that variable.

Unfortunately, many of the special characters used by the shell are also used by other programs—there simply are not enough characters to go around. When the special characters shown in Table 8–2 are used in the shell, they must be quoted. Quoting is used when an assigned value contains a special character, spaces, tabs, or new lines. Without the quotes, the special symbols will be interpreted as shell metacharacters instead of being passed as arguments to programs. The three methods of quoting used in the Bourne shell are described in Table 8–1.

## Table 8–1   Quoting

| \ | backslash | Quotes the next character. |
|---|---|---|
| ' | single quote marks | No interpretation occurs. |
| " | double quotes | All characters enclosed with double quote marks are quoted except back slash, accent grave, double quote, and currency symbol. |

Commands are read from the string between two back ticks (` `` `) and the standard output from these commands may be used to set a variable. No interpretation is done on the string before the string is read, except to remove back slashes (\) used to escape other characters. Escaping back ticks allows nested command substitution like this one:

```
font=`grep font \`cat filelist\``
```

The back slashes inside the imbedded command protect the back ticks from immediate interpretation, so the back tick just before cat fails to match the initial one before grep.

Some characters naturally act as delimiters in the Bourne shell and, when encountered, such characters have the effect of separating one logical word from the next. The characters outlined in Table 8–2 have a special meaning to the shell and cause termination unless quoted.

## Table 8–2   Delimiters

| ; | Command delimiter. Acts as a <return> and executes the commands sequentially. |
|---|---|
| & | Runs commands asynchronously. |
| ( ) | Groups commands into a single logical word. |
| newlines | Separates records (the default). |
| spaces, tabs | Separate fields (the default). |

To display the value of a variable, enter the following at the command prompt (the dollar sign informs the shell that the following name refers to a variable):

```
echo $BC
```

The following is displayed:

```
bill calkins
```

Variables you set are local to the current shell unless you mark them for export. Variables marked for export are called environment variables and will be made available to any commands the shell creates. The following command marks the variable bc for export:

```
export BC
```

Local variables can be listed by typing the set command. Variables that have been marked for export can be listed by typing the env command. The Bourne shell has several pre-defined variables, some of which are described in Table 8–3. These variables get assigned automatically when a user logs on and are defined by the login program, the system initialization file, and the user's initialization files.

## Table 8–3   Default Bourne Shell Variables

| Variable | Description |
| --- | --- |
| ARCH | Sets to the user's system architecture (for example, sun4, sun4c). |
| CDPATH | Sets the search path for the cd command. |
| HOME | Sets the value of the user's home directory |
| LANG | Sets the locale. |
| LOGNAME | Defines the name of the user currently logged in. The default value of LOGNAME is automatically set by the login program to the user name specified in the /etc/passwd file. You should only need to reference (not reset) this variable. |
| LPDEST | Sets the user's default printer. |
| MAIL | If this parameter is set to the name of a mail file and the MAILPATH parameter is not set, the shell informs the user of the arrival of mail in the specified file. |
| MAILCHECK | Specifies how often (in seconds) the shell will check for the arrival of mail in the files specified by the MAILPATH or MAIL parameters. The default value is 600 seconds (10 minutes). If set to 0, the shell will check before each prompt. |
| MAILPATH | Sets the mail path by defining a colon-separated list of file names. If this parameter is set, the shell informs the user of the arrival of mail in any of the specified files. Each file name can be followed by % and a message that will be printed when the modification time changes. The default message is "you have mail." |
| MANPATH | Sets the hierarchies of available man pages. |
| OPENWINHOME | Sets the path to the OpenWindows subsystem. |
| PATH | Lists, in order, the directories the shell searches to find the program to run when the user types a command. If the directory is not in the search path, users must type the complete path name of a command. The default PATH is automatically defined and set as specified in .profile (Bourne or Korn shell) or .cshrc (C shell) as part of the login process.

The order of the search path is important. When identical commands exist in different locations, the first command found with that name is used. For example, suppose that PATH is defined (in Bourne and Korn shell syntax) as PATH=/bin:/usr/bin:/usr/sbin:$HOME/bin and a file named sample resides in both /usr/bin and /home/jean/bin. If the user types the command sample without specifying its full path name, the version found in /usr/bin is used. |
| PS1 | Sets the primary prompt string, by default ``$ ''. |
| PS2 | Sets the secondary prompt string, by default ``> ''. |

## Table 8–3 Default Bourne Shell Variables (continued)

| Variable | Description |
| --- | --- |
| SHELL | Sets the default shell used by `make`, `vi`, and other tools. When the shell is invoked, it scans the environment for this name. |
| TERMINFO | Specifies the path name for an unsupported terminal that has been added to the terminfo database. Use the TERMINFO variable in /etc/profile or /etc/.login. When the TERMINFO environment variable is set, the system first checks the TERMINFO path defined by the user. If it does not find a definition for a terminal in the TERMINFO directory defined by the user, it searches the default directory, /usr/share/lib/terminfo, for a definition. If it does not find a definition in either location, the terminal is identified as "dumb." |
| TERM | Defines the terminal. This variable should be reset in /etc/profile or /etc/.login. When the user invokes an editor, the system looks for a file with the same name as the definition of this environment variable. The system searches the directory referenced by TERMINFO to determine the terminal characteristics. |
| TZ | Sets the time zone used to display dates (for example, in the `ls  -l` command). If TZ is not set in the user's environment, the system setting is used; otherwise, Greenwich Mean Time is used. |

# Built-ins

Built-ins are used in shell programs to make decisions and add intelligence to the task to be performed. Built-ins for the Bourne shell are listed in Tables 8–4 and 8–5. More information on the built-ins described in Table 8–4 is available in the Solaris online manual pages. The shell conditionals listed in Table 8–5 are described in this chapter. Each shell has its own set of built-ins, with the Bourne shell having the fewest. For this reason, it is the smallest and fastest of the three shells.

## Table 8–4 Bourne Shell Built-ins

| | |
| --- | --- |
| break | Exit a `For` or `While` loop |
| continue | Continue next iteration of `For` or `While` loop |
| echo | Write arguments on standard output |
| eval | Evaluate and execute arguments |
| exec | Execute the arguments |
| exit | Exit shell program |
| export | Create a global variable |
| priv | Set or display privileges |

*continues*

---

**Table 8–4    Bourne Shell Built-ins (continued)**

| | |
|---|---|
| read | Read a line from standard input |
| readonly | Change a variable to read only |
| set | Set shell options |
| test | Evaluate conditional expressions |
| times | Display execution times |
| trap | Manage execution signals |
| umask | Set default security for files and directories |
| unset | Unset a local variable |
| wait | Wait for a background process to complete |

---

**Table 8–5    Bourne Shell Conditionals**

| | |
|---|---|
| if-then-else-if | Tests a condition and selects an action based on the results of the test |
| case-esac | Selects an action based on the value of the variable |
| for-do-done | Repeats a sequence of commands until a predetermined condition is met |
| while-do-done | Repeats a sequence of commands until a test condition is no longer true |
| until-do-done | Repeats a sequence of commands until a test condition results in a successful status |

---

## Shell Conditionals

In addition to the built-ins listed in Tables 8–4 and 8–5, the Bourne shell also contains some simple conditionals. A conditional command makes a choice depending on the outcome of some condition. Examples of conditionals are &&, ¦¦, if, and case.

### && and ||

The simplest conditional in the Bourne shell is the double ampersand (&&). When two commands are separated by a double ampersand, the second command executes only if the first command returns a zero exit status (an indication of successful completion).

Example:

```
ls -ld /usr/bin > /dev/null && echo "Directory Found"
```

If the directory /usr/bin exists, the message Directory Found is displayed.

The opposite of && is the double bar (¦¦). When two commands are separated by ¦¦, the second command executes only if the first command returns a non-zero exit status (indicating failure).

Example:

```
ls -d  /usr/foo ¦¦ echo "No directory found"
```

If the directory does not exist, the following message is displayed:

```
/usr/foo: No such file or directory
No directory found
```

The Bourne shell contains the special programs true and false. The only function of the true program is to return a true (zero) exit status. Similarly, the function of the false program is to return a false (non-zero) exit status.

Example:

```
True && echo True
```

The system responds with True

```
False ¦¦ echo False
```

The system responds with False

True and false tests will be discussed later when we discuss if and while conditionals.

The && and ¦¦ are useful conditionals for creating very simple scripts, but additional functionality is sometimes required. The Bourne shell offers two more conditional commands, if and case.

## if

One of the more important built-ins of the Bourne shell is the if conditional. The syntax of the if conditional is

```
if condition-list
      then list
    elif condition-list
      then list
   else list
   if
```

The list following if is executed; if it returns a zero exit status, the list following the first then is executed. Otherwise the list following elif is executed; if its value is zero, the list following the next then is executed. Failing that, the else list is executed. If no list is executed, the `if` command returns a zero exit status. The next example illustrates the use of an `if` conditional statement:

```
if  [ -f  /tmp/errlog ]
    then
        rm /tmp/errlog
        echo "Error log has been removed"
    else
        echo "No errorlog  has been found"
if
```

In the previous example, the program will check for a file named /tmp/errlog. If the file is present, the program removes it. If not present, the file prints out a message.

The previous example uses the `if` test `-f` to evaluate a conditional expression. At the heart of each control structure is a conditional test. The `test` command is commonly used in shell programs to perform various tests and to determine if certain files and directories exist. The test program performs three types of tests:

- It can test files for certain characteristics such as file type and permissions.

- It can perform string comparisons.

- It can make numeric comparisons.

`Test` indicates the success or failure of its testing by its exit status. `Test` evaluates an expression and, if its value is true, sets a zero (true) exit status; otherwise, a non-zero (false) exit status is set. All shell commands return a true (0) value when they complete successfully or a false (1) value when they fail. The exit status of the last shell command can be displayed by looking at the `$?` variable with the `echo` command. Table 8–6 lists some of the common conditions that can be evaluated.

### Table 8–6    Built-in Test Functions

| | |
|---|---|
| -r *filename* | True if the filename exists and is readable. |
| -w *filename* | True if the filename exists and is writable. |
| -x *filename* | True if the filename exists and is executable. |
| -f *filename* | True if the filename exists and is a regular file. |
| -d *filename* | True if the filename exists and is a directory. |
| -h *filename* | True if the filename exists and is a symbolic link. With all other primitives (except -L *file-name*), the symbolic links are followed by default. |
| -c *filename* | True if the filename exists and is a character special file. |
| -b *filename* | True if the filename exists and is a block special file. |

## Table 8–6    Built-in Test Functions (continued)

| | |
|---|---|
| -u *filename* | True if the filename exists and its set-user-ID bit is set. |
| -g *filename* | True if the filename exists and its set-group-ID bit is set. |
| -k *filename* | True if the filename exists and its sticky bit is set. |
| -s *filename* | True if the filename exists and has a size greater than zero. |
| s1 = s2 | True if strings s1 and s2 are identical. |
| s1 != s2 | True if strings s1 and s2 are not identical. |
| n1 -eq n2 | True if the integers n1 and n2 are algebraically equal. Any of the comparisons -ne, -gt, -ge, -lt, and –le may be used in place of -eq. |
| -L filename | True if the filename exists and is a symbolic link. With all other primitives (except -h *file-name*), the symbolic links are followed by default. |

***Operators: These test functions may be combined with the following operators:***

| | |
|---|---|
| ! | Unary negation operator. |
| -a | Binary and operator. |
| -o | Binary or operator (-a has higher precedence than -o). |
| (expression) | Parentheses for grouping. Notice also that parentheses are meaningful to the shell and, therefore, must be quoted. |

Following is an example of where you might use a unary operator:

```
if   [ ! -f  /tmp/errlog ]
    then
          echo "No error log has been found"
if
```

In the example, the statement `[ ! -f /tmp/errlog ]` tests if the file `/tmp/errlog` does not exist.

## Case

Many programs are menu driven; that is, they offer the user a menu of choices from which to select. The `case` statement makes it easy to set up a menu of choices. The general syntax for a `case` statement is as follows:

```
case value in
choice1) commands;;
choice2) commands;;
…….
esac
```

A `case` command executes the list associated with the first pattern that matches the choice. Here's an example to describe how a `case` statement works:

```
echo Please enter the letter next to the command that you want to select:
echo 'a  date'
echo 'b  ls'
echo 'c  who'
read choice
case $choice in
date;;
ls;;
who;;
*)   echo Invalid choice - Bye.
esac
```

The list of choices is scanned to find the one that matches the value input by the user. The choice *) matches any value so it's usually added as a last option—a catchall.

# Repeated Action Commands

The Bourne shell provides three repeated action commands, each of which corresponds to constructs you might have met before in other programming languages:

- `for`

- `while`

- `until`

These commands cause a program to loop or repeat and are described next.

## *For* Loop

A useful shell command is the `for` loop, which is the simplest way to set up repetition in a shell script. The syntax of a `for` loop is as follows:

```
for name [ in word . . . ]
do list
done
```

Each time a `for` command is executed, `name` is set to the next word taken from the `in word` list. If `in word . . .` is omitted, the `for` command executes the `do list` once for each positional parameter that is set. Execution ends when there are no more words in the list. The following example illustrates a simple `for` loop:

```
for i in eat run jump play
do
    echo See spot $i
done
```

When the program is executed, the system responds with

```
See spot eat
See spot run
See spot jump
See spot play
```

If you want to enter data interactively, you can add the shell special command `read`:

```
echo Hello- What\'s your name\?
read name
for i in $name
do
    echo $i
done
```

When executing the program, the user is asked to enter in the word list. Notice the use of the backslash (\) so that the ' and the ? are taken literally and not used as special characters.

## *While* Loop

Another type of loop is the `while` loop. A `while` loop repeats a set of commands continuously until a condition is met. The syntax for a `while` loop is

```
while condition-list
do commands
done
```

First, the condition-list is executed. If it returns a true exit status, the `do` list is executed and the operation restarts from the beginning. If the condition-list returns a false exit status, the conditional is complete. The following illustrates the `while` loop. The program checks to see if the file /tmp/errlog is present. If the file is not present, the program exits the loop. If the file is present, the program prints a message and runs again every 5 seconds until the file is removed.

```
while [ -f /tmp/errlog ]
    do echo The file is still there ; sleep 5
done
```

**N O T E .** *The special command* `sleep 5` *instructs the system to wait 5 seconds before running again.*

## *Until* Loop

The `until` loop is a variant of the `while` statement. Just as the `while` statement repeats as long as the condition-list returns a true value, the `until` statement repeats until the condition-list

returns a false value. The following example continues to display a message every 5 seconds until the file is created.

```
until [ -f  /tmp/errlog ]
    do echo the file is missing; sleep 5
done
```

Conditional structures such as while and until are executed by the shell as if they were a single command. The entire structure is scanned by the shell before any part of it is executed.

## Shell Functions

Any good programming language provides support for functions. A function is a bundle of statements that is executed as a group. The bundles are executed just like a "regular" command and are used to carry out often-required tasks. An advantage of a function is that it is held in the computer's main memory, so execution is much quicker than with a script, which must be retrieved from disk. The current version of the Bourne shell supports shell functions; older versions of the Bourne shell did not. The syntax for shell functions is as follows:

```
name()
{
command-list
}
```

The previous command syntax defines a function named "name". The body of the function is the command-list between { and }. This list is executed whenever name is specified as the name of a command. For example, at the command prompt, type

```
hello()
{
echo hello there
}
```

The function is named "hello" and can be executed by typing hello. The output of the function is hello there. The exit status of a function is the exit status of the last command executed in the body.

Constructing your own commands with scripts and shell programs is a powerful and flexible tool to assist you in system administration. Routine tasks can be simplified and automated to free up your time and allow you to attend to more demanding tasks. Shell programming is a skill that all UNIX systems administrators must have and is one of the keys to becoming a sophisticated UNIX user.

# 9

# The LP Print Service

The following are the test objectives for this chapter:

- Understand the difference between the BSD and SystemV print systems

- Understand the Solaris LP print service

- Describe the print client and print server

- Understand the difference between local and remote printing

- Describe the terminfo database

- Understand how to use Admintool to create, configure, and modify printers

**P**rinters are a standard peripheral for any computer system. One of the first devices added to a new system will be a printer. The multi-user nature of the Solaris operating system means that the Solaris printer software is more complex than that of a single-user operating system. This means that adding a printer to a Solaris system requires more than just plugging it in. This chapter describes all aspects of connecting a printer to a Solaris system. It describes how to setup the printer in the operating system and how to manage the print queues after they're installed.

# The UNIX Print Service

Setting up a Solaris printer involves setting up the hardware: the printer and the printer port. In addition, the system administrator needs to verify that there is at least 8MB of disk space available for /var/spool/lp. Print files will be sent to this location to prepare them for printing. Other configuration files are created but the Solaris operating system takes care of that part for you. When setting up a printer, the Solaris operating system makes the appropriate changes in the system's /etc/printers.conf and /etc/lp directory as required.

## The Print Spooler

*Spool* stands for simultaneous peripheral operations online. The spooler is also referred to as the *queue*. Users execute the print spooler lp program when they want to print something. The print spooler then takes what the user wants to print and places it in the pre-defined /var/spool/lp print spooling directory.

Spooling space is the amount of disk space used to store and process requests in the print queue. The size of the /var directory depends on the size of the disk and how the disk is partitioned. If /var is not created as a separate partition, the /var directory uses some root partition space, which is likely to be quite small. A large spool directory could consume 600MB of disk space. Look at the size and partitioning of the disks available on systems that could be designated as print servers.

When connecting printers, first carefully evaluate the printing needs and usage patterns of the users. If users typically print only short ASCII files without sophisticated formatting requirements, a print server with 20 to 25MB of disk space allocated to /var is probably sufficient. If, however, many users are printing lengthy PostScript files, they probably will fill up the spooling space quite frequently. When /var fills up and users cannot queue their jobs for printing, work flow is interrupted. The size of /var is set when the operating system is loaded and disks are partitioned.

For SunOS users, the SVR4 lp program is equivalent to the BSD lpd print program. In SunOS, the print spooler is located in /usr/spool. When Sun switched from SunOS (which was based on BSD UNIX) to Solaris (which is based on SVR4 UNIX), print systems between BSD and SVR4 were quite different. Throughout this chapter, I'll make reference to the BSD print system for system administrators who might be familiar with that print system. The BSD printing protocol is an industry standard. It is widely used and provides compatibility between different types of systems from various manufacturers. For sites that have a mix of BSD and SVR4 UNIX, Sun has provided compatibility for both print systems in Solaris.

## The Print Daemon

The lp process is the UNIX utility responsible for printing in SVR4 UNIX. The lp print daemon is started by lpsched and is the UNIX process responsible for taking output from the spooling directory and sending it to the correct printer. Again, for SunOS users, lp is equivalent to lpd in BSD UNIX.

Many methods can be used to define a printer on a Solaris system. Table 9–1 describes the tools Solaris provides for adding printers.

### Table 9–1   Solaris Printer Utilities

| | |
|---|---|
| SunSoft Print Client Software | An interface that was previously available only with the Solstice AdminSuite set of administration tools. It is now available as part of the standard Solaris distribution software and is used to set up print clients. |
| Admintool | A graphical user interface used to create, modify, and delete printers on a local system. This is the recommended method of adding printers for novice users. |
| Solstice AdminSuite | A graphical user Print Manager interface used to manage printers in a name service environment and available only with the Solaris 2.6 server software distribution. |
| LP Print Service Commands | The command line utilities used to set up and manage printers. These commands provide complete functionality; Admintool and the AdminSuite packages are somewhat limited for advanced tasks. |

This chapter describes how to set up local printers, set up access to remote printers, and perform some printer administration tasks by using the Admintool GUI or from the command line. Most of the system administrator's needs for setting up printing services, adding printers to servers, or adding access from print clients to remote printers on print servers should be met by Admintool. Setting up a printer from the command line can be a very complex task. We'll examine the hardware issues involved in connecting a printer to a Solaris system before moving on to examine the more complex part of the process—configuring the software.

## Setting Up the Hardware

Connecting printers to a UNIX system is no one's favorite activity, because it can quickly become a time-consuming task. Many printers are on the market, each with a slightly different interface. When connecting a printer locally to a Sun system, you have one of three options:

- Ethernet connection
- Parallel connection
- Serial connection

The type of connection depends on the connectivity options available on the printer itself. If the printer supports the option, an ethernet connection will be the best. If ethernet connectivity is not an option, a parallel connection is the preferred method. Most, if not all, printers have a parallel port. If no parallel option exists, the final choice is a serial connection. The difficulty with a serial connection is in establishing the proper handshake between the computer and the printer. "Handshaking" is a method for communicating simple information between two devices.

## Ethernet Connection

Many new printers come standard with an ethernet interface. A printer with its own ethernet connection is referred to as a network printer. A network printer is a hardware device that provides printing services to print clients without being directly cabled to a print server. It is a print server with its own system name and IP address, and is connected directly to the network. The ethernet interface may be internal or external to the printer. Using an ethernet interface to install a printer is recommended because of its speed.

## Parallel Connection

Most printers, with a few rare exceptions, have a parallel interface. A parallel interface can have a tremendous advantage over a serial interface, especially if it uses a Centronics interface. The Centronics interface completely defines all wires used in the parallel connection between the printer and the computer. Simply connect the printer to the back of the Sun system by using a Centronics parallel cable. Some Sun systems do not have a DB25 parallel connector and require a special cable from Sun. Other older Sun systems do not have a parallel interface, so you must add one by purchasing an SBUS parallel interface from Sun.

## Serial Connection

Some printers support both parallel and serial connections. Sometimes a printer is connected via the serial interface because the Sun station does not have an available parallel interface. To connect a device using a serial interface requires a thorough understanding of serial transmission. This method of connecting a printer is the most difficult because of the complexity in establishing the proper handshake between the computer and the printer.

## Setting Up the Software

For network printers, you use the vendor's software to configure the operating system. After you have completed the vendor software installation, no further software configuration is required. You must obtain software from the printer manufacturer to install the printer on your system. Most are very easy to configure. The HP Jetdirect print server is the most popular but not the only print server available.

The first step is to connect the print server to the network and set the IP address. This process varies on print servers, so follow the manufacturer's guidelines on how to do this. Next, install the print server software and follow the manufacturer's guidelines for configuring the printer. The vendor's software configures everything—no additional software configuration is required.

For printers with a parallel or serial connection, you must use the Solaris tools to configure the operating system to recognize the printer.

## BSD Versus SVR4 Printing Software

The software that drives the UNIX printing process is an area in which the two UNIX versions, BSD and SystemV, are similar and yet very different. The two print systems are similar in that both are based on the concept of spooling. Both SystemV and BSD print services support the concept of an interface program, which acts as a filter through which all output sent to the printer is passed. Example uses of an interface program include

- *Adding a banner page*—Most UNIX systems automatically add a banner page to the front of a print job. The purpose of the page is to identify the owner of the printer output.

- *Adding or removing a line feed character*—UNIX uses just the line feed character to separate lines. The first problem you might encounter when testing a printer is that the text comes out in a stair-step manner. Most printers have a carriage return/line feed and auto line-feed dip switch that controls what the printer will use. The stair-step problem can be fixed by modifying the interface program that performs the necessary translation on all output going to the printer or by setting the printer's dip switch to the setting recommended by the hardware manufacturer.

The differences between BSD and SystemV are in the configuration files and the spooling directories, which are configured automatically by the Solaris operating system. There are also differences in the way the lp daemon handles print jobs as compared to the lpd daemon in BSD.

### BSD Print Service

Each printer connected to a BSD system must have its own spooling directory that is serviced by one lpd daemon. The spool directories are located in the /var/spool/lpd directory. Each printer has its own lpd daemon. In BSD, lpd accesses the file /etc/printcap for any information it requires concerning the printer. The /etc/printcap file is the system's printer database file and stores all of the necessary information about all printers connected to the system. To use a printer, that printer must have an entry in the /etc/printcap file. The lpr function is BSD's equivalent to lp under SystemV. If users want to print something, they use the lpr command, which sends the necessary information to a specified spooling directory.

### SystemV Print Service

In SystemV, one `lp` daemon services all printers. The `lp` daemon is continually running and provides the "power" for the print service. Only one copy of `lp` should be running at any one time. Most of the configuration files are located in the /var/spool/lp directory. The exception is the interface files, which are located in /etc/interface. There should be a SCHEDLOCK file in /var/spool/lp that is responsible for ensuring that only one copy runs. You use the `lpadmin` command to add, configure, and delete printers from the system. Information about printers can be found in the /etc/printers.conf and /etc/lp files. The Solaris Admintool provides a graphical interface to many of the `lp` commands listed in Table 9–2.

**Table 9–2   Solaris *lp* Commands**

| Command | Purpose |
| --- | --- |
| accept/reject | Enables or disables any further requests for a printer or class entering the spooling area. |
| cancel | Enables the user to stop the printing of information. |
| enable/disable | Enables or disables any more output from the spooler to the printer. |
| lpmove | Moves print requests between destinations. |
| lp | The user's print command; places information to be printed into the spooler. |
| lpadmin | Allows the configuration of the print service. |
| lpsched | Starts the print service. |
| lpshut | Stops the print service. |
| lpstat | Displays status of the print service. |

Although Solaris uses the SystemV print model, it still supports BSD-style printing to provide interoperability. The widely used BSD printing protocol provides compatibility between different types of systems from various manufacturers.

## Print Server Versus Print Client

The *print server* is a system that has a local printer connected to it and makes the printer available to other systems on the network. The *print client* is a remote system that can send print requests to a print server. A system becomes a print client when you install the print client software and enable access to remote printers on the system. See Table 9–3 for a listing of the Solaris software packages that need to be installed to support a print-server and print-client installation. If you've worked with an earlier version of Solaris, note that the Solaris 2.6 print software has been redesigned to provide more centralized print administration. If you are installing an earlier version of Solaris, the print package configuration is different.

## Table 9–3    Solaris 2.6 Print Packages

| Package Instance | Package Name |
|---|---|
| SUNWpcr | SunSoft Print - Client |
| SUNWpcu | SunSoft Print - Client |
| SUNWpsr | SunSoft Print - LP server |
| SUNWpsu | SunSoft Print - LP server |
| SUNWpsf | PostScript filters |
| SUNWscplp | SunSoft Print - Source compatibility |
| **Solaris 2.5 packages no longer found in the software distribution:** | |
| SUNWlpr | LP print service |
| SUNWlpu | LP print service - Client |
| SUNWlps | LP print service - Server |

The print client issues print commands that enable the print client to initiate print requests. The print command locates a printer and printer configuration information.

When a print job is sent from the print client, the user issues either the SystemV style lp command or the BSD style lpr command. Any one of the styles shown in Table 9–4 can be used.

## Table 9–4    Valid Print Styles

| | |
|---|---|
| Atomic style | The print command and option followed by the printer name or class; for example: |
| | `lp -d neptune filename` |
| POSIX style | The print command and option followed by server:printer; for example: |
| | `lpr -P galaxy:neptune filename` |
| Context style | Defined in the Federated Naming Service Programming Guide; for example: |
| | `lpr -d thisdept/service/printer/printer-name filename` |

If the user doesn't specify a printer name or class in a valid style, the command checks the user's PRINTER or LPDEST environment variable for a default printer name. These variables can be set in the user's startup file to specify a default printer to use. If neither environment variable for the default printer is defined, the command checks the .printers file in the user's home directory for the _default printer alias. If the command does not find a _default printer alias in the .printers file, it then checks the print client's /etc/printers.conf file for configuration information. If the printer is not found in the /etc/printers.conf file, the command checks the name service (NIS or NIS+), if any.

## Configuring Software for a Solaris Printer

The print client software and the Printer Manager application in Solstice AdminSuite offer a graphical solution for setting up and managing printers on a network. The advantage of the print client software is that it supports a name service (NIS or NIS+) that enables you to centralize print administration for a network. You can also use the lpadmin command on the command line to configure printers on individual systems. Admintool provides an alternative method for installing printers in the Solaris environment. Admintool provides a graphical interface to the lp commands listed in Table 9–2. This section describes how to use Admintool to set up the printer software.

You must run Admintool on the system to which you have attached the printer, because Admintool does not enable you to make changes to a remote system.

When setting up a printer, Admintool makes the appropriate changes in the system's /etc/printers.conf and /etc/lp directories.

**NOTE.** *If you're sitting at systemA and you want to connect a printer to systemB, you don't need to get into the car and drive to that location to run Admintool on systemB. From systemA, simply* rlogin *to systemB and type*

```
admintool -display local_systemA:0.0
```

*SystemB's Admintool should now be displayed on systemA just as if you were sitting at systemB.*

Use the following steps to configure a printer by using Admintool.

1. Type **admintool** to bring up the Admintool menu. The Admintool window appears.

2. Click on the Browse button located in the toolbar and select Printers from the pop-up menu, as shown in Figure 9–1.

**Figure 9–1**

*Selecting printers with Admintool.*

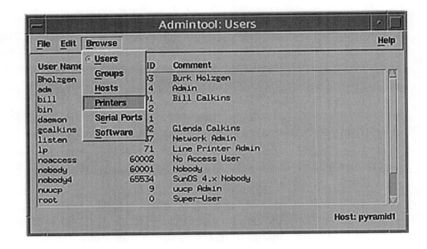

The Printer configuration menu shown in Figure 9–2 appears, with any existing printers displayed in the window.

**Figure 9–2**

*Printer configuration window.*

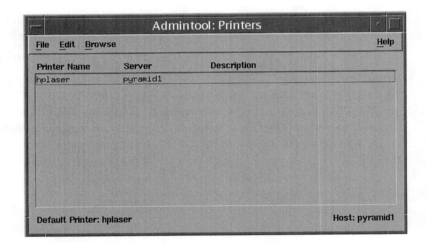

3. Click on Edit, Add.

4. If you're configuring a print client and the print server is located across the network, physically connected to another system, select Access to Printer from the pop-up menu (see Figure 9–3).

**Figure 9–3**

*Printers window pop-up menus.*

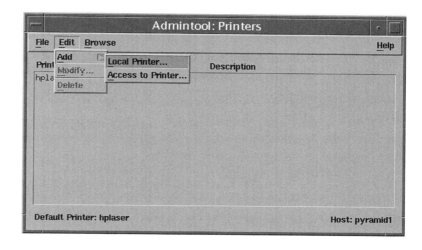

The Add Access to Printer window appears, as shown in Figure 9–4.

**Figure 9–4**

*Add Access to Printer window.*

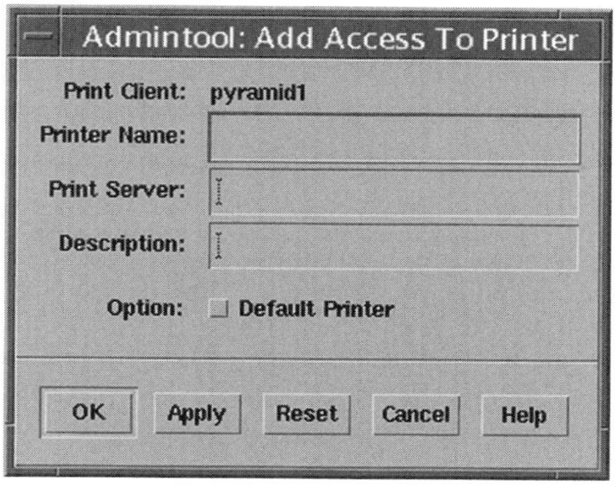

5. Fill in the information in the window as follows:

- *Printer Name*—Enter the name of the printer on the remote system you want to access.

- *Print Server*—Enter the name of the system to which the printer is connected.

- *Description*—If you wish, enter a brief description of the printer.

- *Option*—Check this option if you want to make this the system default printer.

6. Click on the OK button. The window closes and the information is added to the appropriate LP print system files.

7. If you're configuring a print server, and the printer will be connected to the local system, select Local Printer from the pop-up menu shown in Figure 9–3. The window shown in Figure 9–5 is displayed.

8. Fill in the fields as follows:

- *Printer Name*—Enter the name you want to call this printer.

- *Description*—If you wish, enter a brief description of the printer.

- *Printer Port*—Click on the button and select the port to which the printer is connected.

  - /dev/term/a is serial port A.

  - /dev/term/b is serial port B.

  - /dev/bpp0 is the parallel port.

  - Select Other if you've connected an SBUS card with another device name.

- *Printer Type*—Click on the button to select the printer type that matches your printer.

  The printer types here correspond to printers listed in the /usr/share/lib/terminfo directory. The printer type you select must correspond to an entry in the terminfo database. UNIX works best with PostScript printers, because page-formatting of text and graphics from within CDE is for a PostScript printer. If you want to select a PostScript printer, your printer must be able to support PostScript. If you're using an HP LaserJet printer, choose hplaserjet as the print type unless the LaserJet printer supports PostScript.

- *File Contents*—Click on the button to select the format of the files that will be sent to the printer.

- *Fault Notification*—Click on the button to select how to notify the superuser in case of a printer error.

- *Options*—Choose to print a banner or make this the default printer.

**NOTE.** *One printer can be identified as the default printer for the system. If a user does not specify a specific printer when printing, the job will go to the default printer.*

**Figure 9–5**

*The Add Local Printer Window.*

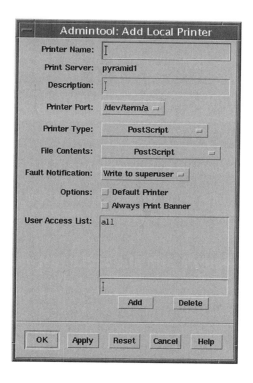

- *User Access List*—If you wish, enter the names of the systems allowed to print to this printer. If none are entered, all clients are allowed access.

9.  After filling in all of the fields, click on the OK button. The window closes and the new printer name appears in the Printer window shown in Figure 9–2.

## Using a Printer Not Listed in the Printer Types Menu

Printer types listed in the Print Manager Window correspond to printers listed in the /usr/share/lib/terminfo directory. If a printer type is not available for the type of printer you are adding, you might need to add an entry in the /usr/share/lib/terminfo database. Each printer is identified in the terminfo database by a short name; for example, an HP LaserJet printer is listed under the /usr/share/lib/terminfo/h directory as hplaserjet. The entries for PostScript printers are in /usr/share/lib/terminfo/P. The name found in the directory is the printer type you specify when setting up a printer.

If you cannot find a terminfo entry for your printer, you can try selecting a similar type of printer; however, you might have trouble keeping the printer set in the correct modes for each print request. If there is no terminfo entry for your type of printer and you want to keep the printer set in the correct modes, you can either customize the interface program used with the printer or add an entry to the terminfo database. You'll find the printer interface program located under the /etc/lp/interfaces directory. Editing an interface file or adding an entry in the terminfo database is beyond the scope of this training guide. A printer entry in the terminfo database contains and defines hundreds of items. Refer to the *Solaris System Administrator's Guide* for information on performing this task.

## Administering Printers

Managing the print system involves monitoring the lp system and uncovering reasons why the system might not be working properly. Other routine tasks involve canceling print jobs and enabling or disabling a printer while it's being serviced. This section provides instructions for the daily tasks you will perform to manage printers and the print scheduler. All of the following commands require superuser access.

### Deleting Printers and Printer Access

Use the Admintool to delete a printer from the system. In the print manager window of Admintool, highlight the printer you want to delete and select Edit, Delete as shown in Figure 9–6. The printer queue will be deleted from the system.

**Figure 9–6**

*Deleting a printer.*

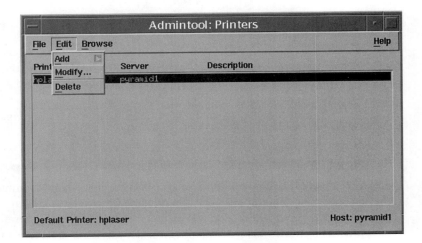

To delete a printer at the command line, issue the following command on the system where the printer is connected:

```
lpadmin -x <printer-name>
```

The printer is deleted from the system.

Maybe you do not want to remove the printer from the print server but you want to keep a particular system from printing to the print server. Issue the following command on the print client from which you want to delete the printer:

```
lpsystem -r <print-server>
```

The print server is deleted from the print client's /etc/lp/Systems file.

Perhaps a printer will be going offline for repairs. To stop accepting print requests on a particular printer, type the following command on the system where the printer is physically connected:

```
reject <printer-name>
```

This step prevents any new requests from entering the printer's queue while you are in the process of removing the printer.

To allow a printer to keep taking requests but to stop the printer from printing the requests, type the following command on the system where the printer is physically connected:

```
disable <printer-name>
```

## Checking Printer Status

The lpstat command is used to verify the status of a printer. You can use this command to determine which printers are available for use or to examine the characteristics of a particular printer. The lpstat command syntax and options are described in Table 9–5.

**Table 9–5   lpstat Command Syntax and Options**

lpstat [-d] [-p printer-name [-D] [-l]] [-t]

| | |
|---|---|
| -d | Shows the system's default printer. |
| -p <printer-name> | Shows if a printer is active or idle, when it was enabled or disabled, and whether it is accepting print requests. You can specify multiple printer names with this command. Use a space or a comma to separate printer names. If you use spaces, enclose the list of printer names in quotes. If you don't specify the printer name, the status of all printers is displayed. |
| -D | Shows the description of the specified printer. |

*continues*

**Table 9–5    *lpstat* Command Syntax and Options (continued)**

**lpstat [-d] [-p printer-name [-D] [-l]] [-t]**

| | |
|---|---|
| -l | Shows the characteristics of the specified printer. |
| -t | Shows status information about the LP print service, including the status of all printers—whether they are active and whether they are accepting print requests. |

Here are a few examples of the lpstat command:

```
lpstat -p hplaser
```

The system responds with

```
printer hplaser is idle. enabled since Jun 16 10:09 1998. available.
```

In the following example, the command requests a description of the printers hplaser1 and hplaser2.

```
lpstat -p "hplaser1 hplaser2" -D
printer hplaser1 faulted. enabled since Jun 16 10:09 1998. available.
unable to print: paper misfeed jam

Description: Printer by finance.
printer hplaser2 is idle. enabled since Jun 16 10:09 1998. available.
Description: Printer in computer room.
```

In the following example, the command requests the characteristics of the printer hplaser.

```
lpstat -p hplaser -l
 printer hplaser is idle. enabled since Jun 16 10:11 1998.
 available.
  Content types: any
  Printer types: unknown
  Description: Printer by computer room.
  Users allowed:
   (all)
  Forms allowed:
   (none)
  Banner not required
  Character sets:
   (none)
  Default is  pitch:
  Default page size:
```

## Restarting the Print Scheduler

The print scheduler, lpsched, handles print requests on print servers. If prints are not coming out of the printer, you might need to restart the print scheduler. To restart the print scheduler,

you use the lpsched command. If a print request was printing when the print scheduler stopped running, that request will be printed in its entirety when you restart the print scheduler.

First, stop the scheduler by typing

`/usr/lib/lp/lpshut`

To restart the scheduler, type

`/usr/lib/lp/lpsched`

## Setting a User's Default Printer

When you added the printer, you were given the option of selecting that printer as the default printer for that particular system. You might want to set the default printer at the user level so that, on a particular system, users can specify their own default printer. If users don't provide a printer name when sending a print job, the print command searches for the default printer in the following order:

First             LPDEST variable

Second            PRINTER variable

Third             System's default printer

These variables can be set in the user's .profile file.

## Modifying the Printer with Admintool

The Solaris Admintool can be used to modify a printer after it was added to the system. Modifications that can be made to a printer via the Admintool include:

- Give the printer description.

- Indicate the printer port.

- List file contents.

- Provide fault notification.

- Select default printer.

- Print a banner.

- Accept and process print requests.

- Provide user access list.

To modify a printer via the Admintool, select Edit, Modify from the Printers window shown in Figure 9–7.

**Figure 9–7**

*The Printers window.*

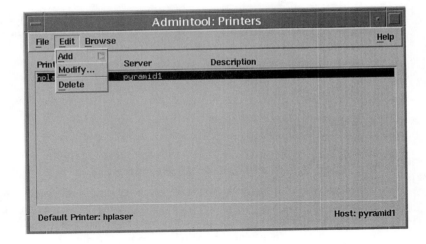

After you select Modify from the drop-down menu, the Modify Printer window appears, as shown in Figure 9–8.

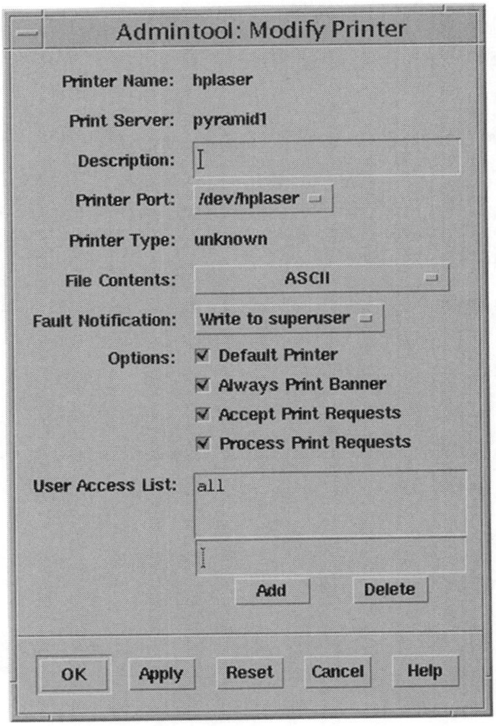

**Figure 9–8**

*The Modify Printer window.*

Modify the selected printer by selecting or filling in the appropriate fields in the Modify Printer window.

A majority of the system problems I respond to are printer related. This chapter introduced you to the Solaris print system and the `lpsched` daemon. Chapter 10, "Process Control," will explore all of the Solaris processes; for a more detailed discussion of the `lpsched` daemon, refer to the *Solaris System Administrator's Guide*.

# C H A P T E R

# 10

# Process Control

The following are the test objectives for this chapter:

- Describe a UNIX process

- Understand how to send a signal to a UNIX process

- Understand how UNIX schedules processes

- Understand how to use the UNIX batch-processing facilities

**S**olaris is a multitasking environment in which a number of programs run at the same time. Each Solaris program is called a *process*. A process is a single program running in its own address space. A process under Solaris consists of an address space and a set of data structures in the kernel to keep track of that process. The address space is a section of memory that contains the code to execute a task. The kernel must keep track of the following data for each process on the system:

- Address space

- Current status of the process

- Execution priority of the process

- Resource usage of the process

- Current signal mask

- Ownership of the process

## Viewing a Process

A process is distinct from a job or command which may be composed of many processes working together to perform a specific task. Each process has a process ID associated with it and is referred to as a *pid*. You can look at processes that are currently executing by using the ps command. A process has certain attributes that directly affect execution. They are listed in Table 10–1.

**Table 10–1    Process Attributes**

| | |
|---|---|
| PID | The process identification, a unique number that defines the process within the kernel |
| PPID | The parent PID (the creator of the process) |
| UID | The user ID number of the user who owns this process |
| EUID | The effective user ID of the process |
| GID | The group ID of the user who owns this process |
| EGID | The effective group ID that owns this process |
| Priority | The priority at which this process runs |

Use the ps command to view processes currently running on the system. Adding the -1 option to the ps command displays a variety of other information about the processes currently running, including the state of each process (listed under S). The codes used to show the various process states are shown in Table 10–2.

## Table 10–2 Process States

| | | |
|---|---|---|
| O | | Process is running on a processor. |
| S | Sleeping | Process is waiting for an event to complete. |
| R | Runnable | Process is on run queue. |
| I | Idle | Process is being created. |
| Z | Zombie state | Process was terminated and parent is not waiting. |
| T | Traced | Process was stopped by a signal because parent is tracing it. |

To see all of the processes that are running on a system, type

```
ps -el
```

The system responds with the following output:

```
F   S  UID  PID  PPID C  PRI NI ADDR     SZ   WCHAN           TTY  TIME CMD
19  T  0    0    0    0  0   SY f0274e38 0    ?               0:01 sched
 8  S  0    1    0    0  41  20 f5af4888 162  f5af4a80 ?      0:01 init
19  S  0    2    0    0  0   SY f5af41c8 0    f02886a4 ?      0:00 pageout
19  S  0    3    0    1  0   SY f5af3b08 0    f028aeb4 ?      9:57 fsflush
 8  S  0    299  1    0  65  20 f5af26c8 368  f597e0ce console 0:00 ttymon
 8  S  0    101  1    0  41  20 f5af3448 340  f5d5bfae ?      0:00 in.route
 8  S  0    298  1    0  41  20 f5af2d88 350  f5982c78 ?      0:00 sac
 8  S  0    111  1    0  41  20 f5af2008 455  f5d5bf5e ?      0:01 rpcbind
 8  S  0    164  1    0  41  20 f5d5e890 691  f5d5ef38 ?      0:01 syslogd
 8  S  0    138  1    0  41  20 f5d5e1d0 450  f5d5be96 ?      0:00 inetd
 8  S  0    113  1    0  79  20 f5d5db10 462  f5d5bee6 ?      0:00 keyserv
 8  S  0    160  1    0  41  20 f5d5d450 650  f5d5bcb6 ?      0:00 automoun
 8  S  0    143  1    0  74  20 f5d5cd90 502  f5d5bebe ?      0:00 statd
 8  S  0    145  1    0  77  20 f5d5c6d0 409  f5d5be1e ?      0:00 lockd
 8  S  0    242  1    0  41  20 f5d5c010 514  f5d5b8a6 ?      0:01 vold
 8  S  0    184  1    0  46  20 f5e4a898 480  f5e4aa90 ?      0:01 nscd
 8  S  0    178  1    0  51  20 f5e4a1d8 360  f5982eb8 ?      0:01 cron
```

The man page for the ps command describes all of the fields displayed with the ps command as well as all of the command options. Table 10–3 lists some important fields.

## Table 10–3 Process Fields

| Field | Description |
|---|---|
| F | Flags associated with the process. |
| S | The state of the process; the two most common values are S for sleeping and R for running. An important value to look for is X, which means the process is waiting for memory to become available. When you see this frequently on your system, you are out of memory. Refer to Table 10–2 for a complete list of the process states. |

## Table 10–3    Process Fields (continued)

| Field | Description |
| --- | --- |
| UID | The user ID of the process owner. For many processes this is 0 because they are run setuid. |
| PID | The process ID of each process. This value should be unique. Generally PIDs are allocated lowest to highest but wrap at some point. This value is necessary for you to send a signal, such as the kill signal, to a process. |
| PPID | The parent process ID. This identifies the parent process that started the process. Using the PPID enables you to trace the sequence of process creation that took place. |
| PRI | The priority of the process. Without the -c option, higher numbers mean lower priority. With the -c option, higher numbers mean higher priority. |
| NI | The nice value, used in priority computation. Not printed when the -c option is used. The process's nice number contributes to its scheduling priority. Making a process nicer means lowering its priority. |
| ADDR | The memory address of the process. |
| SZ | The SIZE field. This is the total number of pages in the process. Each page is 4,096 bytes. |
| WCHAN | The address of an event for which the process is sleeping (if -, the process is running). |
| STIME | The starting time of the process (in hours, minutes, and seconds). |
| TTY | The terminal assigned to your process. |
| TIME | The cumulative CPU time used by the process in minutes and seconds. |
| CMD | The command that generated the process. |

You often want to look at all processes, which you can do using the command ps -el. A number of options available with the ps command control what information is printed out. A few of them are listed in Table 10–4.

## Table 10–4    *ps* Command Options

| | |
| --- | --- |
| -A | Lists information for all processes. Identical to -e. |
| -a | Lists information about all processes most frequently requested. Processes not associated with a terminal will not be listed. |
| -f | Generates a full listing. |
| -P | Prints the number of the processor to which the process is bound, if any, under an additional column header PSR. This is a useful option on systems with multiple processors. |
| -u <username> | Lists only process data for a particular user. In the listing, the numerical user ID will be printed unless you give the -f option, which prints the login name. |

For a complete list of options to the ps command, refer to the Solaris online manual pages.

**NOTE.** *The UNIX* sort *command is useful when you're looking at system processes. Use the* sort *command as the pipe output to sort by size or PID. For example, to sort by SZ field, use the command* ps -el ¦ sort +9 *(remember,* sort *starts numbering fields with zero).*

# Signals

Solaris supports the concept of sending software signals to a process. These signals are ways for other processes to interact with a running process outside the context of the hardware. The kill command is used to send a signal to a process. System administrators most often use the signals SIGHUP, SIGKILL, and SIGSTOP. The SIGHUP signal is used by some utilities as a way to notify the process to do something. For example, the SIGHUP signal is sent to a process if the telephone connection is lost or hangs up. The SIGKILL signal is used to abort a process, and the SIGSTOP signal is used to pause a process. Table 10–5 describes the many signals used.

**Table 10–5　Signals Available Under Solaris**

| Signal | Number | Description |
|--------|--------|-------------|
| SIGHUP | 1 | Hangup; usually means the controlling terminal has been disconnected. |
| SIGINT | 2 | Interrupt; user can generate this signal by pressing Ctrl-C or Delete. |
| SIGQUIT | 3 | Quit process and produce a core dump. |
| SIGILL | 4 | Illegal instruction. |
| SIGTRAP | 5 | Trace or breakpoint trap. |
| SIGABRT | 6 | Abort. |
| SIGEMT | 7 | Emulation trap. |
| SIGFPE | 8 | Arithmetic exception; informs a process of a floating point error. |
| SIGKILL | 9 | Killed; forces the process to terminate. This is a sure kill. |
| SIGBUS | 10 | Bus error. |
| SIGSEGV | 11 | Segmentation fault. |
| SIGSYS | 12 | Bad system call. |
| SIGPIPE | 13 | Broken pipe. |
| SIGALRM | 14 | Alarm clock. |

**Table 10–5    Signals Available Under Solaris (continued)**

| Signal | Number | Description |
| --- | --- | --- |
| SIGTERM | 15 | Terminated; a gentle kill that gives processes a chance to clean up. |
| SIGUSR1 | 16 | User signal 1. |
| SIGUSR2 | 17 | User signal 2. |
| SIGCHLD | 18 | Child status changed. |
| SIGPWR | 19 | Power fail or restart. |
| SIGWINCH | 20 | Window size change. |
| SIGURG | 21 | Urgent socket condition. |
| SIGPOLL | 22 | Pollable event. |
| SIGSTOP | 23 | Stopped (signal); pauses a process. |
| SIGTSTP | 24 | Stopped (user). |
| SIGCONT | 25 | Continued. |
| SIGTTIN | 26 | Stopped (tty input). |
| SIGTTOU | 27 | Stopped (tty output). |
| SIGVTALRM | 28 | Virtual timer expired. |
| SIGPROF | 29 | Profiling timer expired. |
| SIGXCPU | 30 | CPU time limit exceeded. |
| SIGXFSZ | 31 | File size limit exceeded. |
| SIGWAITING | 32 | Concurrency signal reserved by threads library. |
| SIGLWP | 33 | Inter-LWP signal reserved by threads library. |
| SIGFREEZE | 34 | Checkpoint freeze. |
| SIGTHAW | 35 | Checkpoint thaw. |
| SIGCANCEL | 36 | Cancellation signal reserved by threads library. |

In addition, you can write a signal handler in the program to respond to a signal being sent. For example, many system administration utilities, such as the name server, respond to the SIGHUP signal by re-reading their configuration files. This signal can then be used to update the process while running, without having to terminate and restart the process. For many signals, however, nothing can be done other than printing an appropriate error message and terminating the process.

The `kill` command sends a terminate signal (signal 15) to the process and the process is terminated. Signal 15, which is the default when no options are used with the `kill` command, is a gentle kill that allows a process to perform cleanup work before terminating. Signal 9, on the other hand, is called a sure, unconditional kill because it cannot be caught or ignored by a process. If the process is still around after a `kill -9`, it is either hung up in the UNIX kernel waiting for an event such as disk I/O to complete, or you are not the owner of the process. The `kill` command is routinely used to send signals to a process. You can kill any process you own, and superuser can kill all processes in the system except those with process IDs 0, 1, 2, 3, and 4. The `kill` command is poorly named because not every signal sent by it is used to kill a process. The command gets its name from its most common use—terminating a process with the `kill -15` signal.

A common problem occurs when a process continually starts up new copies of itself—referred to as forking or spawning. Users have a limit on the number of new processes they can fork. This limit is set in the kernel with the MAXUP (maximum number of user processes) value. Sometimes, through user error, a process keeps forking new copies of itself until the user hits the MAXUP limit. As a user reaches the MAXUP limit, the system appears to be waiting. If you kill some of the user's processes, the system resumes creating new processes on behalf of the user. It can be a no-win situation. The best way to handle these run-away processes is to send the STOP signal to suspend all processes and then send a KILL signal to terminate the processes. Because the processes were first suspended, they can't create new processes as you kill them off.

You can send a signal to a process you own with the `kill` command. Many signals are available but you only need to worry about two right now—9 and 15. To send a signal to a process, first use the `ps` command to find the process ID (PID) number. For example, type `ps -ef` to list all processes and find the process you wish to terminate.

```
ps -ef
```

| UID | PID | PPID | C | STIME | TTY | TIME | CMD |
|-----|-----|------|---|-------|-----|------|-----|
| root | 0 | 0 | 0 | Nov 27 | ? | 0:01 | sched |
| root | 1 | 0 | 0 | Nov 27 | ? | 0:01 | /etc/init - |
| root | 2 | 0 | 0 | Nov 27 | ? | 0:00 | pageout |
| root | 3 | 0 | 0 | Nov 27 | ? | 12:52 | fsflush |
| root | 101 | 1 | 0 | Nov 27 | ? | 0:00 | /usr/sbin/in.routed -q |
| root | 298 | 1 | 0 | Nov 27 | ? | 0:00 | /usr/lib/saf/sac -t 300 |
| root | 111 | 1 | 0 | Nov 27 | ? | 0:02 | /usr/sbin/rpcbind |
| root | 164 | 1 | 0 | Nov 27 | ? | 0:01 | /usr/sbin/syslogd -n -z 12 |
| root | 138 | 1 | 0 | Nov 27 | ? | 0:00 | /usr/sbin/inetd -s |
| root | 113 | 1 | 0 | Nov 27 | ? | 0:00 | /usr/sbin/keyserv |
| root | 160 | 1 | 0 | Nov 27 | ? | 0:01 | /usr/lib/autofs/automountd |

.
.
.

| UID | PID | PPID | C | STIME | TTY | TIME | CMD |
|-----|-----|------|---|-------|-----|------|-----|
| root | 439 | 424 | 0 | Nov 27 | ? | 0:00 | /bin/cat /tmp/.removable/notify0 |
| root | 5497 | 433 | 1 | 09:58:02 | pts/4 | 0:00 | script psef |

To kill the process with a PID number of 5497, type

```
kill -15 5497
```

# Scheduling Processes

Processes compete for execution time. Scheduling, one of the key elements on a time-sharing system, decides which of the processes will execute next. Although hundreds of processes might be present on the system, only one actually uses the CPU at any given time. Time-sharing on a CPU involves suspending a process and then restarting it at some later time. Because the suspension and resumption of active processes occurs several times each second, it appears to the user that the system is performing many tasks simultaneously.

UNIX attempts to manage the priorities of processes by giving a higher priority to those that have used the least amount of the CPU. In addition, users who are sleeping on an event, such as a keyboard press, get higher priority than processes that are purely CPU driven. On any large system with a number of competing user groups, the task of managing resources falls on the system administrator. This task is both technical and political. As a system administrator, you must understand your company goals in order to manage this task.

When you understand the political implications about who should get priority, you are ready to manage the technical details. As root, you can change the priority of any process on the system by using the `nice` or `priocntl` commands. Before you do this, you must understand how priorities work.

## Scheduling Priorities

All processes have an execution priority assigned to them—an integer value that is dynamically computed and updated on the basis of several different factors. Whenever the CPU is free, the scheduler selects the most favored process to resume executing. The process selected is the process with the lowest priority number, because lower numbers are defined as more favored than higher ones. Multiple processes at the same priority level are placed into the run queue for that priority level. Whenever the CPU is free, the scheduler starts the processes at the head of the lowest-numbered non-empty run queue. When the process at the top of a run queue stops executing, it goes to the end of the line and the next process moves up to the front. After a process begins to run, it continues to execute until it needs to wait for an I/O operation to complete, receives an interrupt signal, or exhausts the maximum execution time-slice defined on that system. A typical time-slice is 10 milliseconds.

UNIX processes have two priority numbers associated with them. One of the priority numbers is its requested execution priority with respect to other processes. This value (its nice number) is set by the process's owner and by root; it appears in the `NI` column in a `ps -l` listing. The other priority assigned to a process is the execution priority. This priority is computed and dynamically updated by the operating system, taking into account such factors as the process's nice number, how much CPU time it has had recently, and what other processes are running and their priorities. The execution priority value appears in the PRI column on a `ps -l` listing.

Although the CPU is the most watched resource on a system, it is not the only one. Memory use, disk use, IO activity, and number of processes all tie together in determining throughput of the computer. For example, consider that you have two groups, A and B. Both groups require large amounts of memory—more than is available when both are running simultaneously. Raising the priority of Group A over Group B might not help if Group B does not fully relinquish the memory it is using. Although the paging system will do this over time, the process of swapping a process out to disk can be intensive and can greatly reduce performance. A better alternative might be to completely stop Group B with a signal and then continue it later when Group A has finished.

## Changing the Priority of a Time-Sharing Process with *nice*

The `nice` command is supported only for backward compatibility to previous Solaris releases. The `priocntl` command provides more flexibility in managing processes. The priority of a process is determined by the policies of its scheduling class and by its nice number. Each time-sharing process has a global priority that is calculated by adding the user-supplied priority, which can be influenced by the `nice` or `priocntl` commands and the system-calculated priority.

The execution priority number of a process is assigned by the operating system and is determined by several factors, including its schedule class, how much CPU time it has used, and its nice number. Each time-sharing process starts with a default nice number, which it inherits from its parent process. The nice number is shown in the NI column of the `ps` report.

A user can lower the priority of a process by increasing its user-supplied priority number. Only the superuser can increase the priority of a process by lowering its nice value. This prevents users from increasing the priorities of their own processes, thereby monopolizing a greater share of the CPU.

In UNIX, nice numbers range from 0 to +19. The highest priority is 0. Two versions of the command are available—the standard version, `/usr/bin/nice`, and a version that is part of the C shell. Use the `nice` command as described in Table 10–6 when submitting a program or command.

### Table 10–6   Setting Priorities with *nice*

*Lowering the priority of a process*

| | |
|---|---|
| `nice command_name` | Increases the nice number by four units (the default). |
| `nice +4 command_name` | Increases the nice number by four units. |
| `nice +10 command_name` | Increases the nice number by 10 units. |

*Increasing the priority on a process*

| | |
|---|---|
| `nice -10 command_name` | Raises the priority of the command by lowering the nice number. |
| `nice - -10 command_name` | Raises the priority of the command by lowering the nice number. The two minus signs are required. The first minus sign is the option sign and the second minus sign indicates a negative number. |

As system administrator, you can use the `renice` command to change the priority of a process after it has been submitted. The `renice` command has the following form:

```
renice priority -n <value> -p <pid>
```

Use the `ps -el` command to find the PID of the process for which you want to change the priority. The process you want to change in the following example is named "largejob":

```
F S   UID   PID  PPID  C PRI NI    ADDR    SZ   WCHAN TTY    TIME  CMD
9 S     0  8200  4100  0  84 20  f0274e38   193          ?    0:00  largejob
```

Issue the following command to increase the priority of PID 8200:

```
renice -n -4 -p 8200
```

Issuing the `ps -el` command again shows the process with a higher priority:

```
F S   UID   PID  PPID  C PRI NI    ADDR    SZ   WCHAN TTY    TIME  CMD
9 S     0  8200  4100  0  60 12  f0274e38   193          ?    0:00  largejob
```

## Changing the Scheduling Priority of Processes with *priocntl*

The standard priority scheme has been improved under Solaris as part of its support for real-time processes. Real-time processes are designed to work in applications areas in which nearly immediate response to events is required. These processes are given nearly complete access to all system resources when they are running. Solaris uses time-sharing priority numbers ranging from –20 to 20. Solaris uses the `priocntl` command, intended as an improvement over the `nice` command, to modify process priorities. To use `priocntl` to change a priority on a process, type

```
priocntl -s -p <new-priority>   -i pid <process-id>
```

where *new-priority* is the new priority for the process and *process-id* is the PID of the process you wish to change. The following example sets the priority level for process 8200 to –5:

```
priocntl -s -p -5 -i pid 8200
```

The following example is used to set the priority (nice value) for every process created by a given parent process:

```
priocntl -s -p -5 -I ppid 8200
```

As a result of this command, all processes forked from process 8200 will have a priority of –5.

Consult the online manual pages for more information about the `priocntl` command.

# Solaris Batch-Processing Facility

A way to divide processes on a busy system is to schedule jobs so they run at different times. A large job, for example, could be scheduled to run at 2 a.m. when the system would normally be idle. Solaris supports two methods of batch-processing—the crontab and at commands. The crontab command schedules multiple system events at regular intervals, and the at command schedules a single system event.

## crontab

The cron daemon schedules system events according to commands found within each crontab file. A crontab file consists of commands, one per line, that will be executed at regular intervals. The beginning of each line contains five date and time fields that tell the cron daemon when to execute the command. The sixth field is the full pathname of the program you wish to run. These fields, described in Table 10–7, are separated by spaces.

**Table 10–7  crontab File**

| Field | Description | Values | |
|---|---|---|---|
| 1 | Minute | 0–59 | An * in this field means every minute. |
| 2 | Hour | 0–23 | An * in this field means every hour. |
| 3 | Day of month | 1–31 | An * in this field means every day of the month. |
| 4 | Month | 1–12 | An * in this field means every month. |
| 5 | Day of week | 0–6 (0=Sunday) | An * in this field means every day of the week. |
| 6 | Command | | |

Follow these guidelines when making entries in the crontab:

- Use a space to separate fields.
- Use a comma to separate multiple values in the time fields.
- Use a hyphen to designate a range of values in the time field.
- Use an asterisk as a wildcard to include all possible values in the time field. For example, an asterisk (*) can be used in the time field to mean all legal values.
- Use a comment mark (#) at the beginning of a line to indicate a comment or a blank line.
- Each command within a crontab file must consist of one line, even if it is very long, because crontab does not recognize extra carriage returns.

The following sample crontab command entry displays a reminder in the user's console window at 5 p.m. on the 1st and 15th of every month.

```
0 17 1,15 * * echo Handing Timesheet > /dev/console
```

crontab files are found in the /var/spool/cron/crontabs directory. Several crontab files besides root are provided during SunOS software installation and are also located in this directory. Other crontab files are named after the user accounts in which they are created, such as bill, glenda, miguel, or nicole. They also are located in the /var/spool/cron/crontabs directory. For example, a crontab file named root is supplied during software installation. Its contents include these command lines:

```
10  3  *  *  0,4 /etc/cron.d/logchecker
10  3  *  *  0   /usr/lib/newsyslog
15  3  *  *  0 /usr/lib/fs/nfs/nfsfind
1   2  *  *  * [ -x /usr/sbin/rtc ] && /usr/sbin/rtc -c > /dev/null 2>&1
```

The first command line instructs the system to run `logchecker` at 3:10 on Sunday and Thursday nights. The second command line schedules the system to run `newsyslog` at 3:10 every Sunday morning. The third command line orders the system to execute `nfsfind` daily at 3:15 in the morning. The fourth command line instructs the system to check for daylight savings time and makes corrections if necessary. If there is no RTC time zone or no /etc/rtc_config file, this entry will do nothing.

The cron daemon handles the automatic scheduling of crontab commands. Its function is to check the /var/spool/cron/crontab directory every 15 minutes for the presence of crontab files. It checks for new crontab files or changes to existing ones, reads the execution times listed within the files, and submits the commands for execution at the proper times.

## How to Create or Edit a crontab File

Creating an entry in the crontab file is as easy as editing a text file using your favorite editor. The procedure is as follows:

1. (Optional) To create or edit a crontab file belonging to root or another user, become superuser.

2. Create a new crontab file, or edit an existing one, by typing

   ```
   crontab -e
   ```

3. Add command lines to the file, following the syntax described in Table 10–7.

4. Save the changes and exit the file. The crontab file is placed in /var/spool/cron/crontabs.

5. Verify the crontab file by typing

   ```
   crontab -l
   ```

   The system responds by listing the contents of the crontab file.

### Controlling Access to crontab

You can control access to crontab by modifying two files in the /etc/cron.d directory: cron.deny and cron.allow. These files permit only specified users to perform crontab tasks such as creating, editing, displaying, or removing their own crontab files. The cron.deny and cron.allow files consist of a list of usernames, one per line. These access control files work together in the following manner:

- If cron.allow exists, only the users listed in this file can create, edit, display, or remove crontab files.

- If cron.allow doesn't exist, all users may submit crontab files, except for users listed in cron.deny.

- If neither cron.allow nor cron.deny exists, superuser privileges are required to run crontab.

Superuser privileges are required to edit or create cron.deny and cron.allow.

During Solaris software installation, a default /etc/cron.d/cron.deny file is provided and contains the following entries:

```
daemon
bin
smtp
nuucp
listen
nobody
noaccess
```

None of the users listed in the cron.deny file can access crontab commands. The system administrator can edit this file to add other users who will be denied access to the crontab command. No default cron.allow file is supplied. This means that, after Solaris software installation, all users (except the ones listed in the default cron.deny file) can access crontab. If you create a cron.allow file, only these users can access crontab commands.

## Scheduling a Single System Event (*at*)

The at command is used to schedule jobs for execution at a later time. Unlike crontab, which schedules a job to happen at regular intervals, a job submitted with at will execute once, at the designated time.

To submit an at job, type **at**. Then specify an execution time and a program to run, as shown in the following example:

```
at 07:45am today
at> who > /tmp/log
at> <Press Control-d>
job 912687240.a at Thu Dec 3 07:14:00 1998
```

When you submit an at job, it is assigned a job identification number, which becomes its filename along with the .a extension. The file is stored in the /var/spool/cron/atjobs directory. In much the same way as it schedules crontab jobs, the cron daemon controls the scheduling of at files.

The at command syntax is listed in Table 10–8.

**Table 10–8** *at* **Command Syntax**

*at -m <time> <date>*

| | |
|---|---|
| -m | Sends you mail after the job is completed. |
| time | The hour when you want to schedule the job. Add am or pm if you do not specify the hours according to a 24-hour clock. "Midnight," "noon," and "now" are acceptable keywords. Minutes are optional. |
| date | The first three or more letters of a month, a day of the week, or the keywords "today" or "tomorrow." |

You can set up a file to control access to the at command, permitting only specified users to create, remove, or display queue information about their at jobs. The file that controls access to at is /etc/cron.d/at.deny and consists of a list of user names, one per line. The users listed in this file cannot access at commands. The at.deny file, created during SunOS software installation, contains the following usernames:

daemon

bin

smtp

nuucp

listen

nobody

noaccess

With superuser privileges, you can edit this file to add other user names whose at access you want to restrict.

To check your jobs that are waiting in the at queue, use the atq command. This command displays status information about the at jobs you created. Use the atq command to verify that you have created an at job. The atq command confirms that at jobs have been submitted to the queue, as shown in the following example:

```
atq
Rank   Execution Date        Owner   Job            Queue   Job Name
1st    Dec  3, 1998 08:00     root    912690000.a     a       stdin
2nd    Dec  3, 1998 08:05     root    912690300.a     a       stdin
```

Another way to check an at job is by issuing the at -1 command. This command shows the status information on all jobs submitted by a user, as shown in this example:

```
at -l
user = root      912690000.a    Thu Dec  3 08:00:00 1998
user = root      912690300.a    Thu Dec  3 08:05:00 1998
```

To remove the at job from the queue before it is executed, type

**at -r [job-id]**

where job-id is the identification number of the job you want to remove.

Verify that the at job is removed by using the at -1 (or the atq) command to display the jobs remaining in the at queue. The job whose identification number you specified should not appear. In the following example, we'll remove an at job that was scheduled to execute at 08:00 a.m. on December 3. First, check the at queue to locate the job identification number.

```
at -l
user = root      912690000.a    Thu Dec  3 08:00:00 1998
user = root      912690300.a    Thu Dec  3 08:05:00 1998
```

Next, remove the job from the at queue:

```
    at -r 912690000.a
```

Finally, verify that this job has been removed from the queue.

```
    at -l
    user = root      912690300.a    Thu Dec  3 08:05:00 1998
```

In summary, the system administrator needs to be aware of the processes that belong to each application. As users report problems, the system administrator can quickly locate the processes being used and look for irregularities. By keeping a close watch on system processes, you'll become familiar with what is normal and what is abnormal. Don't wait for problems to happen—watch system processes daily. Create shell scripts to watch processes for you. By taking a proactive approach to system administration, you'll find problems before they affect the users. In Chapter 11, "Backup and Recovery," we'll move on from system setup and processes to take a look at the system administrator's most important preventive maintenance task, system backups.

# 11

# Backup and Recovery

The following are the test objectives for this chapter:

- Using the Solaris utilities tar, dd, cpio, and pax to copy data

- Using ufsdump and ufsrestore to back up and restore data

**B**acking up a system involves copying data from the system's hard disks onto removable media that can be safeguarded in a secure area. Backups are used to restore data if files get corrupted or data gets destroyed by system failure or a building disaster. Having a fault-tolerant disk array is not enough. Disk mirroring and RAID 5 protect your data in case of a hardware failure, but they do not protect against file corruption, natural disaster, or accidentally deleting a file. Backing up system data—the most important task you will perform—must be carried out on a regular basis. Although even a comprehensive backup scheme can't guarantee against loss of information, you can make sure the loss will be minimal. This chapter describes methods available to perform a backup, types of backups, development of a solid backup strategy, and restoring of data if you encounter a loss. First you'll find an explanation of the tar, dd, cpio, and pax commands, which are used to copy data from disk to disk or from disk to tape. Then the ufsdump and ufsrestore utilities are described as the preferred method of backing up data from a Solaris system to tape on a regular basis.

## Solaris Backup and Restore Utilities

Solaris provides the following utilities that can be used to copy data from disk to removable media and restore it:

| | |
|---|---|
| tar | Used to archive data to another directory, system, or media. |
| dd | Used to copy data quickly. |
| cpio | Used to copy data from one location to another. |
| pax | Use pax to copy files and directory subtrees to a single tape. This command provides better portability than tar or cpio, so it can be used to transport files to other types of UNIX systems. |
| ufsdump | Used to back up all files in a file system. |
| ufsrestore | Used to restore some or all of the files archived with the ufsdump command. |

### *tar*

The primary use of the tar (tape archiver) command is to copy file systems or individual files from a hard disk to a tape or from a tape to a hard disk. You can also use it to create a tar archive on a hard disk or floppy and to extract files from a tar archive on a hard disk or floppy. The tar command is popular because it's available on most UNIX systems; however, it is limited to a single tape. If the data you are backing up requires more than one tape, use the cpio, pax, or ufsdump command.

The tar command has the following syntax:

```
tar <options> <tar filename> <file list>
```

where options is the list of command options listed in Table 11–1. For a more complete listing of options, refer to the Solaris online manual pages. The tar filename is used with the f option and is any name you want to use. The tar filename can also be the name of a device, such as /dev/rmt/0 or /dev/rfd0. The file list is a list of files you want to include in the archive.

## Table 11–1   Command Options for *tar*

| | |
|---|---|
| c | Creates a tar file. |
| t | Table of contents. Lists the names of the specified files each time they occur in the tar filename. If no file argument is given, the names of all files in the tar filename are listed. When used with the v function modifier, it displays additional information for the specified files. |
| x | Extracts or restores files from a tar filename. |
| v | Verbose. Outputs information to the screen as tar reads or writes the archive. |
| f | Uses the tar filename argument as the name of the tar archive. If f is omitted, tar uses the device indicated by the TAPE environment variable, if set. If the TAPE variable is not set, tar uses the default values defined in /etc/default/tar. If the name of the tar file is '-', tar writes to the standard output. |

To create a tape archive on tape device /dev/rmt/0 of everything in the /home/bcalkins directory, type the following:

```
tar cvf /dev/rmt/0 /home/bcalkins
```

To list the files in the archive, type:

```
tar tvf /dev/rmt/0
```

To restore the file /home/bcalkins/.profile from the archive, type:

```
tar xvf /dev/rmt/0 /home/bcalkins/.profile
```

Use tar to create an archive file on disk instead of tape. The tar filename will be files.tar:

```
tar cvf files.tar /home/bcalkins
```

To extract files that were created by using the previous example, type

```
tar xvf files.tar
```

Notice the use of the full pathname. Using the full pathname to create the archive ensures that the files will be restored to their original location in the directory hierarchy. You will not be able to restore them elsewhere.

If you want to be able to restore files with a relative pathname, you could change to the /home/bcalkins directory and specify files to be archived as ./*. This would put the files into the archive using a pathname relative to the current working directory rather than an absolute pathname (one beginning with a forward slash). Files can then be restored into any directory.

## dd

The main advantage of the dd command is that it quickly converts and copies files with different data formats, such as differences in block size or record length.

The most common use of this command is to transfer a complete file system or partition from your hard disk to a tape. You can also use it to copy files from one hard disk to another. When you're copying data, the dd command makes an image copy (an exact byte-for-byte copy) of any media, which can be either tape or disk. The syntax for the dd command, which follows, is described in Table 11–2.

```
dd if=<input-file> of=<output-file> <option=value>
```

### Table 11–2   *dd* Command Syntax

| | |
|---|---|
| if | Used to designate an input file. The input file can be a filename or a device name, such as /dev/rmt/0. If no input file is specified, input for dd is taken from the UNIX standard input. |
| of | Used to designate an output file. The output file can be a filename or a device name, such as /dev/rmt/0. If the output file is omitted, output from dd is sent the UNIX standard output. |

Several other options can follow on the command line to specify buffer sizes, block sizes, and data conversions. See the Solaris online manual pages for a list of these options.

The next few examples illustrate the use of the dd command for copying data. The first example shows how the dd command is used to duplicate tapes. This procedure requires two tape drives: a source tape and a destination tape.

```
dd if=/dev/rmt/0 of=/dev/rmt/1
```

The next example uses dd to copy one entire hard disk to another hard disk. In the example, we need two disks and both must have the same geometry.

```
dd if=/dev/rdsk/c0t1d0s2 of=/dev/rdsk/c0t4d0s4 bs=128
```

In this example, the option bs=128 specifies a block size. A large block size, such as 128KB or 256KB, will decrease the time to copy by buffering large amounts of data. Notice also that the raw device is specified. For this technique to work properly, you must use the raw (character) device to avoid the buffered (block) I/O system.

The dd command can be used with tar to create an archive on a remote tape drive. In the next example, tar is used to create an archive on a remote system by piping the output to a tape drive called /dev/rmt/0 on a remote system named xena.

```
tar cf - files ¦ rsh xena dd of=/dev/rmt/0 obs=128
```

Another example would be to read tar data coming from another UNIX system, such as Silicon Graphics. Silicon Graphics swaps every pair of bytes, making a tar tape unreadable on a Solaris system. To read a tar tape from an SGI system, type

```
dd if=/dev/nrst0 conv=swab ¦ tar xvf -
```

In a similar way, a Solaris system can create a tar tape that is readable by an SGI system:

```
tar cvf - ¦ dd of=/dev/nrst0 conv=swab
```

## cpio

The `cpio` command is used for copying data from one place to another. `cpio` stands for "copy input to output." When copying files with `cpio`, you present a list of files to its standard input and write the file archive to its standard output. The principal advantage of `cpio` is its flexible syntax. The command acts as a filter program, taking input information from the standard input file and delivering its output to the standard output file. The input and output can be manipulated by using the shell to specify redirection and pipelines. The advantages of `cpio` over other UNIX utilities are

- `cpio` can back up and restore individual files, not just whole file systems.

- Backups made by `cpio` are smaller than those created with `tar` because the header is smaller.

- `cpio` can span multiple tapes; `tar` is limited to a single tape.

Because of its flexibility, `cpio` has more options and is perceived as a more complex command than `tar`.

The `cpio` program operates in one of three modes: copy-out (`cpio -o`), copy-in (`cpio -I`), and pass (`cpio -p`). Use copy-out when creating a backup tape and copy-in when restoring or listing files from a tape. The pass mode is generally used to copy files from one location to another on disk. You must always specify one of these three modes. The command syntax for the `cpio` command is

```
cpio <mode> <option>
```

where mode is `-i`, `-o`, or `-p` and option is an option from Table 11–3.

## Table 11–3   Command Options for cpio

| | |
|---|---|
| c | Writes header information in ASCII format for portability. |
| d | Creates as many directories as needed. |
| B | Specifies that the input has a blocking factor of 5,120 bytes to the record instead of the default 512 byte records. You must use the same blocking factor when you retrieve or copy files from the tape to the hard disk as you did when you copied files from the hard disk to the tape. You must use this option whenever you copy files or file systems to and from a tape drive. |

**Table 11–3   Command Options for** *cpio* **(continued)**

v          Verbose. Reports the names of the files as they are processed.

u          Copies unconditionally. Without this option, an older file will not replace a newer file with the same name.

m          Retains previous file modification time. This option is ineffective on directories that are being copied.

The following example shows how to copy the directory /work and its subdirectories to a tape drive with the device name /dev/rmt/0.

```
cd /work
ls -R ¦ cpio -ocB > /dev/rmt/0
```

The next example shows how to copy the files located on a tape back into the directory named /work on a hard disk:

```
cd /work
cpio -icdB < /dev/rmt/0
```

## Backing Up Files with Copy-Out Mode

To use the copy-out mode to make backups, you send a list of files to the `cpio` command via the standard input of `cpio`. In practice, you'll use the UNIX `find` command to generate the list of files to be backed up. Copy-out mode is specified by using the -o option on the `cpio` command line. In the next example, a file named list contains a short list of files to be backed up to tape.

```
cpio -ovB list > /dev/rmt/1
```

Normally, as indicated in Table 11–3, `cpio` writes files to the standard output in 512-byte records. By specifying the -B option, you increase the record size to 5,120 bytes to significantly speed up the transfer rate, as shown in the previous example.

You can use UNIX commands to generate a list of files to be backed up by `cpio` in a number of other ways, as shown in the following examples.

Files can be backed up by entering filenames via the keyboard. Enter Ctrl-D when you have finished typing filenames.

```
cpio -o > /dev/rmt/1
File1.txt
File2.txt
<Ctrl-D>
```

The `ls` command can be used to generate the list of files to be backed up by `cpio`.

```
cd /home/bcalkins
ls * ¦ cpio -o >/dev/rmt/1
```

Use the `find` command to generate a list of files created by the user bcalkins and modified in the last five days. This is the list of files to be backed up.

```
find . -user bcalkins -mtime -5  -print ¦ cpio -o > /dev/rmt/1
```

If the current tape fills up, the `cpio` program prompts you for another tape. You see a message that says:

```
"If you want to go on, type device/file name when ready"
```

You should then change the tape and enter the name of the backup device (for example, /dev/rmt/1).

## Restoring Files with Copy-In Mode

Use the copy-in mode of `cpio` to restore files from tape to disk. The following examples describe methods used to restore files from a `cpio` archive.

This first example restores all files and directories from tape to disk. The `cpio` options specified will restore files unconditionally (-u) to the /users directory and will retain previous file modification times (-m):

```
cd /users
cpio -icvumB < /dev/rmt/1
```

The next example selectively restores files that begin with database. The -d option will create directories as needed.

```
cpio -icvdumB 'database*' < /dev/rmt/1
```

**NOTE.** *Single quotes must be used to pass the wild card argument (\*) on to* cpio.

To get a list of files that are on tape, follow the next example:

```
cpio -ictB < /dev/rmt/1
```

The list of files on /dev/rmt/1 will appear on screen.

## Pass-Mode

Pass-mode generally is not used for backups. The destination must be a directory on a mounted file system, which means pass-mode cannot be used to transfer files to tape. However, you can use pass-mode within `cpio` to copy files from one directory to another. The advantage of using `cpio` over `cp` is that original modification times and ownership are preserved. Specify pass-mode by using the -p option in `cpio`. The following example copies all files from /users to /bkup.

```
cd /users
mkdir /bkup
ls * ¦ cpio -pdumv bkup
```

Files will be listed to the screen as they are copied.

## pax

New in Solaris 2.5 is the pax command, a POSIX conformant archive utility that can read and write tar and cpio archives. It is available on most UNIX systems that are POSIX compliant.

pax can read, write, and list the members of an archive file and copy directory hierarchies. The pax utility supports a wide variety of archive formats, including tar and cpio.

Here's a nice feature: if pax finds an archive that is damaged or corrupted while processing, pax attempts to recover from media defects. It searches through the archive to locate and process the largest possible number of archive members.

The action to be taken depends on the presence of the -r and -w options, which are referred to as the four modes of operation: list, read, write, and copy (described in Table 11–4). The syntax for the pax command is

```
pax <mode> <options>
```

**Table 11–4** *Pax*—**Four Modes of Operation**

| | |
|---|---|
| -r | Read mode (when -r is specified but -w is not). pax extracts the filenames and directories found in the archive file. The archive file is read from disk or tape. If an extracted file is a directory, the file hierarchy is extracted as well. The extracted files are created relative to the current file hierarchy. |
| (none) | List mode (when neither -r nor -w is specified). pax writes the filenames or directories found in the archive file. The archive file is read from disk, tape, or the standard input. The list is written to the standard output. |
| -w | Write mode (when -w is specified but -r is not). pax writes the contents of the file to the standard output in an archive format. If no files are specified, a list of files to copy (one per line) is read from the standard input. A directory includes all of the files in the file hierarchy rooted at the file. |
| -rw | Copy mode (when both -r and -w are specified). pax copies the specified files to the destination directory. |

In addition to selecting a mode of operation, you can select one or more options from Table 11–5. For additional options to the pax command, see the Solaris online manual pages.

## Table 11–5   Command Options for *pax*

| | |
|---|---|
| -r | Reads an archive file from standard input and extracts the specified files. If any intermediate directories are needed for extracting an archive member, these directories are created. |
| -w | Writes files to the standard output in the specified archive format. When no file operands are specified, standard input is read for a list of pathnames—one per line, without any leading or trailing blanks. |
| -a | Appends files to the end of an archive that was previously written. |
| -b | Blocksize. The blocksize must be a multiple of 512 bytes, with a maximum of 32,256 bytes. A blocksize can end with k or b to specify multiplication by 1,024 (1K) or 512, respectively. |
| -c | Matches all file or archive members except those specified by the pattern and file operands. |
| -f <archive> | Specifies archive as the pathname of the input or output archive. A single archive may span multiple files and different archive devices. When required, pax prompts for the pathname of the file or device of the next volume in the archive. |
| -n | Selects the first archive member that matches each pattern operand. No more than one archive member is matched for each pattern. |
| -p <string> | Specifies one or more file characteristic options (privileges). The string option-argument is a string specifying file characteristics to be retained or discarded on extraction. The string consists of the specification characters a, e, m, o, and p. Multiple characteristics can be concatenated within the same string and multiple -p options can be specified. The meanings of the specification characters are as follows:<br><br>a—Do not preserve file access times.<br><br>e—Preserve everything: user ID, group ID, file mode bits, file access times, and file modification times.<br><br>m—Do not preserve file modification times.<br><br>o—Preserve the user ID and group ID.<br><br>p—Preserve the file mode bits. |
| -v | Verbose mode. |
| -x <format> | Specifies the output archive format, with the default format being ustar. pax currently supports cpio, tar, bcpio, ustar, sv4crc, and sv4cpio. |

When using pax, you can also specify file operands along with options from Table 11–5. The operand specifies a destination directory or file pathname. If you specify a directory operand but the directory operand does not exist, is not writable by the user, or is not of type directory, pax exits with a non-zero exit status.

The file operand specifies the pathname of a file to be copied or archived. When a file operand does not select at least one archive member, pax writes these file operand pathnames in a diagnostic message to standard error and then exits with a non-zero exit status.

Another operand is the pattern operand, which is used to select one or more pathnames of archive members. Archive members are selected by using the filename pattern-matching notation described by `fnmatch`(3). Examples of pattern operands are

?          A question mark is a pattern that will match any character.

*          An asterisk is a pattern that will match multiple characters.

[          The open bracket will introduce a pattern bracket expression.

When the pattern operand is not supplied, all members of the archive are selected. When a pattern matches a directory, the entire file hierarchy rooted at that directory is selected. When a pattern operand does not select at least one archive member, `pax` writes these pattern operands in a diagnostic message to standard error and then exits with a non-zero exit status.

The following examples illustrate the use of the `pax` command. For example, to copy files to tape, issue this `pax` command, using `-w` to copy the current directory contents to tape and `-f` to specify the tape device:

```
pax -w -f /dev/rmt/0
```

To list a verbose table of contents for an archive stored on tape device /dev/rmt/0, issue the following command:

```
pax -v -f /dev/rmt/0
```

The tape device in the two previous examples could have been a filename to specify an archive on disk.

The following command can be used to interactively select the files to copy from the current directory to the destination directory:

```
pax -rw -i . <dest_dir>
```

As you become more familiar with the `pax` utility, you'll begin to use it in place of `tar` and `cpio` because of its portability to other UNIX systems, its capability to recover damaged archives, and its capability to span multiple volumes.

## ufsdump

Although the other Solaris utilities discussed in this chapter can be used to copy files from disk to tape, `ufsdump` is designed specifically for backups and is the recommended method for backing up your Solaris file systems. The `ufsdump` command copies files, directories, or entire file systems from a hard disk to a tape. The only drawback to using `ufsdump` is that file systems must be inactive before you can conduct a full backup. If the file system is still active, anything in the memory buffers is not copied to tape.

You should back up any file systems critical to users, including file systems that change frequently. See Table 11–6 for suggestions on what file systems to back up and how often.

**Table 11–6    File Systems to Back Up**

| File System | Frequency |
| --- | --- |
| root (/) | If you frequently add and remove clients and hardware on the network or you have to change important files in root (/), this file system should be backed up. You should do a full backup on the root (/) file system between once a week and once a month. If /var is in the root (/) file system and your site keeps user mail in the /var/mail directory on a mail server, you might want to back up root (/) daily. |
| /usr | The contents of this file system are fairly static and need to be backed up only from once a week to once a month. |
| /export/home | The /export/home file system contains the home directories and subdirectories of all users on the system; its files are volatile and need to be backed up daily. |
| Data | All data directories should be backed up daily. |

The ufsdump command has many built-in features the other archive utilities don't have. These features are described here:

■ The ufsdump command can be used to back up complete or individual file systems to local or remote tape devices. The tape device can be on any system in the network. This command works quickly because it is aware of the structure of the UFS file system type and it works directly through the raw device file.

■ ufsdump has built-in options to create incremental backups that will back up only those files that were changed since a previous backup. This option saves tape space and time.

■ ufsdump has the capability to back up groups of systems over the network from a single system. You can run ufsdump on each remote system through a remote shell or remote login, directing the output to the system on which the drive is located.

■ The system administrator can restrict user access to backup tables.

■ The ufsdump command has a built-in option to verify data on tape against the source file system.

Backing up a file system with ufsdump is referred to as "dumping" a file system. When a file system is dumped, a level between 0 and 9 is specified. A level 0 dump is a full backup and contains everything on the file system. Level 1 through 9 dumps are incremental backups and contain only files that have changed since a previous dump at a lower level.

A good backup schedule involves a recommended three-level dump strategy: a level 0 dump at the start of the month (manually), automated weekly level 5 dumps, and automated daily level 9 dumps. The automated dumps are performed at 4:30 a.m., a time when most systems typically are idle. Automated daily dumps are performed Sunday through Friday mornings. Automated weekly dumps are performed on Saturday mornings. Backups are automated by creating a shell script and using cron to execute the script on a regular basis.

Table 11–7 shows the dump level performed on each day of a typical month. Note that the level 0 dump at the start of the month is performed manually, because the entire system must be idle before you can back up the root file system. One way to ensure that the system is not being used is to take the system into single-user mode. The level 9 and 5 dumps are automated with cron, but also must be conducted when the file systems are not being used.

**Table 11–7  File System Dump Schedule**

|  | Floating | Monday | Tuesday | Wednesday | Thursday | Friday |
|---|---|---|---|---|---|---|
| 1st of month | 0 |  |  |  |  |  |
| Week 1 |  | 9 | 9 | 9 | 9 | 5 |
| Week 2 |  | 9 | 9 | 9 | 9 | 5 |
| Week 3 |  | 9 | 9 | 9 | 9 | 5 |
| Week 4 |  | 9 | 9 | 9 | 9 | 5 |

The backup schedule in Table 11–7 performs the following:

- Each weekday tape accumulates all files changed since the end of the previous week or the initial level 0 for the first week. All files that have changed since the lower-level backup at the end of the previous week are saved each day.

- Each Friday's tape contains all files changed since the last level 0.

This dump schedule requires at least four sets of five tapes, one set for each week and one tape for the level 0 dump. Each set will be rotated each month. The level 0 tapes should not be overwritten and should be saved for at least one year.

Be aware that even with the backup schedule outlined in Table 11–7, data can still be lost. If a hard disk fails at 3 p.m., all modifications since the 4:30 a.m. backup will be lost. Also, files that were deleted mid-week will not appear on the level 5 tapes. Sometimes a user accidentally deletes a file and does not realize it for several weeks. When the user wants to use the file, it is not there. If he asks you to restore it from backup, the only tape it appears on is the level 0, and it could be too far out of date to be useful. If you don't overwrite the daily level 9 tapes so frequently, you can minimize this problem.

The syntax for the `ufsdump` command is

```
/usr/sbin/ufsdump  options  arguments  file systems to backup
```

where

| | |
|---|---|
| options | Is a single string of one-letter option names. |
| arguments | Identifies option arguments and may be multiple strings. The option letters and the arguments that go with them must be in the same order. |
| file systems to back up | Identifies the files to back up. This argument must always come last and specifies the source or contents of the backup. It usually identifies a file system but can also identify individual files or directories. |

For a file system, specify the raw device file for the disk slice where the file system is located.

Table 11–8 describes the options and arguments for the `ufsdump` command.

### Table 11–8    Options for the *ufsdump* Command

| Option | Description |
|---|---|
| 0–9 | Backup level. Specifies level 0 for a full backup of the whole file system specified by *file systems to backup*. Levels 1–9 are for incremental backups of files that have changed since the last lower-level backup. |
| a *archive-file* | Instructs `ufsdump` to create an archive file. Stores a backup table of the tape contents in a specified file on the disk. The file can be understood only by `ufsrestore`. `ufsrestore` uses the table to determine whether a file to be restored is present in a backup file and, if so, on which volume of the media it resides. |
| b factor | Blocking factor. Specifies the number of 512-byte blocks to write to tape per operation. |
| c | Instructs `ufsdump` to back up to cartridge tape. When end-of-media detection applies, this option sets the block size to 126. |
| d bpi | Tape density. Use this option only when `ufsdump` cannot detect the end of the media. |
| D | Disk. Backs up to floppy disk. |
| f *dump-file* | Dump file. Specifies the destination of the backup. The dump-file argument can be one of the following:<br><br>■ Local tape drive or disk drive<br><br>■ Remote tape drive or disk drive<br><br>■ Standard output<br><br>Use this argument when the destination is not the default local tape drive /dev/rmt/0. If you use the f option, you must then specify a value for dump-file. |

## Table 11–8    Options for the *ufsdump* Command (continued)

| Option | Description |
|---|---|
| l | Autoload. Use this option if you have an autoloading (stackloader) tape drive. When the end of a tape is reached, this option takes the drive offline and waits up to two minutes for the tape drive to be ready again. If the drive is ready within two minutes, it continues. If the drive is not ready after two minutes, autoload prompts the operator to load another tape. |
| n | Notify. When intervention is needed, sends a message to all terminals of all users in the sys group. |
| o | Offline. When finished with a tape or disk, takes the drive offline, rewinds (if tape), and removes the media, if possible (for example, ejects disk or removes 8-mm autoloaded tape). |
| s *size* | Size. Specifies the length of tape in feet or size of disk in number of 1024-byte blocks. You need to use this option only when ufsdump cannot detect the end of the media. |
| S | Estimates size of backup. Determines the amount of space needed to perform the backup (without actually doing it) and outputs a single number indicating the estimated size of the backup in bytes. |
| t *tracks* | Tracks. Specifies the number of tracks for 1/4-inch cartridge tape. You need to use this option only when ufsdump cannot detect the end of the media. |
| u | Updates the dump record. For a completed backup of a file system, adds an entry to the file /etc/dumpdates. The entry indicates the device name for the file system's disk slice, the backup level (0–9), and the date. No record is written when you do not use the u option or when you back up individual files or directories. If a record already exists for a backup at the same level, it is replaced. |
| v | Verify. After each tape or disk is written, verifies the contents of the media against the source file system. If any discrepancies occur, prompts the operator to mount new media and then repeats the process. Use this option on an unmounted file system only, because any activity in the file system causes it to report discrepancies. |
| w | Warning. Lists the file systems appearing in /etc/dumpdates that have not been backed up within a day. When you use this option, all other options are ignored. |
| W | Warning with highlight. Shows all file systems that appear in /etc/dumpdates and highlights those file systems that have not been backed up within a day. When you use this option, all other options are ignored. |

The dump command uses these options by default:

```
ufsdump 9uf /dev/rmt/0 files-to-back-up
```

The following is an example of a full backup of the /users file system:

```
ufsdump 0ucf /dev/rmt/0 /users
  DUMP: Writing 63 Kilobyte records
  DUMP: Date of this level 0 dump: Sat Dec 12 13:13:22 1998
  DUMP: Date of last level 0 dump: the epoch
  DUMP: Dumping /dev/rdsk/c0t1d0s0 (pyramid1:/) to /dev/rmt/0.
```

```
DUMP: Mapping (Pass I) [regular files]
DUMP: Mapping (Pass II) [directories]
DUMP: Estimated 10168 blocks (4.96MB).
DUMP: Dumping (Pass III) [directories]
DUMP: Dumping (Pass IV) [regular files]
DUMP: Tape rewinding
DUMP: 10078 blocks (4.92MB) on 1 volume at 107 KB/sec
DUMP: DUMP IS DONE
```

In the following example, the local /export/home file system on a Solaris 2.6 system is backed up to a tape device on a remote Solaris 2.x system called sparc1.

```
ufsdump 0ucf sparc1:/dev/rmt/0 /export/home
DUMP: Date of this level 0 dump: Sat Dec 12 11:50:1 3 1998
DUMP: Date of last level 0 dump: the epoch
DUMP: Dumping /dev/rdsk/c0t3d0s7 (/export/home) to /dev/rmt/0  on host sparc1
DUMP: mapping (Pass I) [regular files]
DUMP: mapping (Pass II) [directories]
DUMP: estimated 19574 blocks (9.56MB)
DUMP: Writing 63 Kilobyte records
DUMP: dumping (Pass III) [directories]
DUMP: dumping (Pass IV) [regular files]
DUMP: level 0 dump on Tue Oct 25 10:30:53 1994
DUMP: Tape rewinding
DUMP: 19574 blocks (9.56MB) on 1 volume
DUMP: DUMP IS DONE
```

## Restoring a File System with *ufsrestore*

Use ufsrestore to restore data from tape to disk. The ufsrestore command copies files from backups created by using the ufsdump command. You can use ufsrestore to reload an entire file system from a level 0 dump and incremental dumps that follow it or to restore one or more single files from any dump tape. If ufsrestore is run by root, files are restored with their original owner, last modification time, and mode (permissions).

The syntax for the ufsrestore command is

```
ufsrestore  options  arguments  filename(s)
```

where

| | |
|---|---|
| options | You must choose one and only one of these options: i, r, R, t, or x. |
| arguments | Follows the option string with the arguments that match the options. |
| filename(s) | Specifies files to be restored as arguments to the x or t options and must always come last. |

Table 11–9 describes some of the more common options and arguments for the `ufsrestore` command. For a full listing, refer to the Solaris online manual pages.

**Table 11–9    Command Options for *ufsrestore***

| Option | Description |
|---|---|
| i | Interactive. Runs ufsrestore in an interactive mode. In this mode, you can use a limited set of shell commands to browse the contents of the media and select individual files or directories to restore. See Table 11–10 for a list of available commands. |
| r | Recursive. Restores the entire contents of the media into the current working directory, which should be the top level of the file system. Information used to restore incremental dumps on top of the full dump is also included. To completely restore a file system, use this option to restore the full (level 0) dump and then for each incremental dump. This is intended for a new file system that was just created with the `newfs` command. |
| x filename(s) | Extract. Selectively restores the files you specify by the filename(s) argument. Filename(s) can be a list of files and directories. All files under a specified directory are restored unless you also use the h option. If you omit filename(s) or enter "." for the root directory, all files on all volumes of the media (or from standard input) are restored. Existing files are overwritten and warnings are displayed. |
| t filename(s) | Table of contents. Checks the files specified in the filename(s) argument against the media. For each file, the full filename and the inode number (if the file is found) is listed. If the filename is not found, `ufsrestore` indicates the file is not on the "volume," meaning any volume in a multi-volume dump. If you do not enter the filename(s) argument, all files on all volumes of the media are listed without distinguishing on which volume the files are located. When you use the h option, only the directory files specified in filename(s)—not their contents—are checked and listed. The table of contents is read from the first volume of the media or (if you use the a option) from the specified archive file. This option is mutually exclusive with the x and r options. |
| b factor | Blocking factor. Specifies the number of 512-byte blocks to write to tape per operation. By default, `ufsrestore` tries to figure out the block size used in writing the tape. |
| m | Restores specified files into the current directory on the disk, regardless of where they are located in the backup hierarchy, and renames them with their inode number. For example, if the current working directory is /files, a file in the backup named ./database/test with inode number 156 is restored as /files/156. This option is useful when you are extracting only a few files. |
| s n | Skips to the nth backup file on the media. This option is useful when you put more than one backup on a single tape. |
| v | Verbose. Displays the names and inode numbers of each file as it is restored. |

Table 11–10 lists the commands that can be used with ufsrestore when selecting interactive mode (ufsrestore -i ).

## Table 11–10 Commands for an Interactive Restore

| Command | Description |
|---|---|
| ls *directory-name* | Lists the contents of either the current directory or the specified directory. Directories are suffixed with a /. Entries in the current list to be restored (extracted) are marked by an * prefix. if the verbose option is in effect, inode numbers are also listed. |
| cd *directory-name* | Changes to the specified directory in the backup hierarchy. |
| add *filename* | Adds the current directory or the specified file or directory to the list of files to extract (restore). If you do not use the h option, all files in a specified directory and its subdirectories are added to the list. Note that all of the files you want to restore to a directory might not be on a single backup tape or disk. You might need to restore from multiple backups at different levels to get all of the files. |
| delete *filename* | Deletes the current directory or the specified file or directory from the list of files to extract (restore). If you do not use the h option, all files in the specified directory and its subdirectories are deleted from the list. Note that the files and directories are deleted only from the extract list you are building. They are not deleted from the media. |
| extract | Extracts the files in the list and restores them to the current working directory on the disk. Specify 1 when asked for a volume number. If you are doing a multi-tape or multi-disk restore and restoring a small number of files, start with the last tape or disk. |
| help | Displays a list of commands you can use in interactive mode. |
| pwd | Displays the pathname of the current working directory in the backup hierarchy. |
| q | Quits interactive mode without restoring any additional files. |
| verbose | Turns on or off the verbose option. Verbose mode can also be entered as v on the command line outside of interactive mode. When verbose is on, the interactive ls command lists inode numbers and the ufsrestore command displays information on each file as it is extracted. |

The following examples illustrate how to restore data from a tape by using ufsrestore.

Use the ufsrestore command to display the contents of the tape.

```
ufsrestore tf /dev/rmt/0
        2       .
     4249       ./users
    12400       ./users/bill
    12401       ./users/bill/.login
    12402       ./users/bill/.cshrc
    12458       ./users/bill/admin
    12459       ./users/bill/junk
```

Use this command to restore a file from a backup that was created by using ufsdump, as follows:

```
ufsrestore f /dev/rmt/0 filename
```

You can restore entire directories from a remote drive located on the system called *sparc1* by adding remote-host: to the front of the tape device name, as illustrated in the next example.

```
ufsrestore rf sparc1:/dev/rmt/0 filename
```

Occasionally a file system becomes so damaged that you must completely restore it from a backup. If you have faithfully backed up file systems, you can restore them to the state of the last backup. The first step in recovering a file system is to delete everything in the damaged file system and re-create the file system by using the newfs command. To recover a damaged file system, follow these steps:

1. First, unmount the file system as follows:

```
umount   /filesystem
```

   where *filesystem* is the name of the corrupted file system.

2. After unmounting the file system, issue the newfs command to create a new file system as follows:

```
newfs /dev/rdsk/disk-partition-name
```

   where *disk-partition-name* is the name of the disk partition containing the corrupted file system.

3. Mount the file system to be restored and change into that directory:

```
mount /dev/dsk/disk-partition-name
cd /filesystem
```

4. Load the tape and issue the following command:

```
ufsrestore rf /dev/rmt/0
```

   The entire contents of the tape will be restored to the file system. All permissions, ownerships, and dates will remain as they were when the last incremental tape was created.

## Additional Notes About Restoring Files

When you restore files in a directory other than the root directory of the file system, ufsrestore re-creates the file hierarchy in the current directory. For example, if you restore files to /home that were backed up from /users/bcalkins/files, the files are restored in the directory /home/bcalkins/files.

When restoring individual files and directories, a good idea is to restore them to a temporary directory such as /var/tmp. After you verify the files, you can move them to their proper locations. You can restore individual files and directories to their original locations; however, if you do so, be sure you are not overwriting newer files with older versions from the backup tape.

Don't forget to make regular backups of your operating system. With all of the customization you've done, such as adding user accounts, setting up printers, and installing application software, losing this information would be disastrous. Whenever you make modifications that affect the root (/), /usr, /opt, and other operating system directories, bring the system down into single-user mode and do a level 0 dump.

This chapter described the standard copy and backup utilities available in Solaris. Although these utilities do a good job of backing up your data, if your company has several servers and large storage pools, you might want to investigate some of the more robust backup packages available from third parties. Most of these packages provide a comprehensive suite of utilities for conducting and managing backups in a complex computing environment. In most cases, they allow single-point backups, not only for Solaris but for other operating systems as well.

# C H A P T E R

# 12

# Device
# Administration

The following are the test objectives
for this chapter:

- Understanding Solaris port
  monitors, the Service Access
  Facility (SAF), and related
  configuration files

- Understanding how to use
  Admintool and the Service
  Access Facility (SAF) commands
  to manage serial ports

- Adding terminals and modems
  to a system and using SAF and
  Admintool

**T**his chapter describes the administration of terminals and modems within Solaris. In that context, we'll explore terminals, modems, port monitors, and services.

Terminals and modems provide access to local and remote system resources; therefore, setting up terminals and modem access is an important responsibility for a system administrator. Most experienced system administrators agree that managing the terminals and modems in UNIX is one of their more complex tasks. Solaris provides support for nearly all models of alphanumeric terminals and modems, but with this flexibility comes complexity. Because of this complexity, Sun has added these tasks to the Admintool to make them easier to perform. As with most Admintool functions, however, they do not provide the complete functionality you get at the command line. Occasionally, you'll encounter tasks that can be performed only from the command line. For this reason, this chapter covers not only the Admintool, but the specific SAF commands as well. I'll begin by describing hardware and software terminology before describing how to manage them.

## Hardware Terminology

This section briefly describes the hardware components involved—ports, terminals, modems, and cabling.

### Ports

A *port* is a channel through which a device communicates with the operating system. A port is a "receptacle" into which a terminal or modem cable may be plugged. The port is controlled by software in the operating system called a device driver. Common types of ports include serial, parallel, small computer systems interface (SCSI), and ethernet. The serial port software must be set up to provide a particular "service" for the device attached to the port. For example, you can set up a serial port to provide bidirectional service for a modem.

A serial port, using a standard communications protocol, transmits a byte of information bit by bit over a single line. Devices that have been designed according to RS-232-C or RS-423 standards—such as modems, alphanumeric terminals, plotters, and some printers—can be plugged into serial ports. Most systems have one or two serial ports. When many serial port devices must be connected to a single computer, you sometimes need to add an adapter board to the system. The adapter board, with its driver software, provides additional serial ports for connecting more devices than could otherwise be accommodated.

### Terminals

Solaris supports two types of displays: the alphanumeric display and the bit-mapped graphics display. The *alphanumeric terminal* and keyboard, referred to as a tty device, connects to a serial port and displays only text. Because the alphanumeric terminal is connected via a serial port, a system can support as many character display terminals as it has serial ports. If you run out of ports, you can add more. The disadvantage with the alphanumeric display is it will not display windows or graphics and does not support a mouse.

The *bit-mapped graphics display* is connected to the system via a graphics adapter of some kind. You simply need to plug the monitor into the system to make it operational. On a bit-mapped graphics display, you don't have to perform any special steps to administer it. The drawback, however, is that most computers support only one graphics display.

## Modems

*Modems* are also connected to a system through a serial port and are used for remote access over telephone lines. Modems can be set up in three basic configurations:

Dial-out

Dial-in

Bidirectional

A modem connected to the local computer might be set up to provide dial-out service, meaning you can access other computers but nobody outside can gain access to this computer. Dial-in service is just the opposite. It allows users to access a system from remote sites, but it does not permit calls to the outside world. Bidirectional access provides both dial-in and dial-out capabilities.

## Cabling

Finally, a few words about *cabling*. The RS-232 standard defines two types of equipment: Data Terminal Equipment (DTE) and Data Communications Equipment (DCE). Most computers are DTE; modems are always DCE. DTE uses pin 2 to transmit data and pin 3 to receive data; DCE does the reverse. To connect a computer to a modem or printer (DTE to DCE), you make the cable connection straight through. To make a connection between two computers (DTE to DTE) or between a computer and a terminal, you need a cable with pins 2 and 3 crossed. This is often called a null-modem or modem-eliminator cable. To save yourself a great deal of frustration, make sure you configured your cables properly before you configure the port monitor and services.

## Software Terminology

Now that I've described the hardware pieces, I will briefly describe the components of the operating system that add functionality to the ports, terminals, and modems.

## Service Access Controller (SAC)

*The Service Access Controller (SAC)* oversees the entire service access facility (SAF). The SAC daemon is started in /etc/inittab by an entry like this one:

```
sc:234:respawn:/usr/lib/saf/sac -t 300
```

The -t option specifies how often the SAC daemon polls the port monitors.

The SAC daemon starts and controls various port monitors. SAC starts all of the port ...tors listed in its configuration file, /etc/saf/_sactab.

## t Monitors

...mechanism for gaining access to a service is through a *port monitor*. A port monitor ...rogram that continuously monitors a port for requests to log in or requests to access ...rs or files.

...a port monitor detects a request, it sets whatever parameters are required to establish communication between the operating system and the device requesting service. Then the port monitor transfers control to other processes that provide the services needed.

A port can be an address on a network, a hard-wired terminal line, or an incoming phone line. The definition of what constitutes a port is strictly a function of the port monitor itself. Port monitors have two main functions: managing ports and monitoring ports for indications of activity.

The first function of a port monitor is to manage a port. The person who defines the port monitor defines how a port is managed. A port monitor is not restricted to handling a single port; it can handle multiple ports simultaneously. An example of port management is setting the line speed on incoming phone connections, reinitializing the port when the service terminates, and outputting a login prompt.

The second function of a port monitor is to watch the port for indications of activity. Two types of activity might be detected. The first is an indication to the port monitor to take some specific port monitor action; for example, pressing the break key to indicate that the line speed should be cycled. Not all port monitors need to recognize and respond to the same indications; the person who defines the port monitor defines the indication used to attract the attention of the port monitor. The second activity a port monitor detects is an incoming service request. When a service request is received, a port monitor must be able to determine which service is being requested from the port. Note that the same service might be available on more than one port.

Solaris has two types of port monitors: ttymon and listen. ttymon connects incoming requests on serial lines to the login service and login program and would be the port monitor to handle modems and terminals. listen connects incoming print jobs to the lp facility. You might be familiar with an older port monitor called getty. In Solaris, getty has been replaced by ttymon. These two programs serve the same function, but a single ttymon can replace multiple occurrences of getty.

### ttymon

Whenever you attempt to log in via a directly connected modem or alphanumeric terminal, the TTY Port Monitor (ttymon) goes to work. ttymon provides Solaris users the same services that getty did under previous versions of SunOS 4.1 software. When someone attempts to log in via an alphanumeric terminal or a modem, the serial port driver passes the operation to the operating system. The ttymon port monitor acknowledges the serial port activity and attempts to establish a communications link. ttymon determines what data transfer rate, line discipline, and handshaking protocol are required to communicate with the device connected to the serial port. Having established the proper handshaking with the modem or terminal, ttymon passes these parameters to the login program.

When SAC invokes an instance of ttymon, ttymon starts to monitor its ports. Each instance of ttymon can monitor multiple ports, which are specified in the port monitor's administrative file. The values used for initializing the port are taken from the appropriate entry in the /etc/ttydefs file. The ttymon port monitor then writes the prompt and waits for user input. When valid input is received from the user, ttymon interprets the configuration file for the port and creates an entry in /etc/utmp. The /etc/utmp file holds accounting information about the user for commands such as who. ttymon then establishes the service environment and invokes the service associated with the port.

After the service terminates, ttymon cleans up the /etc/utmp entry and returns the port to its initial state.

### listen

The network listener service, listen, is a port monitor that runs under SAC. It monitors the network for service requests, accepts requests when they arrive, and invokes servers in response to those service requests.

### Port Monitor Tag (pmtag)

The Port Monitor Tag (pmtag) is the name assigned to an instance of a port monitor. The pmtag is used to define groups of one or more actual port monitor processes. You can name port monitors anything you want, provided the name is unique and is no longer than 14 characters. By default, Solaris assigns names such as zsmon for serial ports. Unless you have a good reason to do otherwise, the system-defined names are the best to use.

## Service Tag (svctag)

Each port assigned to a port monitor has its own service tag. The name used for the service tag is tty followed by the name of the port created in the /dev/term directory. For example, the svctag for /dev/term/a would be ttya.

# Administering Terminals, Modems, and Ports

Three tools are available for administering terminals and modems: Admintool, the Service Access Facility (SAF) commands, and the Solstice AdminSuite's Serial Port Manager. The next section describes how to add a modem to a system by using the Admintool—the preferred method. Second is a description of how to add a modem from the command line. The Solstice AdminSuite's Serial Port Manager is not covered in this manual. AdminSuite is much like the Admintool but is used for configuring systems in a networked, name-service environment.

## Adding a Modem Through the Admintool

Setting up a serial port for a modem is much easier when using the Admintool. This is the recommended method because it eliminates the possibility of a typographical error. Following are the steps used to set up the serial port by using Admintool:

1. Start Admintool, if it's not already running.

2. Select Browse, Serial Ports, as shown in Figure 12–1.

**Figure 12–1**

*The Admintool Browse Menu.*

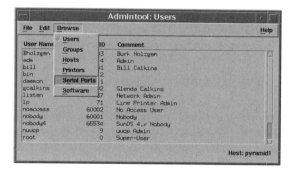

3. In the Serial Ports window, select the port that will be used with a modem, as shown in Figure 12–2.

**Figure 12–2**

*The Serial Ports window.*

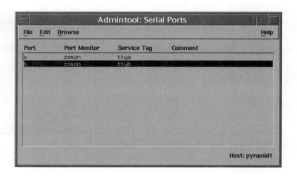

4. Choose Edit, Modify, as shown in Figure 12–3. The Modify Serial Port window appears.

**Figure 12–3**

*The Serial Ports Edit menu.*

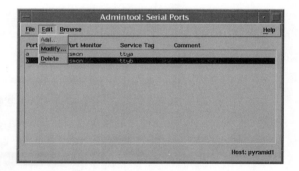

The Modify Serial Port window appears in the Basic Detail mode. To enter additional details, select the More or Expert Detail mode.

5. From the drop-down Template list, choose the modem configuration template that meets—or most closely matches—your modem service (see Figure 12–4).

**Figure 12–4**

*The Modify Serial Port Template list.*

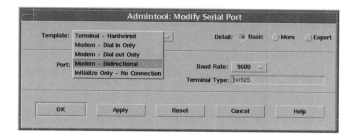

A description of each modem selection can be found in Table 12–1.

---

## Table 12–1 The Modem Template

| Modem Configuration | Description |
|---|---|
| Dial In Only | Users can dial in to the modem but cannot dial out. |
| Dial Out Only | Users can dial out from the modem but cannot dial in. |
| Bidirectional | Users can dial either in or out from the modem. |

---

6. Select the correct baud rate from the Baud Rate drop-down list, as shown in Figure 12–5.

**Figure 12–5**

*The Baud Rate drop-down list.*

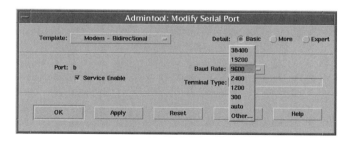

Figure 12–6 shows a completed Modify Serial Port window. The Expert detail mode was selected to show all of the options that can be configured.

**Figure 12–6**

*Completed Modify Serial Port window.*

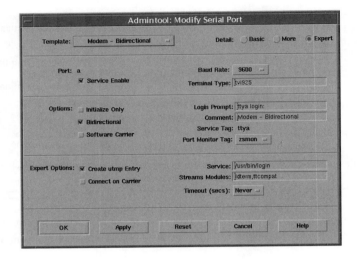

Table 12–2 describes each configurable option shown in Figure 12–6.

**Table 12–2    Modify Serial Port Window Items**

| Item | Description |
| --- | --- |
| Port | Lists the port or ports you selected from the Serial Ports main window. |
| Service | Specifies that the service for the port is turned on (enabled). |
| Baud Rate | Specifies the line speed used to communicate with the terminal. The line speed represents an entry in the /etc/ttydefs file. |
| Terminal Type | Shows the abbreviation for the type of terminal—for example, ansi or vt100. Similar abbreviations are found in /etc/termcap. This value is set in the $TERM environment variable. |
| Option: Initialize Only | Specifies that the port software is initialized but not configured. |
| Option: Bidirectional | Specifies that the port line is used in both directions. |
| Option: Software Carrier | Specifies that the software carrier detection feature is used. If the option is not checked, the hardware carrier detection signal is used. |
| Login Prompt | Shows the prompt displayed to a user after a connection is made. |
| Comment | Shows the comment field for the service. |
| Service Tag | Lists the service tag associated with this port—typically an entry in the /dev/term directory. |

## Table 12–2    Modify Serial Port Window Items (continued)

| Item | Description |
| --- | --- |
| Port Monitor Tag | Specifies the name of the port monitor to be used for this port. The default monitor is typically correct. |
| Create utmp Entry | Specifies that a utmp entry is created in the accounting files upon login. |
| Connect on Carrier | Specifies that a port's associated service is invoked immediately when a connect indication is received. |
| Service | Shows the program that is run upon connection. |
| Streams Modules | Shows the streams modules that are pushed before the service is invoked. |
| Timeout (secs) | Specifies the number of seconds before a port is closed if the open process on the port succeeds and no input data is received. |

7. Click OK to configure the port.

8. Use the `pmadm` command to verify the modem service has been configured for use. To do so, type

```
pmadm -l -s ttya
```

The serial port is now configured and ready for use.

### Service Access Facility (SAF)

The SAF is the tool used for administering terminals, modems, and other network devices. The SAF is an open-systems solution that controls access to system and network resources through tty devices and local-area networks (LANs). SAF is not a program; it is a hierarchy of background processes and administrative commands that include `sacadm`, `pmadm`, `ttyadm`, and `nlsadmin`. See Table 12–3 for a description of these commands.

## Table 12–3    SAF Commands

| Command | Description |
| --- | --- |
| sacadm | Used to add, delete, enable, disable, start, and stop port monitors. |
| pmadm | Configures port monitor services and the associated processes for individual ports. |
| ttyadm | Formats input to pmadm for serial ports. |
| sttydefs | Creates and modifies entries in the /etc/ttydefs file to describe terminal line characteristics. |
| nlsadmin | Formats input to pmadm for remote printing. |

In particular, SAF enables you to

- Set up ttymon and listen port monitors (using the `sacadm` command)
- Set up ttymon port monitor services (using the `pmadm` and `ttyadm` commands)
- Set up listen port monitor services (using the `pmadm` and `nlsadmin` commands)
- Troubleshoot tty devices
- Troubleshoot incoming network requests for printing service
- Troubleshoot the Service Access Controller (using the `sacadm` command)

The configuration files associated with SAF are described in Table 12–4.

### Table 12–4   Files Associated with SAF

| File | Description |
| --- | --- |
| /etc/saf/_sysconfig | Per-system configuration script |
| /etc/saf/_sactab | SAC's administrative file; contains configuration data for the port monitors that the SAC controls |
| /etc/saf/pmtag | Home directory for port monitor pmtag |
| /etc/saf/pmtag/_config | Per-port monitor configuration script for port monitor pmtag if it exists |
| /etc/saf/pmtag/_pmtab | Port monitor pmtag's administrative file; contains port monitor-specific configuration data for the services pmtag provides |
| /etc/saf/pmtag/svctag | Per-service configuration script for service svctag |
| /var/saf/log | SAC's log file |
| /var/saf/pmtag | Directory for files created by pmtag, such as log files |

### *sacadm*

Use the `sacadm` command to add, list, remove, kill, start, enable, or disable a ttymon or listen port monitor. You must be logged in as superuser to use this command. For example, the command syntax used to add a ttymon port monitor is

```
sacadm -a -p mbmon -t ttymon -c /usr/lib/saf/ttymon -v `ttyadm  -V` -y "TTY Ports a & b"
```

Notice the use of the `ttyadm` command.

To view the newly added port monitor, type:

```
sacadm -l -p mbmon
```

The system responds with:

```
PMTAG    PMTYPE    FLGS    RCNT    STATUS      COMMAND
mbmon    ttymon    -       0       STARTING    /usr/lib/saf/ttymon #TTY Ports a & b
```

The sacadm command options used for adding and viewing port monitors are listed in Table 12–5.

## Table 12–5    *sacadm* Command Options

| Command Option | Description |
| --- | --- |
| -a | Adds port monitor option |
| -c | Defines the command string used to start the port monitor |
| -k | Kills port monitor status option |
| -l | Lists port monitor status option |
| -p | Specifies the pmtag mbmon as the port monitor tag |
| -r | Removes port monitor status option |
| -s | Starts port monitor status option |
| -t | Specifies the port monitor type as ttymon |
| -v | Specifies the version number of the port monitor |
| -y | Defines a comment to describe this instance of the port monitor |

To kill a ttymon port   monitor, type

```
sacadm -k -p mbmon
```

To restart a port monitor that has been killed, type

```
sacadm -s -p mbmon
```

To remove a port monitor, type

```
sacadm -r -p mbmon
```

### *pmadm*

The Port Monitor Service Administrator (pmadm) command enables you to administer port monitors' services. Use pmadm to add services, list the services of one or more ports associated with a port monitor, and enable or disable a service. An example would be a terminal service. You can also install or replace per-service configuration scripts or print information about a service.

When you use the pmadm command to administer a service, you specify a particular port monitor via the pmtag argument and a particular port via the svctag argument. For each port monitor type, the SAF requires a specialized command to format port monitor-specific configuration data. This data is used by the pmadm command.

To add a standard terminal service to the mbmon port monitor, type

```
pmadm -a -p mbmon -s a -i root -v `ttyadm -V` -m "`ttyadm -i 'Terminal disabled' -l \
contty —m ldterm,ttcompat -S y -d /dev/term/a -s /usr/bin/login`"
```

Options used in the pmadm command are described in Table 12–6. Note that the above pmadm command contains an embedded ttyadm command.

### Table 12–6   *pmadm* Command Options

| Command Option | Description |
| --- | --- |
| -a | Adds port monitor status option |
| -d | Disables the port monitor service |
| -e | Enables the port monitor service |
| -l | Lists the port monitor service information |
| -p | Specifies the pmtag mbmon as the port monitor tag |
| -s | Specifies the svctag a as the port monitor service tag |
| -i | Specifies the identity to be assigned to svctag when it runs |
| -v | Specifies the version number of the port monitor |
| -m | Specifies the ttymon-specific configuration data formatted by ttyadm |

The next example uses the pmadm command to list the status of a TTY port, or all the ports associated with a port monitor. Type

```
pmadm -l -p mbmon
```

The system outputs the following information:

```
PMTAG     PMTYPE     SVCTAG     FLAGS     ID      <PMSPECIFIC>
mbmon     ttymon     a          -         root    /dev/term/a - - /usr/bin/login \
- contty ldterm,ttcompat login: Terminal disabled - y  #Comment
```

The information reported is described in Table 12–7.

**Table 12–7    Port Monitor Information**

| Service | Description |
|---|---|
| mbmon | The port monitor name, mbmon. |
| ttymon | The port monitor type, ttymon. |
| a | The service tag value. |
| - | Flags following are set by using the `pmadm -f` command. |
| root | The ID assigned to the service when it's started. |

**<PMSPECIFIC> Information:**

| | |
|---|---|
| /dev/term/a | The TTY port pathname. |
| /usr/bin/login | The full pathname of the service to be invoked when a connection is received. |
| contty | The TTY label in the /etc/ttydefs file. |
| ldterm,ttcompat | The streams modules to be pushed. |
| login: Terminal disabled | An inactive message to be displayed when the port is disabled. |
| y | The software carrier value; n indicates software carrier off, y indicates software carrier on. Software carrier is turned on in this example. |
| # | Any comment. There is no comment in this example. |

To disable a port monitor service, type

```
pmadm -d -p mbmon -s a
```

To enable a disabled port monitor service, type

```
pmadm -e -p mbmon -s a
```

## ttyadm

The `ttyadm` command is an administrative command that formats ttymon information and writes it to standard output. `ttyadm` provides a means of presenting formatted port monitor-specific (ttymon-specific) data to the `sacadm` and `pmadm` commands, which are described next in this chapter. `ttyadm` is used, for example, to inform users that a port is disabled. Do so by typing

```
ttyadmin -i
```

The -i option specifies the inactive (disabled) response message sent to a terminal or modem when a user attempts to log in to a disabled port.

To keep the modem connection when a user logs off from a host, type

```
ttyadm -h
```

The system will not hang up on a modem before setting or resetting to the default or specified value. If ttyadm -h is not used, the host will hang up the modem when the user logs out of a host.

Use the -r option with ttyadm to require the user to type a character before the system displays a prompt:

```
ttyadm -r
```

The -r option specifies that ttymon should require the user to type a character or press Return a specified number of times before the login prompt appears. This option prevents a terminal server from issuing a welcome message that the Solaris host might misinterpret as a user trying to log in. Without the -r option, the host and terminal server might begin looping and printing prompts to each other.

Options to the ttyadm command are described in Table 12–8.

### Table 12–8   *ttyadm* Command Options

| Command Option | Description |
| --- | --- |
| -b | The bidirectional port flag. When this flag is set, the line can be used in both directions. |
| -h | Sets the hangup flag for the port. |
| -i | Specifies the inactive (disabled) response message. |
| -l | Specifies which TTY label in /etc/ttydefs to use. |
| -m | Specifies the streams modules to push before invoking this service. |
| -p | Specifies the prompt message, for example, login:. |
| -d | Specifies the full pathname to the device to use for the TTY port. |
| -r *count* | When the -r option is invoked, ttymon waits until it receives data from the port before it displays a prompt. |
| -s | Specifies the full pathname of the service to invoke when a connection request is received. If arguments are required, enclose the command and its arguments in quotation marks ("). |
| -T | Sets the terminal type. |

### nlsadmin

Just as `ttyadm` works for ttymon, so the `nlsadmin` command works for listen. The listen port monitor's administrative file is updated by `sacadm` and `pmadm`, as well as by the `nlsadmin` command. The `nlsadmin` command formats listen-specific information and writes it to the standard output, providing a means of presenting formatted listen-specific data to the `sacadm` and `pmadm` commands. `nlsadmin` does not administer listen directly; rather, it complements the generic administrative commands `sacadm` and `pmadm`.

Each network can have at least one instance of the network listener process associated with it, but each network is configured separately. The `nlsadmin` command controls the operational states of listen port monitors. The `nlsadmin` command can establish a listen port monitor for a given network, configure the specific attributes of that port monitor, and start and kill the monitor. The `nlsadmin` command can also report on the listen port monitors on a machine.

## Setting Up Modems and Terminals by Using SAF

Now that you've learned about `sacadm` and `pmadm`, here's how you put them together to add modems and terminals. To set up bidirectional modem service from the command line, follow these steps:

1. Check to see if a zsmon process is running under SAC. To do so, type the following command:

   ```
   sacadm -l
   ```

   The system responds with

   ```
   PMTAG     PMTYPE    FLGS    RCNT    STATUS      COMMAND
   tcp       listen    -       0       ENABLED     /usr/lib/saf/listen tcp #
   zsmon     ttymon    -       0       ENABLED     /usr/lib/saf/ttymon #
   ```

2. If you do not see a zsmon entry under PMTAG, execute the following command:

   ```
   sacadm -a -p zsmon -t ttymon -c /usr/lib/saf/ttymon -v `ttyadm -V`
   ```

   Check again to see if the zsmon entry is present (status will be STARTING—this is normal).

3. Check to see if a zsmon port monitor is present. To do so, type the following command:

   ```
   pmadm -p zsmon -l
   ```

The system responds with

```
PMTAG      PMTYPE     SVCTAG    FLGS    ID        <PMSPECIFIC>
zsmon      ttymon     ttyb      u       root      /dev/term/b b - /usr/bin/login \
- 9600m ldterm,ttcompat login:  -  - n  #Modem - Bidirectional
```

4. If a port monitor for zsmon is present, remove it by executing the following command:

```
pmadm -r -p zsmon -s <svctag>
```

where the value of *<svctag>* is found by using the output of the previous command. In the above example, this value will be ttyb.

5. Now configure your port monitor. To do so, type

```
pmadm -a -p zsmon  -s ttyb -i root -fu -v `ttyadm -V` -m "`ttyadm -Sn  -d
/dev/term/b -b -m ldterm,ttcompat -l 9600m -s /usr/bin/login`" -y "Modem - \
Bidirectional"
```

ttyb and /dev/term/b specify serial port B; 9600m specifies 9600 baud. Either of these can be modified to reflect a different serial port or baud rate setting.

6. Verify that the port monitor is present by typing

```
pmadm -p zsmon -l
```

The system should respond with output that looks like the following, but the baud rate and service tag might be different:

```
PMTAG      PMTYPE     SVCTAG   FLGS   ID        <PMSPECIFIC>
zsmon      ttymon     ttyb     u      root      /dev/term/b b -
/usr/bin/login    -    9600m       ldterm,ttcompat login:      -     - n  #Modem \
-Bidirectional
```

Serial port B is now configured for a 9600 baud, bidirectional modem. The steps are complex, so you need to be careful not to mistype a command string. Because of the complexity of adding a modem from the command line, Sun has added this task to the Admintool.

## Using the Modem

The following steps outline the process you need to follow to connect and use a modem on a Solaris system.

1. Connect the modem to the correct serial port on the Sun system by plugging the RS-232 cable into either ttya or ttyb. Make sure the RS-232 cable is a "straight through" cable with pins 1–8 and pin 20 provided. Do not use a null modem (cross-over) cable or a null-modem gender-adapter cable.

2. Check for the following line in the /etc/remote file. If it is not there, add it after the `hardwire:\` entry. For the ttyb port, add the following lines:

```
hardwire:\
                :dv=/dev/term/b:br#9600:el=^C^S^Q^U^D:ie=%$:oe=^D:
modem1:\
                :dv=/dev/cua/b:br#9600:
```

Make sure the baud rate matches the baud rate you selected when setting up the serial port.

3. Check the permissions and owner of the modem port. The file /dev/cua/b should be rw-rw-rw- and the owner should be uucp. If not, use the `chmod` command to change the permission and the `chown` command to change the owner.

4. After modifying the /etc/remote file and checking the permission of the port, issue the following command:

```
tip modem1
```

You should get a "connected" message. If you get anything else—for example, "all ports busy"—check the /etc/remote device entry as described in step 2.

5. Verify that the modem is responding to commands. Do so by typing

```
at <cr>
```

You should see an OK displayed.

6. Check the modem register and initialization string. Refer to Table 12–9 for common modem initialization strings and see if the modem type is referenced. If so, follow the manufacturer's instructions for using that string to initialize the modem. For example, the US Robotic Courier Modem string is

```
AT&F1&B1&C1&D2X0S0=1&W
```

If you do not know the initialization string, refer to the manuals supplied with your modem. If you still cannot figure out the initialization string, contact the modem manufacturer's technical support.

7. After setting up the modem, exit the "tip" utility by typing the following sequence:

```
<cr>~.
```

The above sequence is a "carriage return" followed by a "~" character and a "." character.

Table 12–9 shows the strings used to initialize particular modems for use as dial-in and dial-out on Sun Solaris systems.

### Table 12–9    Modem Initialization Strings

| Modem | Initialization String |
| --- | --- |
| US Robotics modems | AT&F1&B1&C1&D2X0S0=1&W |
| Black Box Corporation | ATN0S37=0S0=1Q1&C1&D2&K3&W |
| All other modems | AT&FN0Q2X0&C1&D2S0=1&W |

## Adding a Terminal Through the Admintool

This section describes how to add a terminal by using the Solaris Admintool. Using the Admintool is the easiest way to add a terminal to your system. The steps are as follows:

1. Follow steps 1–4 outlined in the section "Adding a Modem Through the Admintool." When the Modify Serial Port window appears, as shown in Figure 12–7, select Terminal-Hardwired from the Template menu.

**Figure 12–7**

*Modify Serial Port Window.*

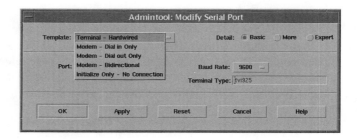

2. Change the values of template entries, if desired. The template entries are described in Table 12–1.

3. Click OK to configure the port and type `pmadm -1 -s ttya` to verify that the service has been added.

Setting up terminals and modems has always been a complicated task in UNIX. When you encounter problems, pinpointing the cause can be difficult. For example, not being able to access the modem could mean an incorrect serial port setting, a cable configuration problem, or an incorrect initialization string on the modem. This is one of those areas where experience and practice can make all the difference in the world. In the early years of UNIX, nearly all peripherals were connected to the serial port. Now, many devices—such as printers and terminals—are connected via the network. Chapter 13, "Networking," will describe how to set up your network and introduce you to some networking fundamentals.

# C H A P T E R

# 13

# Networking

The following are the test objectives for this chapter:

- Defining networking terms

- Identifying and understanding the various network configuration files

- Understanding IP addressing and the various classes of networks

- Understanding name services

- Understanding network commands used to copy files and executing commands on remote systems

- Understanding network commands used to monitor and troubleshoot the network

**O**ne chapter isn't enough to cover network administration; in fact, Sun has developed a certification exam specifically for this area. The basic exam includes some networking fundamentals, however, and this chapter provides you with that basic information. The topics include designing and planning the network, setting up the network, and maintaining the network. As a system administrator, you might be responsible for all of these tasks or you might specialize in a particular area.

# Network Fundamentals

First, we need to define some of the terms used in networking. You'll find an alphabet soup of acronyms, which I'll try to sort out a bit for you. First, I'll describe the types of networks available and then I'll describe the various network protocols. Last, I'll identify the physical components of the network hardware, including the network interfaces and cabling.

## Network Topologies

When we speak of the *network topology*, we describe the overall picture of the network. The topology describes large and small networks as LANs and WANs.

### LAN

A *local area network (LAN)* is a set of hosts, usually in the same building and on the same floor, connected by a high-speed medium such as ethernet. A LAN might be a single IP network, or it might be a collection of networks or subnets connected through high-speed routers.

The cabling or wiring used for computer networks is referred to as network media. A Solaris local area network is connected by some sort of thick or thin coaxial cable, twisted-pair telephone wire, or fiber-optic cable. In the Solaris LAN environment, twisted-pair wire is the most commonly used network media. Other types of network media used in a Solaris LAN include Fiber Distributed Data Interface (FDDI) or Token Ring.

### WAN

A *wide area network (WAN)* is a network that covers a potentially vast geographic area. An example of a WAN is the Internet. Other examples of WANs are enterprise networks linking the separate offices of a single corporation into one network spanning an entire country or perhaps an entire continent.

# Network Protocols

The *network protocol* is the part of the network you configure but cannot see. It's the software portion of the network that controls data transmission between systems across the network.

## Packet

A *packet* is the basic unit of information to be transferred over the network. A packet is organized much like a conventional letter. Each packet has a header that corresponds to an envelope. The header contains the addresses of the recipient and the sender, plus information on how to handle the packet as it travels through each layer of the protocol suite.

The message part of the packet corresponds to the letter itself. Packets can contain only a finite number of bytes of data, depending on the network media in use. Therefore, typical communications such as email messages are sometimes split into packet *fragments*.

## TCP/IP

*Transmission Control Protocol/Internet Protocol (TCP/IP)* is a network communications protocol consisting of a set of formal rules that describe how software and hardware should interact within a network. For the network to function properly, information must be delivered to the intended destination in an intelligible form. Because different types of networking software and hardware need to interact to perform the network function, designers developed the TCP/IP communications protocol, now recognized as a standard by major international standards organizations and used throughout the world. Because it is a set of standards, TCP/IP runs on many different types of computers, making it easy for you to set up a heterogeneous network running any operating system that supports TCP/IP. The Solaris operating system includes the networking software to implement the TCP/IP communications protocol suite.

TCP/IP offers a slew of commands and features that are supported on Solaris and described later in this chapter.

## Ethernet

*Ethernet* is a standard that defines the physical components a machine uses to access the network and the speed at which the network runs. It includes specifications for cabling, connectors, and computer interface components. Ethernet is a LAN technology that transmits information between computers at speeds of up to 10 million bits per second (Mbps). Fast Ethernet pushes the speed up to 100Mbps. Ethernet can be run over four types of physical media:

| | |
|---|---|
| Thick Ethernet | Type 10BASE5 |
| Thin Ethernet | Type 10BASE2 |
| Twisted-pair Ethernet | Type 10BASE-T |
| Fiber-optic Ethernet | Types FOIRL and 10BASE-F |

The 10Base-T type Ethernet is the most popular media in use today.

Ethernet uses a protocol called CSMA/CD for "Carrier Sense, Multiple Access, Collision Detect." The "Multiple Access" part means every station is connected to a single cable. The "Carrier Sense" part means that before transmitting data, a station checks the cable to determine if any other station is already sending something. If the LAN appears to be idle, the station can begin to send data. When several computers connected to the same network need to send data, two computers might try to send at the same time, causing a collision of data. The ethernet protocol senses this collision and notifies the computer to send the data again. How can two computers send data at the same time? Isn't ethernet supposed to check the network for other systems that might be transmitting before sending out data across the network? Here's what happens: An ethernet station sends data at a rate of 10 megabits per second. This means it allows 100 nanoseconds per bit of information that is transmitted. The signal travels about one foot in a nanosecond. After the electric signal for the first bit has traveled about 100 feet down the wire, the station begins to send the second bit. An ethernet cable can run for hundreds of feet. If two stations are located 250 feet apart on the same cable and both begin transmitting at the same time, they will be in the middle of the third bit before the signal from each reaches the other station. This explains the need for the "Collision Detect" part of CSMA/CD. Two stations can begin to send data at the same time and their signals will "collide" nanoseconds later. When such a collision occurs, the two stations stop transmitting and try again later after a randomly chosen delay period.

Although an ethernet network can be built using one common signal wire, such an arrangement is not flexible enough to wire most buildings. Unlike an ordinary telephone circuit, ethernet wire cannot be spliced to connect one copper wire to another. Instead, ethernet requires a *repeater*, a simple station that is connected to two wires. When the repeater receives data on one wire, it repeats the data bit-for-bit on the other wire. When collisions occur, the repeater repeats the collision as well. In buildings that have two or more types of ethernet cable, a common practice is to use repeaters to convert the ethernet signal from one type of wire to another.

## FDDI

*Fiber Distributed Data Interface (FDDI)* is a standard for data transmission on fiber-optic lines in a local area network that can extend in range up to 200KM (124 miles). The FDDI protocol is based on the token-ring protocol. In addition to being large geographically, an FDDI local area network can support thousands of users. FDDI also allows for larger packet sizes than lower-speed LANs using ethernet.

An FDDI network can contain two token rings: a primary token ring and a secondary token ring for possible backup in case the primary ring fails. The primary ring offers up to 100Mbps capacity. If the secondary ring is not needed for backup, it can also carry data, doubling the capacity to 200Mbps.

## ISDN

*Integrated Services Digital Network (ISDN)* is a high-quality digital communications product that gives a single phone line the capability to transmit voice and packet data simultaneously.

Transmission speeds can be either 64Kbps (using one channel) or 128Kbps (with the two 64Kbps channels linked). Some ISDN adapters offer compression, with speeds to the Internet and dial-up networking approaching 512Kbps.

## Network Hardware

The *network hardware* is the physical part of the network you can actually see. The physical components connect the systems together and include the NIC, host, cabling, connectors, hubs, and routers.

### NIC

The computer hardware that enables you to connect it to a network is known as a *Network Interface (NIC)* or network adapter. The network interface can support one or more communication protocols to specify how computers use the physical media—the network cable—to exchange data. Many computers come with a preinstalled network interface; others require you to purchase the network interface separately.

Each LAN media type has its own associated network interface. For example, if you want to use ethernet as your network media, you must have an ethernet interface installed in each host that is to be part of the network. The connectors on the board to which you attach the ethernet cable are referred to as ethernet ports. The same is true if you plan to use FDDI, and so on.

### Host

If you are an experienced Solaris user, you are no doubt familiar with the term *host*, often used as a synonym for "computer" or "machine." From a TCP/IP perspective, only two types of entities exist on a network: routers and hosts. When a host initiates communication, it is called a sending host, or the sender. For example, a host initiates communications when the user types `ping` or sends an email message to another user. The host that is the target of the communication is called the receiving host, or recipient.

Each host has the following three characteristics that help identify it to its peers on the network:

Hostname
: Every system on the network has a unique hostname. Hostnames enable users to refer to any computer on the network by using a short, easily remembered name rather than the host's network IP address.

Internet address or IP address
: Each machine on a TCP/IP network has an Internet address that identifies the machine to its peers on the network.

Hardware address
: Each host on a network has a hardware address that also identifies it to its peers. This address is physically assigned to the machine's CPU or network interface by the manufacturer. Each hardware address is unique.

### Hub

Ethernet cabling is run to each system from a *hub*. The hub connects all of the ethernet cables together. Hubs can support from two to several hundred systems.

### Router

A *router* is a machine that forwards ethernet packets from one network to another. To do this, the router must have at least two network interfaces. A machine with only one network interface cannot forward packets; it is considered a host. Most of the machines you set up on a network will be hosts.

# Planning the Network

You need to do a great deal of planning before you set up your network. As part of the planning process, you must go through the following steps:

1. Obtain a network number and, if applicable, register your network domain with the InterNIC.

2. After you receive your IP network number, devise an IP addressing scheme for your hosts.

3. Create a list containing the IP addresses and hostnames of all machines to comprise your network. You will use this list as you build network databases.

4. Determine which name service to use on your network: NIS, NIS+, DNS, or the network databases in the local /etc directory. Name services are discussed later in this chapter.

5. Establish administrative subdivisions, if appropriate, for your network.

6. Determine if your network is large enough to require routers. If appropriate, create a network topology that supports them.

7. Set up subnets, if appropriate, for your network.

Only after carefully planning your network are you ready to start setting it up.

# Setting Up the Network

During the installation of the operating system you'll use the Solaris software installation program to configure your network. The network configuration files set up by the Solaris installation program are

/etc/hostname.interface

/etc/nodename file

/etc/defaultdomain

/etc/inet/hosts

## /etc/hostname.interface

This file defines the network interfaces on the local host. At least one /etc/hostname.interface file should exist on the local machine. The Solaris installation program creates this file for you. In the filename, *interface* is replaced by the device name of the primary network interface.

The file contains only one entry: the hostname or IP address associated with the network interface. For example, suppose le0 is the primary network interface for a machine called system1. The filename file would be called /etc/hostname.le0 and the file would contain the entry `system1`.

## /etc/nodename

This file should contain one entry: the hostname of the local machine. For example, on a computer named xena, the file /etc/nodename would contain the entry `xena`.

## /etc/defaultdomain

This file is present only if your network uses a name service (described later in this chapter). This file should contain one entry: the fully qualified domain name of the administrative domain to which the local host's network belongs. You can supply this name to the Solaris installation program or edit the file at a later date.

For example, if the host is part of the domain pyramid, which is classified as a .com domain, the /etc/defaultdomain should contain the entry `pyramid.com`.

## /etc/inet/hosts

The hosts database contains the IP addresses and hostnames of machines on your network. This file contains the hostnames and IP addresses of the primary network interface and any other network addresses the machine must know about. When a user enters a command such as `ping xena`, the system needs to know how to get to the host named xena. The /etc/hosts file provides a cross-reference for the system to look up xena and find xena's network IP address. For compatibility with BSD-based operating systems, the file /etc/hosts is a symbolic link to /etc/inet/hosts.

The /etc/inet/hosts file uses the format described in Table 13–1.

## Table 13–1  /etc/inet/hosts File Format

***address hostname <nickname> [#comment]***

| | |
|---|---|
| address | The IP address for each interface the local host must know about. |
| hostname | The hostname assigned to the machine at setup and the hostnames assigned to additional network interfaces the local host must know about. |
| [*nickname*] | An optional field containing a nickname or alias for the host. |
| [*# comment*] | An optional field where you can include a comment. |

When you run the Solaris installation program on a system, it sets up the initial /etc/inet/hosts file. This file contains the minimum entries the local host requires: its loopback address, its IP address, and its hostname.

For example, the Solaris installation program might create the following entries in the /etc/inet/hosts file for a system called xena:

```
127.0.0.1        localhost        loghost     #loopback address
192.9.200.3      ahaggar                       #host name
```

In the /etc/inet/hosts file for machine xena, the IP address 127.0.0.1 is the loopback address, the reserved network interface used by the local machine to allow interprocess communication so it sends packets to itself. The operating system, through the `ifconfig` command, uses the loopback address for configuration and testing. Every machine on a TCP/IP must have an entry for the localhost and must use the IP address 127.0.0.1.

If you've already installed your operating system and answered no to installing a network, you can either edit the network configuration files manually or reissue the network configuration portion of the installation program.

To reissue the program portion, you must first be superuser. Then type **sys-unconfig** at the command line to restore the system's configuration to an "as-manufactured" state. After you run the command, the system starts up again and prompts you for the following information:

| | |
|---|---|
| Hostname | Input a unique name for the computer. |
| The name service you will use | Select NIS, NIS+, DNS, or a local file. |
| Time zone | Input your local time zone. |
| IP address | Input the unique IP address for this host. |
| IP subnet mask | If your network uses subnets, input the subnet mask. |
| Root password | Enter a root password. |

When the system is finished prompting for input, it continues the startup process. When the system is started, the network has been configured.

## Network Security Files

Chapter 4, "System Security," included coverage of network security. If necessary, refer to that section to review the discussion on configuring the network security files /etc/hosts.equiv and /.rhosts.

## IP Addressing

Each host on the TCP/IP network has a network address—referred to as the IP address—that is unique for each host on the network. If the host will participate on the Internet, this address must also be unique to the Internet. For this reason, Internet IP addresses are controlled by an administrative agency, such as the InterNIC.

The IP address is a sequence of four bytes and is written in the form of four decimal integers separated by periods (for example, 0.0.0.0). Each integer is 8 bits long and ranges from 0 to 255. The IP address consists of two parts: a network ID assigned by the InterNIC administrative agency and the host ID assigned by the local administrator. The first integer of the address (0.0.0.0) determines the address type and is referred to as its class. There are five classes of IP addresses: A, B, C, D, and E. Without going into great detail, the following is a brief description of each class.

Class A networks are used for very large networks with millions of hosts, such as the Internet. A class A network number uses the first eight bits of the IP address as its network ID. The remaining 24 bits comprise the host part of the IP address. The values assigned to the first byte of class A network numbers fall within the range 0–127. For example, consider the IP address 75.4.10.4. The value 75 in the first byte indicates that the host is on a class A network. The remaining bytes, 4.10.4, establish the host address. The InterNIC assigns only the first byte of a class A number. Use of the remaining three bytes is left to the discretion of the owner of the network number. Only 127 class A networks can exist; each of these networks can accommodate up to 16,777,214 hosts.

Class B networks are medium-size networks, such as universities and large businesses with many hosts. A class B network number uses 16 bits for the network number and 16 bits for host numbers. The first byte of a class B network number is in the range 128–191. In the number 129.144.50.56, the first two bytes, 129.144, are assigned by the InterNIC and comprise the network address. The last two bytes, 50.56, make up the host address and are assigned at the discretion of the owner of the network.

Class C networks are used for small networks containing fewer than 254 hosts. Class C network numbers use 24 bits for the network number and 8 bits for host numbers. A class C network number occupies the first three bytes of an IP address, and only the fourth byte is assigned at the discretion of the network owners. The first byte of a class C network number

covers the range 192–223. The second and third bytes each cover the range 1–255. A typical class C address might be 192.5.2.5, with the first three bytes, 192.5.2, forming the network number. The final byte in this example, 5, is the host number.

Class D addresses are used for IP multicasting as defined in RFC 988, and class E addresses are reserved for experimental use.

The first step in planning for IP addressing on your network is to determine which network class is appropriate for your network. After you have done this, you can obtain the network number from the InterNIC addressing authority. When you receive your network number, you can plan how you will assign the host parts of the IP address. You can reach the InterNIC Registration Services in several ways.

The United States mailing address is

Network Solutions
Attn: InterNIC Registration Services
505 Huntmar Park Drive
Herndon, Virginia 22070

You can send email regarding network registration to `hostmaster@rs.internic.net`.

The InterNIC phone number is 703-742-4777. Phone service is available from 7 a.m. to 7 p.m. (Eastern Standard Time).

**N O T E .** *Do not arbitrarily assign network numbers to your network, even if you do not plan to attach it to other existing TCP/IP networks. As your network grows, you might decide to connect it to other networks. Changing IP addresses at that time can be a great deal of work and can cause downtime.*

## Name Service

When a user enters a command such as `ping xena`, one of the first things that must happen is translation of the hostname xena to an IP address. This can happen in either of two ways.

The IP address can be determined from the /etc/inet/hosts file or it can be resolved through the domain name service (DNS). For a small network, using just /etc/hosts is not a problem. For a larger network, trying to keep the /etc/inet/hosts file in sync on all hosts can result in a great deal of work, because these files must be exactly the same on each host. If the same address gets used on two different systems, the network could fail.

DNS relies on the named server to provide hostname-to-IP address translations. The named server is a host that permanently stores hostname and IP address information for a specific domain. A domain name is the network equivalent of a hostname. A hostname refers to a specific system on the network, and a domain name refers to a specific network. Sites and institutions are assigned a domain name for their network; they, in turn, assign hostnames to systems within their domain. The Internet domain name system provides a scheme by which every site in the world has a unique name.

# TCP/IP Commands

TCP/IP offers several commands and features that are supported on the Solaris operating system. These commands are part of the TCP/IP networking package and are available on most UNIX systems.

## telnet

telnet is used to log into another system on the network. The following is a sample session:

```
# telnet pyramid1
Trying 192.9.200.4...
Connected to pyramid1.
Escape character is '^]'.

SunOS 5.6
login: bill
Password:
Last login: Sat Jan 16 07:55:03 from 192.9.200.1
Sun Microsystems Inc.   SunOS 5.6      Generic August 1997
pyramid1%
```

## rlogin

rlogin is also a command for logging into another system on the network. Unlike telnet, rlogin has a mechanism whereby you don't have to enter a login name and password.

## ftp

The File Transfer Protocol (FTP) is used to transfer one or more files between two systems on the network. Here is a sample ftp session:

```
pyramid1% ftp pyramid1
Connected to pyramid1.
220 pyramid1 FTP server (SunOS 5.6) ready.
Name (pyramid1:bill): <cr>
331 Password required for bill.
Password: <enter password>
230 User bill logged in.
ftp> pwd
257 "/users/bill" is current directory.
ftp> ls
200 PORT command successful.
150 ASCII data connection for /bin/ls (192.9.200.4,47131) (0 bytes).
admin
file1
data
226 ASCII Transfer complete.
19 bytes received in 0.049 seconds (0.38 Kbytes/s)
```

```
ftp> get file1 /tmp/file1
200 PORT command successful.
150 ASCII data connection for file1 (192.9.200.4,47132) (31311 bytes).
226 ASCII Transfer complete.
local: /tmp/file1 remote: file1
31441 bytes received in 0.12 seconds (266.82 Kbytes/s)
ftp> bye
221 Goodbye.
pyramid1%
```

## rcp

You can also use the rcp (remote copy) command to transfer one or more files between two hosts on a network. The other system must trust your ID on the current host. This trust relationship was discussed in Chapter 4.

The rcp command is more convenient than ftp. First, rcp does not require a login or password if the proper trust relationship exists between the systems, which makes it suitable for scripts. Second, rcp allows complete directory trees to be copied from one system to another. However, ftp has more options and is considered more secure. An example use of rcp is

```
rcp /etc/hosts systemB:/etc/hosts
```

The example uses rcp to copy the file /etc/hosts from the local system to systemB.

## rsh

You use the rsh (remote shell) command to execute a shell on another system on the network. The other system must trust your ID on the current system. The following example uses rsh to get a long listing of the directory /etc on systemB:

```
rsh systemB ls -la /etc
```

## rexec

The rexec command is also used to execute a shell on a remote system. The command differs from rsh in that you must enter a password. At many sites, rsh is disabled for security reasons and rexec is used as a replacement.

## rwho

The rwho command produces output similar to the who command but for all systems on the network.

## *finger*

The `finger` command displays information about users logged on the local or other systems. If `finger` is used without an argument, it gives information concerning users currently logged in. If `finger` is used with an argument (for example, the user name *glenda*) it displays information about all users matching the argument. You can also use the `finger` command to look up users on a remote system by specifying the user as username@host. To protect user privacy, many remote systems do not allow remote fingering of their systems.

## Network Maintenance

In addition to the TCP/IP set of commands, Solaris provides several network commands the system administrator can use to check and troubleshoot the network. To verify that the network is operational, follow these steps:

1. Check the network connection to another system by typing:

   **ping** *<options> <ip address>*

   For example, to check the network between systemA and systemB, type
   **ping systemB** from systemA. If the check is successful, the remote system replies

   ```
   systemB is alive
   ```

   If the network is not active, you get this message:

   ```
   no answer from systemB
   ```

   If this is the response, check your cabling and make sure the remote system is configured properly.

2. Check for network traffic by typing:

   ```
   netstat -i 5
   ```

   The system responds with:

   | input | le0 | output | | | input | (Total) | output | | |
   |---|---|---|---|---|---|---|---|---|---|
   | packets | errs | packets | errs | colls | packets | errs | packets | errs | colls |
   | 95218 | 49983 | 189 | 1 | 0 | 218706 | 49983 | 123677 | 1 | 0 |
   | 0 | 0 | 0 | 0 | 0 | 3 | 0 | 3 | 0 | 0 |
   | 0 | 0 | 0 | 0 | 0 | 4 | 0 | 4 | 0 | 0 |
   | 1 | 1 | 0 | 0 | 0 | 144 | 1 | 143 | 0 | 0 |
   | 0 | 0 | 0 | 0 | 0 | 256 | 0 | 256 | 0 | 0 |
   | 0 | 0 | 0 | 0 | 0 | 95 | 0 | 95 | 0 | 0 |
   | 0 | 0 | 0 | 0 | 0 | 1171 | 0 | 1171 | 0 | 0 |

   The `netstat` command is used to monitor the system's TCP/IP network activity and is described in more detail in Volume 2. `netstat` can provide some basic data about how much and what kind of network activity is happening. The `-i` option shows the state of the network interface used for TCP/IP traffic. The last option, `-5`, reissues the `netstat`

command every five seconds to get a good sampling of network activity. Type `ctrl-c` to break out of the `netstat` command.

4. Look in the *colls* column for a high number of collisions. To calculate the network collision rate, divide the number of output collisions (Output Colls) by the number of output packets. A network-wide collision rate of greater than 10% can indicate an overloaded network, a poorly configured network, or hardware problems.

5. Examine the *errs* column for a high number of errors. To calculate the input packet error rate, divide the number of input errors by the total number of input packets. If the input error rate is high—more than 25%—the host might be dropping packets due to transmission problems. Transmission problems can be caused by other hardware on the network as well as heavy traffic and low-level hardware problems. Routers can drop packets, forcing retransmissions and causing degraded performance.

6. Type `ping -sRv <hostname>` from the client to determine how long it takes a packet to make a round trip on the network. If the round trip takes more than a few milliseconds, there are slow routers on the network or the network is very busy. Issue the `ping` command twice and ignore the first set of results. The `ping -sRv` command also displays packet losses. If you suspect a physical problem, use `ping -sRv` to find the response time of several hosts on the network. If the response time (ms) from one host is not what you expect, investigate that host.

In a networked environment, system performance depends on how well you've maintained your network. An overloaded network will disguise itself as a slow system and can even cause downtime. Monitor your network continuously; you need to know how the network looks when things are running well so you know what to look for when the network is performing poorly. The network commands described in this chapter only report numbers. You're the one who decides if these numbers are acceptable for your environment. As stated before, when it comes to system administration, practice and experience will make you excel as a system administrator. The same holds true for administering a network.

# APPENDIX

# A

# The History of
UNIX

**U**NIX is plural. It is not one operating system but many implementations of an idea that originated in 1965. As a system administrator, you'll want to understand the history of the UNIX operating system—where it came from, how it was built, and where it is now. Understanding the various versions of UNIX and its origins makes it clear why UNIX became known as a somewhat hostile operating system. For example, UNIX was not developed by a single company with a large marketing organization driving the user interface. (In other words, it did not follow the development path of, say, Microsoft Windows.) On the other hand, UNIX was not invented by hackers who were fooling around; it grew out of strong academic roots. The primary contributors to UNIX were highly educated mathematicians and computer scientists employed by what many people feel is the world's premier industrial research center, Bell Laboratories. Although knowledgeable and experienced in their own right, these developers maintained professional contacts with researchers in academia, leading to an exchange of ideas that proved beneficial for both sides. Understanding the symbiotic relationship between UNIX and the academic community means understanding the background of the system's inventors and the history of interactions between universities and Bell Laboratories.

## How It All Began

It all began at Bell Labs, the research lab of AT&T, one of the largest and most powerful companies of our time. Ironically, AT&T was not interested in developing and selling computers or operating systems. In fact, the U.S. Department of Justice did not allow AT&T to sell software. However, AT&T's existing systems, made up of people and paper, were in danger of being overwhelmed in the boom of the 1960s. By the 1970s, the phone business was in jeopardy. Out of desperation and need, Ken Thompson of AT&T set out to develop what no computer company was ready to provide—a multiuser, multiprocessing operating system to be used in-house for its own information processing department. Specifically, the goal was an operating system to support several programmers simultaneously in a more hospitable environment.

What follows is an account of major dates and events in the development cycle of the UNIX operating system.

## 1965–1969

In 1965, Bell Labs joins with MIT and General Electric in a cooperative development of Multics, a multiuser interactive operating system running on a GE 645 mainframe computer. However, unhappy with the progress in the development of a system that is experiencing many delays and high costs, Bell Labs drops out of the development of Multics in 1969.

# 1970

Ken Thompson, exposed to Multics at Bell Labs, meets up with Dennis Ritchie, who provides a Digital Equipment Corporation PDP-7 minicomputer to continue the development of an operating system capable of supporting a team of programmers in a research environment. After they create a prototype, Thompson returns to Bell Labs to propose the use of this new operating system as a document preparation tool in the Bell Labs patent department. The new operating system is named UNIX to distinguish it from the complexity of MULTICS. Efforts to develop UNIX continue, and UNIX becomes operational at Bell Labs in 1971.

The first version of UNIX is written in assembly language on a PDP-11/20. It includes the file system, `fork()`, `roff`, and `ed`, and is used as a text-processing tool for preparation of patents.

# 1970–1972

During the early 1970s, UNIX begins to gain popularity throughout Bell Labs, and as word of the new operating system spreads, universities embrace it. However, although it is looked on favorably by the academic and high technology sectors, it is met with skepticism by the business community. In a move to heighten the popularity of UNIX, AT&T begins to license the UNIX source code to universities at a minimal cost. AT&T provides many licensees with the software code and manuals, but doesn't provide technical support. By the late 1970s, 70% of all colleges and universities have UNIX. Computer science graduates are using it, even modifying the code to make it more robust. Up to this point, UNIX was written in assembly language and ran primarily on DEC hardware—first on the PDP-7, then the PDP-11/40, the 11/45, and finally the 11/70, on which it gained wide popularity.

# 1973–1979

This period will become the most significant in the development of UNIX. Ritchie and Thompson had developed the C programming language between 1969 and 1973 and now rewrite the UNIX kernel in the high-level C language. Now the OS can be compiled to run on different computers and, within months, UNIX can be ported to new hardware. Modifications to the OS are easy. Again, Thompson resonates with the academic community already using UNIX in many of its system design courses. UNIX, now written in a general-purpose language featuring modern commands, begins to take off in the areas of word processing and programming.

By now, UNIX is at version 6, the first release of UNIX to be picked up by a commercial firm, Whitesmiths, Inc., who create a commercial copy of version 6 called Idris.

In 1973, Ken Thompson visits Berkeley while on sabbatical and installs version 6 on a PDP-11/70. Two graduate students, Bill Joy and Chuck Haley, get involved with version 6

and later play an important role in the development of the UNIX system at Berkeley. The first project they work on is the development of the UNIX ex editor.

Joy and Haley begin to take interest in the internal operations of UNIX, specifically the kernel. Bill Joy puts together a distribution of UNIX called the "Berkeley Software Distribution," or BSD. He includes enhancements such as the C shell (a C-like interface to UNIX) and the VI editor. 1BSd is released in 1975. By the second release of BSD (1978), Joy has added virtual memory support, which allows programs to run even if they require more physical memory than is available at the time. This second edition of BSD has a strong influence on the release of Bell Lab's Version 7 of UNIX, which is released in 1979 and is the last of the "clean" versions of UNIX.

In the late 1970s, the United States Department of Defense's Advanced Research Projects Agency (DARPA) decides to base its universal computing environment on Berkeley's version of UNIX. In the 4.1 release of BSD, DARPA provides some important performance tune-ups. The fast file system, which provides a method of improving performance of the file system and preventing file fragmentation, is added in release 4.2.

## 1982–1983

AT&T formally releases a beta version of UNIX to the commercial sector in 1982, but in 1983, AT&T releases the first true production version of UNIX, naming it System III (Systems I and II never existed). Although based on version 7 of UNIX and, thus, including some BSD utilities, the release of System III does not include the VI editor or the C shell. Instead, AT&T includes the programmer's workbench.

With the release of System III, AT&T sees a future in UNIX and soon releases System V. (System IV is never seen outside of AT&T.) System V includes the editor, curses (the screen-oriented software libraries), and the init program, which is used to start up processes at UNIX boot-up.

In the early 1980s, Bill Joy leaves Berkeley with a master's degree in electrical engineering and becomes co-founder of Sun Microsystems (Sun stands for Stanford University Network). Sun's implementation of BSD is called SunOS. Sun extends the networking tools of the operating system to include the Networked File System (NFS) that is to become an industry standard. Sun also does some of the early work in developing windowing software for UNIX. SunOS first gets released in 1983. With workstation products now being offered by Sun, UNIX begins to gain acceptance in the high-technology arena, especially computer-aided design and engineering (CAD/CAE) environments. The early 1980s see CAD/CAE become popular. Additional workstation vendors such as HP and Apollo begin to exploit CAD/CAE capabilities, and performance gains over the popular personal computers of the time. These UNIX workstations could out-perform PCs and, with UNIX as an operating system, could provide a multiuser environment.

In other business computing environments, however, UNIX is still considered a hostile environment and does not pose a threat to the mainframes of the time. UNIX has yet to define itself as a user-friendly, tried-and-tested operating system. It is, however, gaining ground in the areas of multitasking and networking. More important, UNIX is being touted as the operating system that provides portability between different hardware architectures, and as a consequence, software developers are getting excited about UNIX. In theory, a program written in C for UNIX would be portable to any hardware platform running the UNIX operating system.

## 1984–1987

In 1984, AT&T releases System V, release 2, and in 1987, release 3. Release 2 introduces the terminal capability database `termcap` file, named `terminfo`, which provides support for various CRT terminals connected to the UNIX system. Other changes include the addition of `streams` and Remote File Systems.

## 1988–1992

In 1988, AT&T shocks the UNIX community by purchasing a percentage of Sun Microsystems, already a leader in the industry. Other hardware vendors see this as an unfair advantage for Sun, so they quickly form a consortium group called Open Software Foundation (OSF). Together they raise millions of dollars to develop a new UNIX standard to compete against Sun's.

In a counter-strike, AT&T, Sun, Data General, and Unisys join forces to start their own organization to fight OSF. This consortium of companies, called UNIX International (UI), is formed to oversee the development of System V standards.

OSF and UI will turn out to be the two major competing commercial standards for UNIX.

By the late 1980s, AT&T concludes that UNIX is a distraction from the company's focus on producing hardware. As a result, AT&T forms the UNIX Software LAB (USL), ultimately purchased by Novell in 1992.

In 1992, at the summer UseNIX conference, Berkeley announces it will conclude its development activities at 4.4 of BSD. Several people who were involved with BSD form smaller companies to try to continue development of BSD, but without Berkeley and ARPA, it is not the same.

In the 1990s, BSD and System V dominate the industry, with several vendors providing their versions of one of the two operating systems. Soon UNIX, an operating system meant to provide portability of applications between multiple hardware platforms, is getting out of control. Applications are not portable between UNIX System V, release 3, and BSD. To create even more confusion, hardware vendors are enhancing their versions of BSD and System V.

# 1993

Sun announces that SunOS, release 4, will be its last release of an operating system based on BSD. Sun sees the writing on the wall and is moving to System V, release 4, which they name Solaris. System V, release 4 (SRV4), would be a merger of System V and BSD, incorporating the important features found in SunOS.

As more hardware vendors, such as Sun, begin to come into the picture, a proliferation of UNIX versions emerges. Although these hardware vendors have to purchase the source code from AT&T and port UNIX to their hardware platforms, AT&T's policy toward licensing the UNIX brand name allows nearly any hardware vendor willing to pay for a license to pick up UNIX. Because UNIX is a trademark, hardware vendors have to give their operating systems a unique name. A few of the more popular versions of UNIX that have survived over the years are

- *SCO UNIX*—SCO Open Desktop and SCO Open Server from the Santa Cruz Operation for the Intel platform.

- *SunOS*—Sun's early OS and the best known BSD operating system.

- *Solaris*—Sun's SRV4 implementation, also referred to as SunOS 5.x.

- *HP-UX*—Hewlett-Packard's version of UNIX. HP-UX 9.x was System V, release 3, and HP-UX 10 is based on the System V, release 4 OS.

- *Digital UNIX*—Digital Equipment's version of OSF/1.

- *IRIX*—The Silicon Graphics version of UNIX. Early versions were BSD-based; version 6 is System V, release 4.

- *AIX*—IBM's System V-based UNIX.

- *Linux*—A free UNIX operating system for the INTEL platform.

With the uncontrolled proliferation of UNIX versions, standards become a major issue. In 1993, Sun announces they are moving to System V in an effort to promote standards in the UNIX community. With two major flavors of UNIX, standards cannot become a reality. Without standards, UNIX would never be taken seriously as a business computing system. Thus, Sun develops BSD but provides its users with System V, release 4, shrink-wrapped directly from AT&T. In addition, any applications developed by Sun to be added onto UNIX are to be SRV4-compliant. Sun challenges its competitors to provide true portability for the user community.

The Graphical User Interface (GUI) is the next wave in the development of the UNIX operating system. As each hardware vendor tries to outdo the other, ease of use becomes an issue. Again, in this area especially, standards are important. Applications that are to be portable need a GUI standard. Therefore, Sun and AT&T start promoting OPEN LOOK, which they jointly developed. Their goal is to create a consistent look and feel for all flavors of UNIX, but unfortunately, OSF has its own GUI called OSF/MOTIF. Thus, round two of the fight for standards begins, with MOTIF beating out OPEN LOOK.

MOTIF is based on a GUI developed at MIT, named X-Windows, which enables a user sitting at one machine to run programs on a remote machine while still interacting with the program locally. X is, in effect, one way for different systems to interface with each other. X-Windows lets a program run on one computer and display its output on another computer, even when the other computer is of a different operating system and hardware architecture. The program displays its output on the local machine, accepts keyboard and mouse input from the local machine, but executes on the CPU of the remote machine.

The local machine is typically a workstation or terminal called a dedicated X terminal and built specifically to run X-Windows. The remote machine may be a minicomputer or server, a mainframe, or even a supercomputer. In some cases, the local machine and the remote machine might, in fact, be the same. In summary, X is a distributed, intelligent, device-independent, operating-system–independent windowing system.

As stated earlier, MOTIF beat OPEN LOOK in the standards war. Sun concedes and starts to provide a package that contains both OPEN LOOK and MOTIF—called the Common Desktop Environment (CDE)—as standard equipment in the Solaris OS.

## Late 1990s

Today many hardware vendors have "buried the hatchet" and, for the sake of users, are moving their implementations of UNIX to be SRV4-compliant. SVR4 will clearly be the dominant flavor of UNIX across most major platforms. As all vendors begin to implement SVR4 along with the Common Desktop Environment, users will begin to see a more consistent implementation of UNIX. In addition, software providers can be assured that applications written to be SVR4 compliant will be portable across many hardware platforms.

### Solaris

We have discussed the history of UNIX and made predictions. No other flavor of UNIX is more popular or has enjoyed a wider user base and cultural following than Sun Microsystem's Solaris. Sun Microsystem's focus has been on UNIX since it was founded in 1982, and it appears to have no intention of moving away from the UNIX operating system. Sun's user base has a strong loyalty for the company as well as for the operating system. Sun's most recent version is Solaris 2.6, based on System V, release 4. The Solaris operating system is available for the SPARC architecture, Sun's own processor, and the Intel platform.

## Milestones in the Development of UNIX

1965     Bell Laboratories joins with MIT and General Electric to develop Multics.

1970     Ken Thompson and Dennis Ritchie develop UNIX.

1971     The B-language version of the OS runs on a PDP-11.

1973     UNIX is rewritten in the C language.

| | |
|---|---|
| 1974 | Thompson and Ritchie publish a paper and generate enthusiasm in the academic community. Berkeley starts the BSD program. |
| 1975 | The first licensed version of BSD UNIX is released. |
| 1979 | Bill Joy introduces "Berkeley Enhancements" as BSD 4.1. |
| 1982 | AT&T first markets UNIX. Sun Microsystems is founded. |
| 1983 | Sun Microsystems introduces SunOS. |
| 1984 | About 100,000 UNIX sites exist worldwide. |
| 1988 | AT&T and Sun start work on SVR4, a unified version of UNIX. |
| 1988 | OSF and UI are formed. |
| 1989 | AT&T releases System V, release 4. |
| 1990 | OSF releases OSF/1. |
| 1993 | Novell buys UNIX from AT&T. |
| 1993 | Sun introduces Solaris, which is based on System V, release 4. SunOS, which is based on BSDF UNIX, will be phased out. |
| 1995 | Santa Cruz Operation buys UNIXware from Novell. SCO and HP announce a relationship to develop a 64-bit version of UNIX. |
| 1997 | International Data Corp estimates that approximately three million UNIX systems will be shipped worldwide. |

# B

# The Fundamentals of Client-Server Computing

W hen speaking of client-server, open systems, and distributed computing environments, UNIX comes up in the same conversation. UNIX provides the foundation required to support these environments. This section describes the roll of UNIX in the world of client-server computing.

## The First UNIX Server

Before 1990, UNIX was used exclusively by scientists, mathematicians, engineers, and graduate students. During this period, UNIX ran only on minicomputers, smaller than a mainframe but larger than a PC. A typical mini was equipped with 300MB of disk space and 2–4MB of RAM. A minicomputer usually supported one to twelve users and was accessed via dumb alphanumeric terminals.

### An OS Designed for Speed

Disks operate in milliseconds and RAM operates in nanoseconds. UNIX was designed to take advantage of RAM; thus, the more RAM, the better the performance. When RAM was limited, disk space was substituted for physical RAM. As the number of users on a server grew, performance degraded and another server was added. As users were moved to the new server, data was shared via the network. Soon, graphical terminals became available and replaced the character-based terminals; before long, these graphical terminals had their own CPUs and RAM. Because they had no disk drive and relied on the minicomputer or "server" for storage, the terminals were termed "diskless clients." With their own processing capability, the terminals could off-load the task of processing from the server which, by this time, was simply used for storage of applications and data. At power-on, the client downloaded UNIX into its local memory and—except for retrieving data—operated in a standalone mode.

## The Birth of the Workstation

As disk drives became less expensive, disks were added to the client and UNIX could be loaded locally. The term "diskfull" client was coined, but these were soon referred to as "workstations" to differentiate them from the less expensive personal computers. Workstations operating with the UNIX OS were multitasking, multiuser systems, but the PC was still a single-tasking, single-user environment.

Workstations were fueled by cheaper memory and faster CPUs. Servers and workstations were equipped with 16–32MB of RAM, and applications could be loaded directly on the workstations to further improve performance. Workstations could access data across several servers and share processing tasks with other workstations, allowing the processing load to be distributed across a network of computers.

Workstation costs averaged between $35,000 to $55,000, with servers in the $100,000 range. Use of these systems was mainly in high-tech and engineering environments. The systems were standalone units, and system management was not a big issue for this group of users; however, workstation vendors looking for new opportunities knew they must break out of the technical arena. They looked toward general business applications such as accounting, finance, and business information systems—environments requiring larger systems, supporting hundreds of users and large data pools. Up-time was required 24 hours per day, 7 days per week, and system failures and data loss were disastrous to these environments.

## Distributed Computing

Something else was happening in the computer world that changed the course of UNIX: mainframes were running out of power because of the large numbers of users and the more complex applications they were supporting. With more users came more data and the need to access this data in a timely fashion. To further complicate matters, businesses were no longer centralized, and many users needed to connect to the mainframe over telephone lines. When the mainframe failed, all users were affected.

UNIX fit perfectly in this environment. It already had the network functionality for computers to communicate, and it acted as a single system while providing a distributed computing environment. Local systems could run processes on other, less loaded systems, and data access was transparent across multiple networks. As performance degraded, another server could be added to lighten the load. The UNIX system now had a chance to infiltrate the mainframe world. A typical scenario placed multiple UNIX servers on a network. Workstations, called clients, were placed at the users' desks. Applications ran on the users' desktops, accessing data on the servers. In a nutshell, this was client-server computing and the advantage UNIX used to gain new markets.

In recent years, PCs and workstations have grown more powerful and less expensive. At first, cost and performance constituted the difference between a workstation and a personal computer. Today, the distinction between a workstation and a PC is less obvious. Whatever we call the desktop system, users no longer need to rely on the mainframe when they have high performance and adequate storage on their desktop computers. Application developers are porting their applications to these high-performance desktops, using the mainframe for storage and large database transactions. By moving the application to the local desktop, the load of users and their applications is distributed over the network and off the mainframe. Unfortunately, this means the network takes a beating and soon becomes the performance bottleneck.

Many advances in network technology are addressing this network bottleneck. Ethernet switches and network interfaces that support 100-megabit to 1-gigabit transfer rates are being implemented, adding complexity to the system administrator's job. Network management is as important as managing the UNIX system. The system administrator not only needs to understand the UNIX operating system and hardware but must be knowledgeable in network design and management as well.

## UNIX Administration in a Mainframe Environment

Today many businesses are replacing mainframes with several less expensive, more power-ful UNIX servers. The mainframe world, however, requires consistency and robust system management utilities. With 25 years of development under its belt, UNIX provides much of the functionality a user would expect. In fact, the last few releases of SVR4 have not seen much more development in this area, other than the development of GUIs and the window-ing system. User enhancements that provide general functionality within the OS have been developed and tested and are as solid as any OS in existence. Development now lies in the area of performance, high availability, and system administration. Hardware vendors com-peting against mainframes are rapidly developing applications and utilities to compete in this arena. To appear open and SVR4-compliant, vendors usually refer to features as exten-sions or enhancements. In addition, third-party software developers daily create new appli-cations as additional "extensions" to UNIX, to meet the demands of the server community. This area is rapidly changing for the UNIX system administrator.

Unfortunately, even when a system is SVR4-compliant, system administration is not consis-tent between hardware vendors. As standards are developed for the UNIX operating system, the area of system administration is often overlooked. Although everyone is moving toward SVR4, and to the general user, UNIX is UNIX, be aware that system administration on HP, IBM, DEC, and such is very different and will probably always remain that way.

# Overview of
# SCSI Devices

**S**CSI (pronounced "scuzzy") is an acronym for the Small Computer Systems Interface. This interface is an American National Standards Institute (ANSI) standard for high-speed parallel data communication between computers and their peripheral devices. The SCSI standard can be divided into SCSI-1, SCSI-2, and SCSI-3. SCSI-3 is the most recent version of the SCSI command specification and is also called Fast/Wide SCSI. SCSI-2 and SCSI-3 allow scanners, hard disk drives, CD-ROM players, tapes, and many other devices to connect to a computer.

You might be familiar with IDE disk drives but not SCSI drives. IDE drives are much more prevalent on PCs. The IDE/ATAPI is also a data interface that often is provided by PC manufacturers and is generally included when you purchase a new personal computer. Usually, the computer motherboard comes with a primary and secondary IDE bus. Up to two IDE/ATAPI devices, a master and slave, can be connected to each bus. Because this interface is less sophisticated than the SCSI one, ATAPI devices are usually more affordable. Note, however, that IDE/ATAPI devices are often slower and—particularly in the case of CD-Readers—less accurate. The benefits of SCSI are probably best identified by listing the reasons why anyone would use SCSI:

- SCSI makes adding new peripheral devices to a computer system easy.

- Because the development cycle for SCSI devices is very short, the latest generation of SCSI peripherals keeps pace with the latest generation of computer systems. SCSI disk drives usually out-perform IDE disk drives.

- SCSI maintains high performance standards, which is why SCSI is still the dominant interface for medium and large systems.

- SCSI is a smarter bus than IDE. On operating systems that allow multitasking, the SCSI drive is a better choice because the extra intelligence of the SCSI bus is used. IDE also uses controllers on each device, but they cannot operate at the same time and they do not support command queuing. The performance overhead of SCSI over IDE comes from the structure of the bus, not the drive. The nature of the SCSI bus provides much better performance when you're doing data-hungry tasks such as multitasking. The SCSI bus controller is capable of controlling the drives without any work by the processor. Also, all drives on a SCSI chain are capable of operating at the same time. With IDE, you're limited to two drives in a chain, and these drives cannot work at the same time (in essence, they must "take turns").

- SCSI is an intelligent interface, which means the intelligence about I/O operations is moved from the host CPU to the peripheral device. Data can then be transferred at high speeds between the devices without taking any CPU power. Also, computer systems can use a standard set of commands to accomplish the moving of data between the host and device. Adding to the simplicity of the SCSI interface, you can connect a new peripheral device to an existing system with no hardware changes or additional hardware parts.

- SCSI has a demonstrated track record of keeping pace with the growing and evolving requirements of desktop and server systems.

- Using SCSI both preserves the investment of installed-base environments and maintains a platform for future enhancements of SCSI systems.

Here are the definitions of a few SCSI terms you'll come across:

- *Host adapter*   The host adapter, or SCSI controller, is the card that connects your computer to the SCSI bus.

- *SCSI device*   Any device that attaches to the SCSI host adapter, such as a tape drive or disk drive.

- *SCSI ID*   Also referred to as the target ID, this is a unique ID assigned to each SCSI device. It is usually selectable on the rear of the device. No two devices on the same SCSI chain can share the same ID.

- *SCSI chain*   Devices such as disk drives and tape drives are daisy-chained from the host adapter. This chain of devices is referred to as a SCSI chain.

- *SCSI terminator*   The last device on the SCSI chain must be terminated. Termination must be present at only two positions on the SCSI bus—the beginning and the end. Termination at the beginning of the SCSI bus is done on the motherboard automatically. The system administrator usually has to install a terminator on the last SCSI device. There must be two terminators on the bus—not more or less. The terminator is either passive or active and is usually labeled as such; some active terminators have a small LED as well. A passive terminator is a group of resistors on the physical end of a single-ended SCSI bus that dampens reflected signals from the ends of the bus. Passive terminators do not use a voltage regulator and might not be exactly +5 volts. Active terminators use a voltage regulator to make sure the voltage is exactly +5 volts. You need to determine what type of termination to use, so follow the instructions in the hardware installation guide that comes with the equipment. Some peripherals are auto-terminating; terminating these devices twice can cause undesirable results.

- *Single-ended SCSI*   An early type of SCSI-1 device. The maximum length for a SCSI-1 SCSI chain is 6 meters and the maximum number of devices is eight.

- *Differential SCSI*   The next-generation SCSI type. Allows a maximum cable length of 25 meters and is electrically incompatible with single-ended devices. Differential SCSI supports a maximum of 16 devices.

- *Asynchronous SCSI*   A way of sending data over the SCSI bus. The initiator sends a command or data over the bus and then waits until it receives a reply.

- *Synchronous SCSI*   Rather than waiting for a reply, connected devices that both support synchronous SCSI can send multiple bytes over the bus. This improves throughput, especially if you use long cables.

- *Fast SCSI (SCSI-2)* Fast SCSI allows faster timing on the bus; 10MHz instead of 5MHz. On an 8-bit SCSI bus, this increases the maximum speed from 5MBps to 10MBps.

- *Ultra SCSI* Allows up to 20MHz signals on the bus to achieve speeds of up to 20MBps.

- *Wide SCSI (SCSI-3)* Uses an extra cable (or 68-pin P cable) to send the data 16 or 32 bits wide. This allows for double or quadruple speed over the SCSI-1 bus. Currently, no single drive reaches these speeds, but groups of several drives can.

Following is a visual guide for SCSI connectors.

Most SCSI Slow (5MBps) computers and host adapters use the Centronics-type 50-pin connector shown in Figure C–1.

**Figure C–1**

*50-pin Centronics SCSI connector.*

Many 8-bit SCSI Fast (up to 10MBps) computers and host adapters use the 50-pin high-density connector shown in) Figure C–2.

**Figure C–2**

*50-pin high-density SCSI connector.*

All Fast or Wide (16-bit) SCSI-3 computers and host adapters, as well as old DEC single-ended SCSIs, use the 68-pin high-density ) connector shown in Figure C–3.

**Figure C–3**

*68-pin high-density SCSI connector.*

A less common SCSI connector, the New SCA 80-pin connector is shown in Figure C–4.

**Figure C–4**

*SCA 80-pin SCSI connector.*

As when adding any other peripheral or equipment to your system, consult with the manufacturer first. When adding equipment to your Sun system, first call Sun and make sure the equipment is supported under Solaris and that you can obtain instructions for connecting the equipment. Again, a few minutes of planning will save hours of grief and downtime. Most system administrators are more comfortable having their hardware maintenance person install the equipment.

# D

## On the Web

T he Internet is a great source of information, especially for system administrators. You might be interested in the following Web sites and newsgroups to further your knowledge in UNIX. These sites are valuable as you search for information regarding Solaris and Sun Microsystems. All of these links are also available from my Web site at `www.pdesigninc.com`.

## Mailing Lists

`sun-managers-request@ra.mcs.anl.gov`

Sun managers' mailing list.

`sun-nets-requests@umicas.umd.edu`

A mailing list devoted to networking Sun systems.

`sun-spots-request@rice.edu`

A mailing list discussing Sun workstations.

`suns-at-home-request@ea.ucn.purdue.edu`

A mailing list dedicated to users who have Sun systems at home.

## Newsgroups

`comp.sys.sun.admin`

A newsgroup for Sun system administration issues and questions.

`comp.sys.sun.announce`

A newsgroup used for Sun announcements and Sunergy mailings.

`comp.sys.sun.apps`

A newsgroup covering software applications for Sun computer systems.

`comp.sys.sun.hardware`

A newsgroup for Sun Microsystems hardware.

`comp.sys.sun.misc`

A newsgroup of miscellaneous discussions about Sun products.

`comp.sys.sun.wanted`

A newsgroup for people looking for Sun products and support.

```
comp.unix.admin
```

A general UNIX system administration newsgroup.

```
comp.unix.solaris
```

Discussions about the Solaris operating system.

## Web Sites

```
www.pdesigninc.com
```

My Web page. This site provides links to all of the sites mentioned in this book, as well as other sites as they become available.

```
www.sun.com
```

Sun's official Web site.

```
www.netline.com/sunex
```

*SunExpert.* A free magazine with UNIX tips and news and technology from the world of Sun.

```
www.sun.com/sunworldonline
```

*SunWorld.* Sun's own online magazine for the Sun Community.

```
www.ugu.com
```

The UNIX Guru Universe. The great home page for UNIX system administrators, providing links to useful sites for nearly all versions of UNIX.

```
sunsolve.sun.com
```

A source for free and recommended security support information. This Web site contains collections of informational documents, patch descriptions, a symptom/resolution database, and download access to the latest system patches.

```
http://docs.sun.com
```

This Web site contains all of the Sun product documentation, including manuals, guides, and AnswerBooks.

```
http://sun.icsnet.com
```

A site providing links to Solaris FAQs, software, and manual pages.

```
www.latech.edu/sunman.html
```

The archive to summaries of questions posted to the Sun managers' mailing list.

`www.sunfreeware.com`

Lots of freeware, precompiled in package format for Solaris running on SPARCs and x86.

`http://www.net-kitchen.com/~sah/`

Suns-at-Home is a mailing list devoted to folks who have Sun Workstations at home.

# UNIX-Related Publications Available on the Web

`www.zdjournals.com/sun`

*Inside Solaris*

`http://sun.expert.com`

*SunExpert Magazine*

`www.samag.com`

*SysAdmin Magazine*

`www.performance-computing.com`

*Performance Computing. UNIX Review* magazine is now *Performance Computing.* You'll find back issues of UNIX Review at this site.

`www.networkcomputing.com/unixworld`

*UNIX World*

# I N D E X

# A

# I - J - K

## Technical Support:

If you cannot get the CD to install properly, or if you need assistance with a particular situation in the book, please feel free to check out the Knowledge Base on our Web site at `http://www.superlibrary.com/general/support`. We have answers to our most Frequently Asked Questions listed there. If you do not find your specific question answered, please contact Macmillan Technical Support at (317) 581-3833. We also can be reached via email at `support@mcp.com`.